Contorno

Contorno

Literary Engagement
in Post-Peronist Argentina

William H. Katra

Rutherford ● Madison ● Teaneck
Fairleigh Dickinson University Press
London and Toronto: Associated University Presses

Associated University Presses
440 Forsgate Drive
Cranbury, NJ 08512

Associated University Presses
25 Sicilian Avenue
London WC1A 2QH, England

Associated University Presses
2133 Royal Windsor Drive
Unit 1
Mississauga, Ontario
Canada L5J 1K5

The paper used in this publication meets the requirements
of the American National Standard for Permanence of Paper
for Printed Library Materials Z39.48-1984.

Library of Congress Cataloging-in-Publication Data

Katra, William H.
    Contorno: literary engagement in post-Peronist Argentina.

    Includes index.
    1. Argentina—Intellectual life—20th century.
    2. Argentina—Politics and government—1955–1983.
    3. Contorno (Buenos Aires, Argentina)—History.
    4. Argentine literature—History and criticism.
    I. Title.
    F2849.2.K38   1988   982'.063   86-46407
    ISBN 0-8386-3316-1 (alk. paper)

PRINTED IN THE UNITED STATES OF AMERICA

Los pueblos han de vivir criticándose, porque la crítica es la salud. . . . ¡Con el fuego del corazón deshelar la América coagulada!

José Martí

Contents

Preface

THE SOCIOPOLITICAL AS WELL AS LITERARY AND CULTURAL FOCUS OF THE
Argentine journal *Contorno* during its relatively brief publishing life from
1953 to 1959 accounts for the two objectives of this study. First, I intend
to utilize the writings published in this journal in order to present an
interpretation of the social and political events—in addition to the predominant groups and their corresponding ideologies—for the period
that spanned the end of Perón's government and the beginning of
approximately a decade that is now generally considered to be a golden
age of Argentine cultural activity (the period between approximately
1957 and 1966). The appearance of journals such as *Contorno* generally
have responded to periods of institutional and social crisis, a factor that
accounts in large part for their brief and sporadic publishing record.
However, *Contorno* was pivotal because of its relationship to the Peronist
phenomenon, which has colored the entire past forty years of Argentine
social history and its cultural reflection.

As Argentina's national crises multiply and project their shadows into
the uncertain future, the concerned reader inevitably inquires about
their roots in the past. *Contorno* initially responded to a wide-spread
feeling of rejection, incomprehension, and frustration on the part of the
educated middle class in the waning years of the Peronist decade. As
national leadership passed from Perón to military bosses, and then to
Frondizi, the *Contorno* writers, in successive issues, treated time and
again the causes for the growing uneasiness experienced by Argentina's
population and attempted to offer new perspectives on the country's
problems. The primary focus in early issues was literature, while social
and political concerns later came to predominate. But even when their
inquiries began with literary issues, the attention of these writers constantly ranged beyond the limits of the text into social and political
analysis. Indeed, these writings continue to interest researchers today
on account of their authoritative analyses of the fluid social and political
events that marked the end of the Peronist decade and the country's
emergence into its most recent period of institutional crisis. In short, this
study intends to offer more than the analysis of a historically important
literary publication; it is also an interpretation of a sociocultural phenomenon viewed through the perspective of a major intellectual journal.

In addition to offering an informed testimony of the crucial social and political events of the late and post-Peronist years, this study focuses on a key chapter of Argentine, and more broadly, Latin American, intellectual and cultural history. It was a period when the ideas of post–World War II European (but primarily French) existentialism predominated in intellectual circles throughout the West. This body of ideas in the philosophical sphere was transformed into a prescription for the *Contorno* writers' *engaged* writing practice in Argentina.

Existentialism was the philosophical, and at times methodological, foundation for their "Third World" orientation. This meant that they attempted to define in theory and follow in practice a role for intellectual involvement that avoided the extremes of both the elitist individualism of their country's cultural establishment and the authoritarian collectivism of the parties of the institutionalized Left. This also meant that in philosophical orientation they sought a middle course between the bourgeois liberalism of the first and the Stalinist materialism of the second. They followed the lead of Jean-Paul Sartre and others in combining ideas associated with phenomenology, as learned from their readings in Husserl and Heidegger, with a Hegelianized version of Marxism. One strength of the *Contorno* participants was their success in adapting these ideas to the exigencies of their own situation. The pages of their journal attest to these writers' continued attempts, throughout nearly a decade of dramatic changes in the social and political landscape of the country, to reconcile theory and practice. Their engagement, therefore, cannot be defined in terms of a doctrinaire plan for intellectual and writing activity; instead, it was a disposition for involvement, a dynamic process of adapting objectives and actions to their constantly evolving situation.

Through their journal, the *Contorno* writers strove to develop effective means whereby their cultural intervention would become relevant to the most urgent social and political questions affecting their countrymen. In this regard, they clearly followed in the national tradition of Alberdi, Echeverría, Sarmiento, Lugones, Ugarte, Castelnuovo, Martínez Estrada, and others, who, in their own ways, sought a synthesis of cultural and political goals. What is of particular interest about *Contorno*, however, is the carefully documented and detailed record—as preserved in the pages of their journal—of the development of their consciousness as social critics and the trials, successes, and failures of their socially inspired writing practice.

The *Contorno* blend of sociopolitical and cultural concerns sets the stage for the critical focus of the present work. Although such studies are common in Latin America, only recently are they emerging as a vital research focus in the United States. Detailed studies of specific sociocultural phenomena in Latin America are rarely published in English.

Literary scholars tend to circumscribe their research by focusing on purely formal criteria and therefore rely too heavily on the work of social scientists for an interpretation of the social and cultural contexts into which their own findings become inserted. As such, the present study hopes to partially remedy the acute need for analyses of the ideology of Latin American culture in general and of specific national ones in particular.

A final justification for this detailed analysis of the journal *Contorno*, now almost thirty years after its publication, is its role as the initial generational experience for several individuals who are now recognized as leading figures in their respective fields of intellectual inquiry. David Viñas, in addition to his fame as one of Argentina's most repected novelists, has won broad recognition as essayist and political commentator. Tulio Halperín Donghi, presently at the University of California at Berkeley, is, without a doubt, among the most widely published and esteemed historians writing today on Argentina and Latin America. Noé Jitrik and, to a lesser degree, Adolfo Prieto, presently at the University of Florida, are among today's most respected critics of Argentine and Latin American literature and culture. Lastly, every new work by Juan José Sebreli that critically examines heretofore under-explored aspects of Argentine social and political life raises new clouds of polemic and wins the begrudging admiration even of his critics. In essence, then, *Contorno's* greatest legacy is what it initiated. The inquiry of its pages pointed beyond its pages; the journal's relatively short life set the tone and established the pattern for the subsequent writings of its participants. Their lasting contributions to Argentina's and Latin America's cultural life still lay in the future when, in 1955, a decade of Peronist government came to a close.

The present work also compiles extensive and up-to-date bibliographies of the writers associated with *Contorno* for the purpose of familiarizing the reading public with their important contributions.

Acknowledgments

I APPRECIATE THE ASSISTANCE OF WASHINGTON STATE UNIVERSITY'S RE-
search and Arts Committee and its Humanities Research Center. Much
of the initial research was accomplished during a fruitful summer spent
as guest of the Berkeley-Stanford Joint Center for Latin American Studies. Thanks is due to Frances Wyers for directing my Ph.D. dissertation,
that touched on many of the themes treated here, and Lori Nyegaard,
who researched much of the information presented in the bibliographies. Jean Bonde, of the University of Wisconsin–La Cross's Library,
and Betty Heyder, copy editor for Associated University Presses, provided indispensable services. Gratitude is also due to David William
Foster who, during several years, has prodded me into completing the
written testimony of a largely mental construct. I am indebted to David
Viñas, Noé Jitrik, Adolfo Prieto, and the other past writers of *Contorno*,
for timely guidance and constant, indirect inspiration; after all, every
written enterprise traces to some degree—and in this case to a great
degree—the spiritual autobiography of its writer. Most of all, I wish to
thank my wife and companion, Sara, and my two children, Dani and
Esti; through them I become aware of how a project such as this, which
looks to the past, also resonates with future meaning. Here, I repeat the
homage offered in my dissertation some nine years ago: this work is
dedicated to my friends in and around Mal Abrigo, Uruguay, who
taught me to share in love, dreams, and struggle. It is my hope for them
and for others throughout the Río de la Plata region that the dreams and
projections of the *Contorno* writers will not be forgotten.

Contorno

1
Introduction

CONTORNO APPEARED AT A SIGNIFICANT MOMENT IN CONTEMPORARY AR-
gentine history: its first issue in 1953 preceded the fall of Perón by two
years, and its irregular publications up through 1959 gave evidence of
Argentina's chaotic entrance into a new period of turmoil, hopes, and
frustrations. Peronism was like a benchmark separating two distinct
historical periods. Events have subsequently born out the insight of the
young intellectuals then writing for that journal, that the ambiguities
and confusions they themselves experienced with regard to the nation's
recent transformations and its tumultuous political life were indeed
representative of a broad sector of the country's educated middle class.

On the one hand, they believed necessary many of the reforms which
Peronism had brought to the country, such as the incorporation of the
working class into the nation's social and political life and the accelerated
expansion of Argentina's industrial infrastructure. On the other hand,
however, they felt a profound disgust for the corruption, demagoguery,
and bossism that had come to characterize, in their eyes, the preceding
decade of Peronist predominance. Their confusions extended into the
fields of culture and literature as well. They had little in common with,
and therefore hardly respected, the writers of the country who had
supported Perón in his rise to power—Marechal, Wast, Gálvez—and had
a similar lack of enthusiasm for later Peronist supporters such as essayists Hernández Arregui, Jauretche, and J. A. Ramos. At the same
time, they criticized the writers of the "liberal" intelligentsia—Borges,
Mallea, and, at times, Martínez Estrada—for refusing to confront in their
literature the issues most relevant to the national crisis, or for merely
repeating the tired, ahistorical formulas that years ago had ceased to
pertain to relevant issues.

Their journal, *Contorno,* was established largely as a response to these
confusions. Through its ten issues over the next several years, they
gained the respect of their contemporaries for their attempts at conceptualizing the multiple crises of Argentina's cultural and political life.
Most valuable was their articulation of widespread needs. First, there
was the imperative of revitalizing a political elite that would build upon

the strengths of the Peronist experience in order to guide the country in an era of progress and stability. And second, there was the need for a rejuvenated national culture which respected the nation's traditions and historical past, while at the same time indicating new directions based on the most important ideological and artistic currents in the West.

The *Contorno* participants all hailed from middle-class families. Neither bathing in opulence nor besieged by poverty, most grew up in the sheltered environment offered by their genteel professional circle.[1] Most could trace parental origins to the European immigration that had arrived on Argentine soil in the late nineteenth or early twentieth centuries. A few—one example is Adolfo Prieto, whose family was from San Juan—had moved recently to Buenos Aires from provincial capitals, but the majority had been born and raised in the cosmopolitan environment of the nation's capital.

Ismael and David Viñas, in addition to Juan José Sebreli, Noé Jitrik, and León Rozitchner, had grown up under the humiliating glances of the majority population on account of their Jewish heritage. To grow up Jewish meant to be aware of social and cultural differences and, on occasion, to experience ostracism and insult. In an atmosphere relatively free of social intolerance, they learned to accept their Jewishness neither as an embarrassment nor as a right of vindication, but merely as one among several aspects of their social origins.[2] In later years, several of them would publish significant works treating Jews and Judaism in Argentina.[3] During the *Contorno* years, however, their Judaism was accepted less as a class or ethnic distinction and more as a metaphor for idealistic youths such as themselves, whose actions were impeded by an intransigent social system. In *Dar la cara* David Viñas would call "judíos del alma" those progressive youths of the country whose good will and social concern motivated them to dream about and struggle for a better future.

At the beginning of the *Contorno* experience, the principal contributing writers had already finished or would shortly end their course work in the Facultad de Filosofía y Letras in the Universidad Nacional de Buenos Aires.[4] Ismael Viñas, a graduate of the Facultad de Derecho of the same university, was the only one of the group's nucleus not to pursue formal studies in the humanities. A few had already completed advanced studies in different fields before opting for the humanities-centered curriculum: Ramón Alcalde had undergone seven years of study in a Jesuit seminary, and Tulio Halperín Donghi had successfully completed the requirements for a law degree in 1950. Considered as a group, they united several different orientations or fields of inquiry: León Rozitchner, who had graduated from the Faculté de Lettres in the Sorbonne, and Alcalde both specialized in philosophy. Oscar Masotta would dedicate himself to psychoanalytical studies. Juan José Sebreli excelled as a sociologist. Halperín's area of competence was national history. David Viñas, Adelaida Gigli, Noé Jitrik, and Adolfo Prieto decided upon Argentine literature and the national cultural tradition as their areas of intellectual endeavor. Alcalde, Rozitchner, I. Viñas, and Halperín, undoubtedly because of their age advantage (they were born in 1923, 1924, 1925 and 1925, respectively, while the other principal participants were born between 1927 and 1930) and, in the case of the first two, because of their limited but nevertheless valuable experience in labor and politics, initially instructed the group in the arts of social and political analysis. These differences in academic orientation and background proved to be relatively inconsequential in the light of the objectives and critical perspectives they shared in editing their journal.

The women associated with the journal were, for the most part, friends and associates of the nucleus surrounding the Viñas brothers. Adelaida Gigli was, from the second issue on, a member of the Directive Committee. On occasion articles by her, as well as a few by Marta Molinari and Regina Gibaja, were printed in *Contorno*'s pages. Others, for instance Susana Fiorito, provided essential services in its typing, editing, and layout.[5] The relatively low profile of women in the journal's preparation bothered some of the participants. One fairly ineffectual remedy, which has been mystified by *Contorno* critics wholly out of proportion to its scant importance at the time, was David Viñas's decision to sign two essays published in different issues of the journal with the pseudonym, Raquel Weinbaum.

One set of critics called attention to the three different subgroups that came together in the common task of editing the journal.[6] First, there was the nucleus around the Viñas brothers, which brought to the journal a strong criticism of liberalism in its political and historiographical aspects and emphasized the need of studying the literature of the country from this "revisionist" perspective. Second, there were F. J. Solero and Rodolfo Kusch, who embraced the orientation of national reality offered by Martínez Estrada and Murena in its more irrationalist and intuitive aspects. And third, there were Sebreli, Masotta, and Carlos Correa, with an "existentialist-populist-leftist" orientation—according to Sebreli[7]— who most fervently applied the ideas of Sartre in combination with Hegelian and Marxist tendencies. These last three were strong supporters of Peronism, an allegiance that was hardly evident in their essays, but which was manifested in actions such as their exhibition of photographs of Juan and Evita Perón in places frequented by members of opposition student and intellectual groups. Their political convictions caused a constant tension to exist between them and the other *Contorno* participants.

These differences in political orientation do not invalidate certain common interests and identities of the group as a whole. Initially, the group of ambitious youths came together because of their shared concern and, at times, confusion with regard to the dramatically altered social and political lanscape of the country. Most of them were both attracted and repelled by the revolt of the colonels in 1943, and perhaps even more so by the workers' massive rally in support of Juan Domingo Perón in the Plaza de Mayo on 17 October 1945. In their majority, they came from families which had traditionally supported the old Radical Party; as a group they were attracted to socialist ideas, although few, if any, felt an affinity for the Socialist or Communist Parties. All of them, however, considered themselves "leftist." Although many were repulsed by Perón's politics of corruption, they nevertheless identified strongly with his nationalist and anti-imperialist rhetoric, his plans for the country's industrial development, and his vague but strident attacks on the old "oligarchy" of the country. For ten years, the *Contorno* writers would admit in 1956,[8] most of them had waited on the sidelines because they were unwilling to support in full the revolution that was occurring in their midst. At the same time, they were not disposed to oppose it, as many of the country's older writers had chosen to do. Peronism, they would write, became for them a period of frustrated waiting and suffering. This was because it signified the erosion of the previously stable ideological fabric that had been imparted to them as a matter of course through society's institutionalized organs of cultural dissemination.

The Ideological Terrain

During the long decade of Peronism, while a majority of the future *Contorno* writers were engaged in their respective courses of study in the Facultad de Filosofía y Letras in the Universidad Nacional de Buenos Aires, they found ample opportunities for broadening their knowledge, and in a few cases experience, in the politics of the country. The hallmark of their generation was the realization that university and career specialization could not be separated from a consideration of the most urgent social and political questions of their time. All realized the need for a broad theoretical preparation in such issues that would be a prelude to future involvement. A few among their ranks sought early political experience in the university student organizations. Alcalde, Jitrik, and David Viñas, for example, served terms at the head of the Centro de Estudiantes Reformistas de la Facultad de la Universidad de Buenos Aires (FUBA); Rozitchner, in his turn, was later elected president of the Centro de Estudiantes de Filosofía. This involvement occurred primarily during periods of relative calm, with few student strikes and a relatively low level of militancy.

In spite of this early involvement in student groups notorious for their political activism, none of the future *Contorno* writers had as yet become affiliated with any political group; indeed, few, if any, had developed a well-defined political or ideological agenda. This was initially interpreted by the participants themselves as a problem: they aspired to activism, yet could identify with no established group which would channel their energies and good will into effective praxis. Ismael Viñas explained that this noninvolvement during the early years of Peronism was a result of their origins and social links to the indecisive and ideologically confused middle class of the country.[9] Indeed, the young intellectuals' response to Perón's overwhelming triumph at the polls had been, like that of their middle-class brethren, a mixture of disgust and apprehension. On the negative side, they, like the other progressive members of their class, despised the military and clerical officials, two of the mainstays of Perón's governing coalition. They knew that these same two groups had provided the essential support for the conservative reaction of the 1930s and they hastened to make unfavorable comparisons. As the years progressed, Peronism continued to repulse them, but now for different reasons: the opportunism of its followers, the demagoguery of its leaders, and the general corruption of values and institutions that was evident throughout the society.

On the positive side, the young *Contorno* writers slowly began to accept the more favorable aspects of the working class's new influence. Originally, worker militancy had been perhaps the greatest source of their ambiguity. Not unlike the generations of intellectuals before them, they had been educated in the romanticized liberal perspective that in great part ignored the role of the masses and focused on the cultural heroes of middle- and upper middle-class extraction. Not unexpectedly, then, the workers' inflammatory rhetoric and massive demonstrations initially caught them off guard. If this was the long-anticipated social revolution promised by leftist theorists, then where were its articulate spokesmen and intellectual leaders? But they slowly became convinced that worker militancy promised social changes which were long overdue for the country. They were similarly captivated by the movement's rhetoric of anti-oligarchic militancy, its slogans of anti-imperialism, and its commitment to develop the nation's industrial infrastructure. These promises overstepped even the progressive programs for national renovation advanced by the country's most important political groupings and in time would coincide with their own audacious dreams for national progress.

Like the middle class in general, they were confused by the Peronist phenomenon and the changes it had wrought upon the country. Their first response was negative. When the policies of the regime touched them directly, it was not always benignly. First of all, there was the venomous rhetoric of the regime that singled them out—them, the intellectuals of middle-class extraction—as its chosen enemies. The future *Contorno* writers could tolerate this only in part, since at this stage their own vaguely defined criteria for social involvement coincided precisely with these verbal attacks: they were in agreement with the militant voices of Peronism, that the predominant orientations of the country's elitist intellectuals were generally based on an already superseded, and therefore largely dysfunctional, image of a heirarchical social order.

Perón's actions with the goal of transforming the university affected them in a more direct fashion. In 1950 and 1951 the FUBA went out on strike in a show of solidarity with the union of railway workers. Jitrik, with other student leaders, was imprisoned in Villa Devoto for eight days; several were tortured. Although these events left lasting impressions in the minds of the participants, they were hardly the rule. Beyond minor acts of police registration and the denial of good conduct certificates, the Peronist leadership was little bothered by the student movement, except when the latter attempted to act in conjunction with the workers. But the regime's acts did provide reason for the young intellectuals' growing dissatisfaction. They chafed under the forced incorporation of Catholic professors into the ranks of university faculties. Also, there was the government-orchestrated ostracism, and at times persecution, that caused several esteemed instructors of liberal orientation to leave the country in search of more favorable teaching and research conditions elsewhere.[10] Similarly aggravating were the new curricular prohibitions, especially of topics related to Marxist politico-economic theory and philosophy, that motivated many students to organize informal, clandestine study groups. A number of the *Contorno* participants, then members of the Centro de Estudiantes, met together on a regular basis for several months in the basement of a house on the Avenida Las Heras in order to study the political ideas which had been proscribed in the official classroom. But with the general prohibition of strikes and the depoliticization of the curriculum, the university environment entered into what Halperín Donghi has recently described as "una provinciana motononía, y la tibia solidaridad de los marginados."[11] The future *Contorno* writers alternated between the offense they felt on account of the "blindness" of the ideological Right upon invading the university,[12] and their perplexity as relatively uninvolved spectators who were reluctant to take part in the "eternal fiesta" which Peronism offered to the masses. While repulsed by many facets of the Peronist movement, their intensely sensed social responsibility led them to support more and more the overall changes that it was bringing upon the country.[13]

Reluctance to get involved in the urgent social and political issues of their time might have been part of the legacy shared with the older writers of the country, but there was one major difference: whereas the writing mission of the country's liberal intelligentsia was based on the conviction that one should situate oneself at the margin of events, the *Contorno* participants sensed the necessity for active involvement. According to Ismael Viñas, that impulse for activity went far deeper than an intellectual conviction about the possible social or personal benefits that could result. For the members of his group, that commitment was also born of a *passion* for involvement: "no bastan la honradez y el conocimiento de la tarea, ni la reivindicación puramente intelectual de la vida. Contando con que es necesario el afán, la pasión de actuar, de actuar con la vida. Pues nos parece haber sido demostrado que la sola fidelidad al espíritu, es traición al espíritu. Y que, sin juegos de palabras, termina en traición al espíritu."[14] Their hesitance to become politically involved, either for or against the Peronist movement, had resulted from their confusion with regard to their political convictions at the time and not from a disposition against involvement. If this ambiguity was the source of frustration, they also realized its positive role in discouraging premature action that could have resulted in a treason of the spirit.

Their confusion was understandable: the political landscape was in complete disarray. The Peronist coalition was splitting apart, and the parties of the ideological Left had united with those of the Right in opposition to the government in power. The field of political groupings was fluid and contradictory, with old alliances disintegrating and new ones springing up. The traditional parties—the Radicals and the Communists, for example—threatened new divisions within their ranks. The political orbit of the country was in crisis. The *Contorno* writers realized that this instability was the outward sign of a situation in the throes of a radical realignment, where old labels and names no longer corresponded faithfully to the interests and values previously represented. All of this bred confusion, but they were of the belief that careful action on their part could serve to guide the country into a new period of equilibrium. Their first generational task, then, was to study the national reality and comprehend its confused contours. This task had to come before any possible political action. But they also realized that their own program for national transformation could only be formulated as a response to the inadequacies of the programs set forth by the existing social and political groupings. Either way, their immediate need was the same: they realized that successful political action in the future had to be preceded by a thorough study of the ideological terrain.

It was particularly frustrating, but at the same time exhilarating, to realize that as individuals and as a group their values and expectations did not coincide with those of any existing group. They rejected out of hand the traditional, status-quo orientation of the proponents of aristocratic nationalism,[15] but they came together on many substantive issues defended by the progressive nationalists.[16] While they concurred with several issues normally associated with Marxism, there were, nevertheless, serious and substantial issues which alienated them from the parties of the organized Left.[17] While they shared with the liberal intellectuals common experiences related to class origin, professional development and cultural orientation, there were still major points of contention.[18] In short, the *Contorno* writers realized their own separateness; they experienced alienation from the established ideological currents and political configurations that their situation presented to them. They rejected the diagnosis that it was they who were out of step with their reality. Instead, they were convinced that the nation's cultural and political landscape no longer adequately represented the real needs—social, economic, political, psychological, technological—of its people. A major contribution (the documentation of this falls outside of the scope of this study)[19] was the *Contorno* writers' articulation of the lack of synchronization between the prevailing currents of social discourse and their society's active forces. They recognized that their own confusion, which resulted from this inadequate social articulation, was shared by a great many other youths throughout their country. With humility, they admitted that in the absence of sure solutions their principal qualification for generational leadership was this disposition for involvement, which would be tempered by a "fidelidad al espíritu." Through determined analysis and study, they would attempt to define, both in theory and in action, a new and appropriate position within the social and ideological whole.[20]

They realized the inadequacy of the existing schemes for understanding the social and political forces around them: the Left versus the Right, progressives versus conservatives, liberals versus fascists, nationalism versus internationalism, religious intolerance versus anticlericalism. None of these tired oppositions could not be applied in clear and uncertain terms for describing the most relevant issues affecting the nation. Nor did these worn oppositions faithfully serve for situating a particular group or individual within the ideological whole.[21] They painfully realized that not only had the social landscape become definitively altered after nearly a decade of Peronist transformations, but that the ideological construction of that reality which they inherited from previous generations had completely collapsed.

This was not nearly so acute a problem for other nation groups, whose members had experienced relatively few problems in defining their allegiances on the basis of class and individual interests. At one extreme of the ideological equation, the agro-oligarchy and the country's liberal cultural elite had no difficulty in arriving at the conclusion that Peronism was in almost every respect evil and that it represented the disturbing fall of a society from prosperity and decency to perennial crisis, stagnation, and moral degradation. At the other extreme, the workers overwhelmingly viewed Peronism as an opportunity for social and economic ascension; it was their compensation for decades, if not centuries, of exploitation and condescension at the hands of society's power brokers. For the upper and lower classes, then, Peronism offered relatively few dilemmas with regard to allegiances: one was either for or against. With the middle class, however, the situation was different. Adolfo Prieto explained:

> Sólo la clase media vivió el peronismo con caracter conflictual, y las fisuras internas, las encontradas derivaciones del choque de intereses económicos y de clarificaciones sociales, la sorda violencia con que se manejaron los símbolos de acusación y de defensa, sólo tiene paragón en la historia de la sociedad argentina con la experiencia del rosismo.[22]

The middle class, which had neither gained nor lost in status or economic position throughout the Peronist decade, was trapped between the two social extremes and was effectively marginalized from the exercise of power by Perón's corporate state. It was the members of the middle class who felt most keenly the contradictions of Peronism on a personal level, because they had been kept waiting on the sidelines of events and had been unable to fulfill what many had projected as their historical mission of guiding the country toward growth, wealth, and stability.[23]

The ambiguities of the middle class became even more emphasized in the consciousness of the intellectuals, especially those who aspired to effective social and political action. Intellectuals dealt with ideas. Day in and day out, their tasks of formulating explanations and then casting them into writing demanded a firm understanding of their situation. Given the reigning confusion with regard to ideological labels, and given the fluid status of social and political alliances, socially oriented intellectuals such as the *Contorno* writers understandably expressed frustration in the face of the society's uncertainties and contradictions and in the light of their inability to formulate coherent explanations for the social crisis. They were agonizingly aware that the degree of such difficulties for them was hardly experienced by the other middle-class youths, who had chosen technical or mechanical livelihoods or jobs in state or company bureaucracies. Nor did those new confusions with regard to the ideological landscape of their culture offer undue problems for the writers of the older generations whose self-assumed task was the creation of esoteric labyrinths and extraworldly fantasies. Their intellectual task as critics of culture consequently had to begin with a clear understanding of their own relationship as intellectuals to the social and political process.

Contorno's Three Stages

Contorno therefore came into being as a personal and group response to questions that were overwhelmingly social and political in nature. This was the essential contradiction affecting the majority of the journal's participants: Whereas their formal university preparation and writing orientations were primarily in the fields of literature, philosophy, and culture, in general with each succeeding issue they focused their attention more and more on social and political questions. This accounts for the three more or less distinct periods of their journal's publishing activity.

The first stage is characterized by the analysis in the pages of their journal of the country's cultural legacy, especially that which was inherited from the writers of the generation immediately preceding them. Thus, one can find in *Contorno*'s early issues some of the most penetrating criticism written from a social or political perspective that exists anywhere on the work of Arlt, Lugones, Mallea, Borges, and other "consecrated" figures of the country's cultural tradition.[24] This "committed" critical enterprise was closely associated with a second task, that of defining or situating themselves—their values, political orientations, and objectives—with relation to the larger society. Criticism and self-definition went hand-in-hand, since they believed that their study of the country's literature and intellectual tradition was an effective means for developing a criterion for their own involvement in society. As such, they saw the necessity of venturing beyond a narrowly defined conception of fiction or literature by offering a type of criticism that attempted a marriage of artistic and political, aesthetic and ethical considerations. Similarly, they sought to integrate their own, admittedly subjective, perspectives with considerations originating in historical, psychological, sociological, and political disciplines. Writing, for them, was a form of social action, because it inevitably influenced the perceptions and motivations of the public.

In the early issues of *Contorno*, what stands out is the young writers' need to "ejercer la negativa" against the cultural tradition they inherited from the older generations of intellectuals in their country.[25] In a series of articles published in *Marcha,* and later collected in book form, Uruguayan critic Emir Rodríguez Monegal bestowed upon them the name "parricides" on account of this critical position regarding their country's writing establishment. He called attention to the young writers' "actitud de crítica de rechazo, o de aceptación condicionada" that resulted from their personal experiences with Peronism.[26] Inherent in their criticism of the older generations of intellectuals was their own system of values, emphasizing literature's relevance to social and political issues, and the writer's necessary involvement in the urgent questions of his time.

From their journal's first issue, it was evident that the *Contorno* writers followed closely the ideas and assimilated the spirit of literary *engagement,* as popularized by the leading French intellectuals of the time, in particular, Jean-Paul Sartre, Maurice Merleau-Ponty, and Albert Camus. The very name of their journal indicates that Sartre's ethical message to the writer had been enthusiastically received: Sartre's *situation* was their *contorno,* and to talk of writing was to talk of committing oneself to one's historical circumstances. "Nuestra literatura tendrá algún sentido cuando sea una literatura de agitación," wrote David Viñas, reflecting Sartre's dual concerns of cultural relevancy and historical or political efficacy.[27] The ideas of engagement offered an attractive solution for a principal concern of the young *Contorno* writers: how the intellectual, through his writing and moral example, could best influence and hopefully guide society's active forces in the creation of a more just order.

Sartre's example was particularly instructive for the young writers in Argentina throughout the decade of the 1950s. In terms of temperament, all-the youthful militants plus their older French mentor—were writers by calling who felt the need to involve themselves in the social and political issues of their time. In terms of sociopolitical background, all were intellectuals of middle-class extraction who realized that the most important chapters of their respective national histories were being written by the groups of organized workers. Their own mission, the young writers realized, was the creation of bridges of communication between middle- and working-class experiences, such as those Sartre and his group had attempted to bring into existence in post-war France.

Also of interest to the *Contorno* writers were Sartre's attempts to forge new channels of communication in philosophical circles. They enthusiastically read and absorbed the fundamental thrusts of the French existentialist school, which rejected the rigid materialism of Stalinist fundamentalism in favor of an eclectic combination of Freudian, phenomenological, and Hegelianized Marxist categories. Like the French existentialists, the *Contorno* militants were repulsed by the dogmatically rendered principles espoused by the bureaucratized Marxists of their respective cultures. They therefore willingly accepted existentialism's new flexibility in social, historical, and philosophical thought, although rarely, if ever, did their writings reveal them as committed ideological theorists.

The fall of Perón in 1955 initiated the second moment in the *Contorno* writers' ideological and critical trajectory which would end two years later with the election of Frondizi to the presidency of the country. During this period the *Contorno* writers' concern with political issues took precedence over the previous emphasis on literary questions, and they utilized their journal for analyzing the possibilities for overcoming the political crisis that had descended upon the country. The first six issues of *Contorno*, which included the double issue of September 1955, had largely treated literary questions from the social, or committed, perspective. Now, beginning with the double issue of 1956, these writers concerned themselves primarily with questions of a politico-cultural nature. They dealt with issues such as what type of leadership a humanistic intelligentsia could offer the working class and through what means they could bring about an electoral alliance between intellectuals of university extraction and the organized workers. Similarly, they published two issues of *Contorno cuadernos*, in 1957 and 1958, that treated social and political issues relevant to the approaching national election. In addition, several of the *Contorno* writers became directly involved in organizing activity among students' and workers' groups. They applied their intellectual theories to social reality in their attempt to develop a political, as well as a cultural, praxis. They struggled to define for themselves an acceptable social role that united intellectual theorization and political activism.

The third stage of *Contorno* activity was signaled by Frondizi's election to the presidency and the young writers' subsequent disillusionment with the national political process, as it then existed, for achieving significant progressive reforms. In this last period, that ended with the journal's demise after the combined number 9/10 issue in 1959, their journal placed overwhelming emphasis on issues relevant to the politics and political economy of the country. Previous concern with literary and cultural matters was left aside, and the social-scientific orientation now predominated.

Contorno had now completed its trajectory; it had begun as a literary and cultural journal, and now ended as a sociopolitical and economic organ of expression. This dramatic change in emphasis undoubtedly reflected the writers' path of growing awareness that cultural activism could do little, by itself, to bring into existence the necessary conditions for progressive social and political action.

2
Engagement and the Responsibility of the Intellectual in Society

THE INITIAL WORDS OF ISMAEL VIÑAS'S ESSAY THAT HEADED *CONTORNO*'S first issue defined the collective state of mind of the journal's principle participants at the time: "Rebeldía, rechazo, desconcierto." Rebelliousness, rejection, uncertainty—with regard to the political situation of their country, with regard to the dramatic social and economic transformations that had occurred in their society in the last few decades, with regard to the literature that their *maestros* held in front of them as worthy models of imitation, and lastly, with regard to their own relationship to these changes and modes of social participation. However, those three words must be read in conjunction with the concluding sentence of Viñas's initial paragraph: "El mundo, este mundo inmediato, nuestro país, nuestra ciudad, nos aprietan como algo de que somos responsables." This sentence announces that their many confusions, as they launched themselves into public life, would be the motor for further involvement and not an invitation into escapisms. They felt responsible—for the multiple crises affecting their society as well as for their own alienation. It was the sign of their generation that the two areas became condensed into one single struggle. Their own realization as individuals was integrally related to their country's emergence from the present impasse.

The *Contorno* group's lexicon of rebellion and responsibility quickly suggested in the minds of followers and detractors alike an association between the *Contorno* trajectory and the engagement experience of the French intellectual Left. The writings of Albert Camus, Jean-Paul Sartre, Maurice Merleau-Ponty, and Simone de Beauvoir, perhaps the foremost proponents of engagement in postwar France, were best-sellers throughout Europe and even, in Spanish translation, on the streets of Buenos Aires. The *Contorno* youths, as well as thousands of young writers and intellectuals across Europe and the Americas, were attracted to these writings because they communicated the common experience of disillusionment with a world order gravitating toward chaos. They enthusiastically embraced the exhortation of those writers to become involved in their society's affairs and thereby struggle to salvage what was possible, and then to rebuild it according to more humanistic and solid principles.

The *Contorno* writers, like other members of the young generation of writers throughout Latin America, were especially drawn to the deliberations of Jean-Paul Sartre, because it was he who articulated most clearly the urgent concerns of their age. They were familiar with Sartre's philosophical quest to establish a coherent body of thought that provided a conceptual understanding of both social and personal experience. From their readings of *Nausea* and *Being and Nothingness,* they became aware of Sartre's powerful attacks on bourgeois mentality and his philosophy of negation. In the articles of *Les Temps Modernes,* which began publication in 1945, they read further about Sartre's struggles on behalf of freedom and dignity for all people. Similarly, they responded favorably to his attempts at establishing a conceptual and political meeting ground that would justify a multi-party alliance uniting intellectuals and workers.

With regard to philosophical issues, they learned of his dual loves, one for the "Subject," as defined by Descartes, and the other for the "Collective," which received its sharpest affirmation in the writings of Marx. They and other youthful intellectuals throughout the West eagerly followed Sartre's progress in defining the common ground linking one's pursuit of individual or subjective freedom with the equally important responsibility of the concerned citizen for his society. What would become of his attempt to seek compatible theoretical ground between the phenomenological thought of Husserl and Scheler and the sociological inquiries of Marx, Weber, and Lukács? Sartre also attempted to bridge the liberal and Marxist traditions by combining the analytical method of defining, classifying, and categorizing individuals, with the dialectical method whereby man revealed himself mutually as shaped by and giving shape to the milieu in which he lived.

There were instances when the *Contorno* writers borrowed the conceptual baggage of their French mentors directly. More often than not, however—as I. Viñas explains—their engagement orientation grew up as a logical response to the personal and national needs that they themselves experienced:

> Como siempre, tal hecho obedeció a diversas causas, naturales unas, artificiales otras, dada nuestra particular situación dentro de la órbita de la civilización europea, hecha tanto de participación y de interrelación como de dependencia. Hubo así imitación pura y simple, por una parte. Por la otra, participación en un proceso de revisión, desintegración y creación de valores, característico del

medio siglo último en todo el ámbito de la cultura blanca. Y, final-
mente, causas internas.[1]

The *Contorno* writers' situation highly resembled that of the French
intellectuals, a fact which explains in part how the ideas and orientations
of the latter lent themselves so readily to Argentina in the waning years
of Peronism. A first similarity was the social crisis experienced by both
groups. For the French in the aftermath of World War II, there were the
psychological scars resulting from Nazi German's brutal Occupation.
Although hardly comparable, most *Contorno* participants recognized the
Peronist government's legacy of trauma and fear, especially as experienced by the upper and middle classes (from 1953 and on most of the
population, in addition, experienced the fear of impending conflict and
the risk of overt violence). In their respective situations, the French
intellectuals as well as the young *Contorno* writers saw before them the
dead weight of the existing social and political institutions that had failed
to change with the times or whose leadership had become discredited
on account of corruption or ineffectiveness. On a more optimistic side,
young Argentine intellectuals, similar to their French mentors, viewed
the present as pregnant with untried possibilities: it was a moment of
change that pointed toward a new and hopefully more positive alignment of social and political forces.

On the subjective level, there were also notable points of comparison.
Sartre, Camus, Merleau-Ponty, and de Beauvoir, like the *Contorno* writers, were all intellectuals and writers of petit-bourgeois extraction. All
were strongly repulsed by the influential cultural elites of their respective countries (for Sartre, it was the bourgeoisie; for the *Contorno* writers,
it was the group of liberal writers associated with *Sur*). All felt a vague
attraction to the popular classes, which they would attempt to transform
into involvement on the latters' behalf. All possessed a common disposition that oriented them toward a life of social activity and involvement.
All shared the need of feeling themselves essential to the collectivity. In
their own way, they were all theoreticians who attempted to channel
ideas into action; they all sought ways to utilize their intellectual talents
as a means of transforming their respective societies.

With regard to ideological orientation, the two groups were also very
similar. Both the French existentialists and the young *Contorno* intellectuals, since their early years, had been influenced by the revolutionary
promise of Marxism. For Sartre, this transferred directly into his roman-
tic advocacy of a workers' revolution during the early 1950s, that went
hand in hand with his strident opposition to capitalism. The *Contorno*
writers, although embracing Marxist principles throughout the life of

their journal, never went as far as Sartre. Perhaps because they recognized the underdeveloped class consciousness of Argentina's working class, their most radical advocacy during the 1950s was for an intellectual-led worker electoral force that, through democratic and constitutional means, would bring about the desired transformation of the nation's social and economic structures.

Although the French intellectuals and the writers of *Contorno* closely followed Marxist principles as a guide for social criticism as well as praxis, neither group openly and wholeheartedly endorsed the political parties of the Left or the latter's Marxist dogmas. On the contrary, both groups, throughout their respective periods of intense activity, persistently attacked the fossilized theories and outlooks of traditional Marxism and attempted through their own intellectual labors to infuse the latter with a newly humanized version of mankind dialectically interacting with the material forces of history. This issue is discussed in greater detail below.

The *Contorno* writers were wholly aware of these similarities between their own situation and that of the postwar French intellectuals of the Left. As a result, they followed closely such developments as Albert Camus's progressive distancing from Sartre and his erstwhile colleagues of *Les Temps Modernes* and, while doing so, attempted to glean from those developments a guide for their own activity. Although they could only admire the high principles that motivated Camus's moral exhortations and placed him above the social and political fray, they cooled to the comparison they saw between the author of *The Rebel* and the Olympian liberal writers of their own country. Like Sartre, Jeanson, and other French militants, they criticized Camus's immoderate faith in reason and his fall into a dark "absurdism," as exemplified in *The Myth of Sisyphus* and *The Rebel*.[2] They followed the lead of Sartre and his closest associates in contrasting Camus's view that absurdity typified human behavior *per se* to Sartre's, where absurdity was primarily characteristic of things in themselves when they invaded man's consciousness and usurped his initiative or will to determine his own existence. They also became disheartened with Camus's growing pessimism concerning the possibilities for the social activist to achieve lasting and significant changes in his society. Camus believed that injustices could only be diminished "arithmetically," since "the injustices and suffering of the world will remain and, no matter how limited they are, they will not cease to be an outrage."[3] Thus, he promoted "revolt" rather than "revolution." The *Contorno* writers were aware that similar sentiments of moral outrage had led several liberal writers of Argentina's older generations only to resignation in front of their respective situations. Camus, like those Argentine writers, seemingly placed a higher priority on his own moral purity and would not risk compromising dearly held values in the vicissitudes of social and political action. In effect, this attitude discredited the goals of social revolution in favor of a sterile interchange of pure ideas.

Spiritually, the *Contorno* writers were therefore more akin to Sartre in their ambitions for social and political activism and in their dramatic search for confrontation. They therefore followed with passionate interest Sartre's successive attempts to bring into existence a coalition of leftist political forces and then his stormy love-hate relationship with the French Communist party. Politics, for Sartre, as well as for themselves, was the art of the possible: one constantly had to make choices among sometimes unlikely or undesirable alternatives. A commitment to one's situation meant that the promotion of a higher social or political vision often meant the tolerance of one's own "dirty hands" in the short run.[4] Sartre had chosen to ally himself with the Communist party, in spite of his loathing for their pretentious claim to theoretical truth and their inflexible—and therefore anti-Marxist—methodologies of inquiry. Even though the iron discipline of the Party and its vertical authoritarianism in opinion and decision making was anathema to Sartre's own critical spirit, he had, nevertheless, come to realize that it offered to the workers their best hope of political and social leadership. For the *Contorno* writers, their equally unpleasant alliance would soon be with the nationalist and leftist holdovers of the Peronist coalition who would join together in electing Frondizi to the Presidency in 1958.

Another orientation that the *Contorno* writers shared with Sartre was the instinctive—and later intellectual—dissatisfaction with both the ideological Right and the Left, that inevitably forced them into the role of precursors. Sartre's early disgust with the French bourgeoisie can be compared to the *Contorno* writers' dissatisfaction with their country's agro-bourgoisie, on the one hand, and the conservative liberal writers on the other. In spite of the dramatic differences between postwar France and Peronist Argentina, there were still points of comparison. Sartre and the *Contorno* writers came together in the appraisal that laissez-faire economic practices largely accounted for the predominance of the elites in their respective countries. For both, this politico-economic fact became the basis for their cultural critique. Sartre's bête noire was abstract, analytical bourgeois humanism that rationalized social inequalities and "justified" the mistreatment of the Jew and of the colonized native. The *Contorno* writers, in their turn, argued that liberalism's excessive emphasis on individualism was integrally related to the solipcistic, pessimistic discourse of Argentina's older writers. These and other related orientations, the *Contorno* writers argued, served to either cloud or evade a comprehensive understanding of social and individual realities. They argued, like Sartre, that the culture of liberalism functioned on behalf of the economic and social elites whose interest was to preserve the status quo.

Intellectual "Responsibility"

The *Contorno* writers' respect for Sartre as a guide in attitudinal and theoretical matters also carried over to his role as philosopher of existentialism. Their writings reveal that they passionately embraced his principal ideas on engagement, even though at times they failed to capture entirely the spirit of his message. Sartre's influence is clearly seen in their rhetorical affirmation of their social guilt, out of which their sense of "responsibility" was derived. Sartre's treatment of this issue in his early writings is not entirely unambiguous. In the 1944 work, *Anti-Semite and Jew,* he established responsibility as a collective situation: "To be a Jew is . . . to be abandoned to the situation of being a Jew and at the same time . . . to be responsible in and through one's own person for the destiny and the very nature of the Jewish people."[5] Who was a Jew? "The Jew is one whom other men consider a Jew."[6] Sartre argued that members of an exploited or persecuted group had the responsibility of defending that group. The argument took an "existentialist-moralist" turn when he then argued that anyone should consider himself "responsible" if the glance of the other revealed that he was taken to be a member of such a group.

The other side of the issue was the responsibility that one should feel for having perpetrated such oppression. Sartre argued that all Germans, whether or not they knew of their government's actions with relation to the Holocaust, should hold themselves responsible for the deaths of untold thousands of Jews. His rather extreme logic was that the fact that they were citizens of that state made them either direct or indirect accomplices of those atrocities.

Sartre's arguments about responsibility took a Marxist-determinist direction a few years later, when, at the height of the Algerian crisis, he published a series of essays in *Les Temps Modernes* and in *L'Express,* in addition to the prefaces to two books (the more famous was for Fanon's *The Wretched of the Earth*), had the object of moving his country's stolid bourgeoisie to admit its complicity in the dirty work of colonial warfare. He proposed that all settlers in Algeria, whether good or bad or whether innocent beneficiaries or victims of that system, were guilty because they were participants in an exploitative system. Furthermore, all Frenchmen were equally liable on account of the colonial policy that their government had pursued for generations in their name. In brief, Sartre's early writings conceptually combine several types of "guilt" (a rational reconstruction of these positions would occur later in his work) in a rhetorical and at times demagogic fashion, with the goal of sensitizing the middle-class reader to the sufferings of society's persecuted minorities and exploited lower classes.[7]

What, then, was the social or political objective that triggered the "responsibility" felt in Argentina by the *Contorno* writers in their first years of public writing activity? Ismael Viñas, writing in the initial issue of *Contorno*, was decidedly vague about the issue: "El mundo, este mundo immediato, nuestro país, nuestra ciudad, nos aprietan como algo de que somos responsables." Prieto, in his 1954 book-length study on Borges, demonstrated a similar lack of specificity: it was the imminent crisis in society that triggered their concern and their involvement: they were "hombres insertos en un devenir histórico, que saben que tienen que hacer algo y aceptan el trabajo como una carga ineludible."[8]

Further on in his essay, I. Viñas provided a second and equally imprecise reason for their group responsibility: the lack of relevance in the writing of the established liberal writers of the country. He wrote: "Sentimos que el espíritu es una responsabilidad. . . . Sentimos que de algún modo somos responsables por lo que los representantes del intelecto, por lo que los hombres del espíritu no han hecho. Aun más por sus omisiones que por sus actos nos sentimos culpables." His observation about the lack of sociological or historical relevance in the writing production of the older, liberal writers was well taken, and one must respect the ambition of the *Contorno* writers to fill that gap in their country's cultural expression. However, the credibility of the disinterested reader is stretched by the argument that this omission was *the cause* for the *Contorno* writers' social guilt. The elder writers of the country could not be blamed for the multiple problems of their country simply because they had refused to concern themselves with such issues. In short order, David Viñas would build upon the exaggerated and disproportionate guilt singled out by his brother and by Prieto and convert it into an ontology of the concerned intellectual: he would urge his fellows to always "escribir como culpables."[9]

In the European context, Sartrian "guilt," no matter how one chose to define it, had the impact of sensitizing the French bourgeois or petit-bourgeois reader to the deplorable plight of society's victims: guilt for Sartre was the essential state of mind that grew into concern and action on behalf of those who were less fortunate than oneself. In contrast, the guilt articulated by the *Contorno* writers did not—at least not yet—enter into a conscious mental play that would result in a greater sensitization and sympathy for Argentina's social underdogs. Instead, it ambiguously reflected the degree of discomfort that the young writers themselves felt as petit-bourgeois intellectuals in a system that had relegated them to a marginal position. This type of self-pity could hardly be compared to the altruistic "guilt" of Sartre. It is as if they treated the issue of "guilt" as a deliberate afterthought. Their concern as involved or potentially involved citizens was real; their initial ambiguity with regard to social and political values, and their alienation from the existing social groups, were also real. But Sartrian guilt and responsibility were concerns that were still foreign to their personal situations. Those imperfectly understood terms were part of the new party jargon that in one way or another had to be incorporated into their evolving description of the reality in which they lived. It was an instance of a superficial "copying" of the lexicon of French engagement.

Rather than condemn the *Contorno* writers for having ignored the essence of Sartrian "guilt" and "responsibility," one must attempt to understand this shortcoming in the light of their particular relationship to the country's exploited groups. In truth, their situation in this regard contrasted decidedly with that of Sartre. In France, the advanced degree of proletarian class conscience, worker organization, and education accounted for an essentially similar cultural outlook that Sartre shared with working class leaders there. At the same time, the collaboration of workers and vanguard intellectuals of the Left in France had a wartime legacy upon which to build of shared suffering and united resistance to fascism; intra-class collaboration was therefore a viable option there. In comparison, Argentina's workers had a relatively short history of organization, and there was no prior instance when intellectuals had been called upon to join ranks with the workers on behalf of the nation as a whole. Therefore, vast cultural and historical differences still separated Argentine workers from intellectuals with regard to education, political orientation, and class values. An overt worker orientation to the intelligentsia's social goals had little if any precedent in the country's history.

One therefore understands in part the difficulty of the *Contorno* writers, and therefore their resulting confusion, in living up to the spirit of Sartrian guilt and responsibility. Attracted as they were to the Sartrian spirit of sacrifice, they were hardly aware of its political implications. In any event, their superficial imitation of engagement terminology does not call into question their moral integrity. Indeed, they later came to realize the theoretical shortcomings in their social and political vision, and moved to correct them accordingly. Sartre's message of responsibility, although misunderstood in the first moment, later became their faithful guile in the painful process of re-education. They accepted their French mentor's example in continually reassessing their progress toward self-imposed moral, social, and political standards. So, although they initially misunderstood the Sartrian message of guilt and responsibility, they nevertheless demonstrated something more important: like

Sartre, their vital orientation complemented an intellectual conviction that their realization as individuals was inextricably linked to the destiny of their society.

The Re-evaluation of Traditional Marxism

The *Contorno* writers' dissatisfaction with their country's liberal heritage was accompanied by their distrust of traditional or "vulgar" Marxism. Liberalism's principal shortcoming was that the emphasis on individual freedom led its followers to totally ignore the concerns of the collectivity; Marxism's liability was that its adherents' exclusive concern for the salvation of society—in their study of material forces and relations of production—blinded them to the essential role of the individual in history and the subjective needs of even the most socially involved activists. The *Contorno* writers recognized that Sartre's philosophical dilemma was their own: while accepting liberalism's essential advocation of personal liberty, in addition to Marxism's quest to save collectivity, they rejected out of hand the mainstream practice of both. Was a middle road between liberalism and Marxism philosophically and politically possible?

Sartre never believed there to be an irresolvable contradiction between liberalism, with its existentialist focus, and Marxism, with its goal of social liberation.[10] Instead, the two complemented each other. He was attracted to a Hegelian or idealistically flavored Marxism that, while emphasizing the formative role of material forces in society's historical development, never fell into a crass determinism which relegated man to the role of a passive recipient of culture. Herein lay his emphasis on existentialism, which instructed that man's foremost attribute was freedom to act and therefore to determine the course of his own existence. As a consequence, Sartre depicted human history as the dialectical interplay between socioeconomic and cultural forces, on the one hand, and the individual's freedom, on the other. Historical materialism was his preferred mode of inquiry for understanding the former; existentialism was the ideology that Sartre chose for understanding the latter.

It is inconsequential whether the *Contorno* writers considered themselves Marxists at this early stage in their intellectual trajectories—or whether or not their critics considered them to be so—but it is unmistakable that their subsequent writings would later serve to broaden substantially the, until then, narrow limits of Marxist social and cultural inquiry on their continent. In this regard, their thinking did not differ essentially from that of their mentor Sartre. However, it would be a mistake to believe that they were merely Latin American imitators of European or Sartrian thought, for that judgment does not do justice to their personal and group response to the ideological and cultural currents then dominant in Argentina. Better understood, the *Contorno* writers traveled along the same theoretical path as that traveled by Sartre. They, like Sartre in Europe, were protagonists on their own continent in the emergence of a new Hegelian or "Neo-Marxist" critical tradition.

The focal point of the *Contorno* writers' critique of traditional or "vulgar" Marxism was its adherents' inflexible application of materialist and dialectical categories. They believed that the self-proclaimed followers of Marx had buried the human subject under the mechanistic interpretation of social and economic determinism. Theirs was the depiction of a crude play of materialistic forces that relegated the human to the passive role of a social receptacle which was completely devoid of an affective or interior dimension.[11] The theorists of the organized Left, themselves of submissive spirit and with minds conditioned to accept party dogmas, could not comprehend that material causes were always accompanied by subjective motives which obeyed factors related to the individual's temperament, passions, and cultural orientations.[12]

Undoubtedly there was a certain amount of self-interest invested in the *Contorno* writers' attacks, for they, as middle-class intellectuals, nurtured the ambition of achieving through political action and intellectual labor a significant transformation in Argentina's social and political landscape. Their idealism, coupled with their desire to guide those changes, therefore contradicted the deterministic tenets of vulgar Marxism. In their initial years of writing activity, they fell into the error of overemphasizing the role of the individual in effecting social change. Nevertheless, their early critiques must still be read as perhaps the earliest manifestation in Latin America of this dramatic renovation of Marxist theory that Sartre had initiated some years earlier in Europe: the humanization of Marxism according to the comprehensive understanding of man dialectically inserted within a social reality and acting in accordance with a defined situation.

In their critiques of Argentina's socio-economic and cultural contexts, the *Contorno* writers anticipated another dramatic re-evaluation of traditional Marxist categories: what was then taken by Marxist thinkers to be the determination of superstructures on the basis of the existing base (economic) structures. The *Contorno* thinkers did not have to read in the pages of Sartre, nor would they have to wait for the intelligent deliberations of the Althusserian school, in order to realize that the political structures of their own country very inadequately represented the distribution of productive or economic power, or that the various forms of cultural expression hardly reflected the underlying socioeconomic structures. Indeed, they realized that the confusions they experienced at the beginning of their writing careers were directly related to the *lack of correspondence* between these various levels. In subsequent years, their analysis of this phenomenon would break ground that even Sartre did not and could not adequately enter: the effects of economic dependency upon the social, political, and cultural life of their country. In this theoretical labor, the future works of Juan José Sebreli, David Viñas, Ismael Viñas, León Rozitchner, Tulio Halperín Donghi, Noé Jitrik, and Adolfo Prieto would occupy a foremost position in the cultural heritage of their continent.[13]

The *Contorno* writers avidly read in the publications of Sartre about how existentialism's "marriage" to Marxism pointed to a conceptualization of the revolutionary role of the intellectual within the social totality. In Sartre's "Materialism and Revolution" (1946) they harkened to the interpretation of "revolution" as a process of *going beyond* the present situation, a process that utilized the information gained from one's familiarity with lived reality in order to transform society's material structures. Sartre posed the idea that the new philosopher embodied "the thinking of the oppressed insofar as they rebel together against oppression."[14] As discussed above, before 1955, the *Contorno* writers had not as yet made their pact with the socially oppressed of the country. Nevertheless, they still warmed to the idea that by uniting both thought and action they would be able to decisively influence the composition of political forces in the country and, as a result, set into motion profound economic and social changes. It is significant that by 1959, in their last issue of *Contorno*, the young writers would sharply criticize the overly idealistic thrust of this position, just as Sartre would do in *The Words* (1964) with regard to his early existentialist advocations.

Engagement in Theory

The concept of engagement—that theoretical center of the *Contorno* writers' enterprise—owed its popularization to Sartre's *Literature and Existentialism*.[15] This work, originally published in 1947, signaled the emergence of a social ontology in Sartre's thought that was structured upon the awareness of the social issues he had previously discussed in *Being and Nothingness* (1943). The work therefore provided a conceptual link between the existential anthropology that had characterized his earlier period and his brand of Marxism that would predominate later. Briefly stated, engagement projected that the middle-class intellectual resolved the conflict between his need for individual fulfillment and his responsibility to the collectivity by totally committing himself to a socially oriented writing praxis. It is not necessary to outline the philosophical roots of Sartre's engagement, since this issue is treated extensively by the existing criticism.[16] My intention here is merely to highlight some of the major aspects of that philosophical position that particularly affected the outlook of the young Argentine writers.

Even though the *Contorno* writers never demonstrated an intense involvement in the complex philosophical issues underlying Sartre's activist intellectual vocation, they nevertheless read carefully and discussed his successive works. It is evident that they attempted to integrate many of his ideas into their individual and collective writing agendas. Although the *Contorno* writers did not elaborate on the philosophical underpinnings for their own role in the post-Peronist political scene, their projected mission as facilitators for a political coalition uniting the different middle-class groups of the Left and the working class bears a resemblance to the political mission defined by Sartre for himself and other concerned writers of the French Left.

The Sartrian conception of *situation* elucidates especially well the convergence of existentialist and Marxist tendencies that attracted the young Argentine writers. A brief definition for *situation*, given by Sartre himself, is "the common product of the contingency of the in-itself and of freedom . . ."[17] The "in-itself," or *en-soi*, pertains to that aspect of being that is innate or material and, as such, is formed or determined for the most part by the forces of production. Man modifies a given reality, including his own, through *praxis*, which can be defined as the application of a deliberated plan of action to a given object or material reality. Existentialist theorists highlighted the role of activity, whereby man manifests his freedom in "personalizing" the world. Thus, "there is freedom only in a *situation* and there is a situation only through freedom," affirmed Sartre.[18] He argued that man best familiarizes himself with the factual nature of his situation through a Marxist analysis of the social and economic forces surrounding him. Through his exercise of reason, he formulates the "objective possibilities" for action; then, through action, he realizes his *pro-ject*, which confers meaning on *en-soi*, that is, on the factual nature of his situation.

The key to this operation is language. Sartre followed a distinguished philosophical tradition in affirming that the basic instrument for man's appropriation of the world is language, itself a product of man's dialectical encounter with his situation. Man necessarily recurs to language to conceptualize his reality and to formulate his project. In this respect, he depends upon the historical legacy of his society, because it is his society that over the years has formulated that instrument of conceptualization and has instructed the individual in its use. "Freedom is the only possible foundation of the laws of language," wrote Sartre,[19] but it is also true that language can be actualized in the present only through man's exercise of freedom. Man's confrontation with his situation occurs only through his use of language, which is another way of stating that the truth of language is speech. Speech, by actualizing language, conceptualizes experience; it presupposes man and his identity as a collective being.

All men draw upon the verticality of the human experience through time in their appropriation of speech and its application in freedom. However, the intellectual has the social function of extending this trans-individualized function of language in its horizontal dimensions, that is, among the different people and population groups that exist in any given moment. Herein lies the central role of the intellectual: his function is to educate people with regard to those aspects of individual experience that are shared by other members of their group; he therefore helps to break down the barriers of social isolation and promote a shared consciousness of collective identity.

In *Being and Nothingness* Sartre discusses a further importance of the intellectual in constituting the group or in imparting a sense of community. In that work he emphasizes the normal condition of estrangement and lack of interaction between individuals because each, in the process of comprehension, necessarily "objectifies" the people he encounters, and thereby denies their subjective dimension. Through one's glance, and then in a subsequent act of conceptualization, a second being achieves at best an "objective" standing, just as that first person himself becomes reduced to an objective status in the perception of the second. In this situation of mutual ignorance, it is only the perception of a third individual that can create an *us-object* identity between the original two beings: they become *us* objects through the glance and subsequent conceptualization of this third observer.[20] As mutual objects in the experience of the third, the first and the second people suddenly become unified. This third person, whether friend or enemy, God, or the projected consciousness of the first two in intimate relationship with another, encourages reciprocity and a pact of generosity between the two formerly hostile or mutually independent wills.

Although Sartre's detailed discussion of this generosity pact and its implications for society would be found only in his 1960 work, *Critique of Dialectical Reason*, he anticipated many of its themes in *Literature and Existentialism*. In essence, Sartre argued that it is the concerned middle-class intellectual who can best provide this essential "third" perspective that unites the separate members of the working class. Because the intellectual is "different," he is able to perceive and reveal the shared traits of the distinct workers that become the basis for a collective identity. The intellectual therefore confers objective status upon the workers and creates the conceptual configuration of "working class." He synthesizes the multiplicity of performances and activities and highlights the similarities in orientation, while minimizing their differences. The intellectual, then, discovers the human dimension of the workers' world. He is essential for creating the *us-object* feeling which unites the workers in a common historical destiny.

Sartre took personal pride in his identity as petit-bourgeois intellectual because of this function, as he envisioned it, of uniting workers around a common set of objectives and instructing them in their shared identity. In a quasi manifesto marking his entry into national politics in 1948, he affirmed the central role of this type of intellectual activity in creating a common ground between theoreticians of the communist and the noncommunist Left.[21]

"Synthetic" or "Totalizing" Criticism

Sartre, in addition to his characterization of the middle-class intellectual's essential role in achieving working-class harmony and group identity, posited that the intellectual occupied an ideal position for providing an accurate overview of the diverse interests and orientations that constituted a given society. He argued that the worker possessed only a limited capacity for "totalizing" or conceptualizing the "whole" of his intricate interrelationships with the world, and that was due in part to the fact that the worker combined action with thought in applying his labor to a preconceived task. The action-oriented intellectual, however, could go beyond the limitations of the worker because he had access to the written historical legacy of the entire society and could offer an even broader perspective of the plurality of factors that constituted his situation. Furthermore, the intellectual who structured his analysis upon the Hegelian and Marxian notion of the dialectic would be best capable of integrating into a unified vision the complex multiplicity of factors related to a given society. He would take into account the fact that the act of analysis was only a moment within the dialectical movement. One who studies a given reality must constantly reconsider his original hypothesis in relation to the data generated by his analysis. He has to take into account the interrelatedness (in the words of Sartre) of "the inert with the inorganic, negation, contradictions overcome, negation of negation, in short, totalization in action."[22] Sartre's "synthetic" or holistic method for analyzing the other in relation to self, or the text in relation to the writer (Chapter Three discusses in detail the impact of phenomenology upon Sartre's conception of a desirable form of literary criticism), contrasted with the analytical focus that typified the writing of the bourgeois or liberal intelligentsia. Sartre criticized the latter for their implicit denial of social classes and for what at times became a nearly exclusive study of psychological relationships. For example, in the eyes of the liberal writer, only individual workers existed, not a working class. In contrast, totalizing or synthetic (later Sartre would reject these two terms in favor of a third: *dialectical*) thinking went beyond this shortcoming by ascribing to all beings a subjectivity and by demonstrating that proletarians are "united by internal solidarity" that goes far beyond "external bonds of resemblance."[23] In short, the intellectual, who was schooled in the synthetic approach to social reality and who was aware of how the past acted upon the present, could project how the present constituted a program of future possibilities. This last aspect of "totalization" was foremost in both Sartre's and the *Contorno* writers' minds: the engaged intellectual who was immersed in the problems relevant to his situation could theorize with respect to possible activity and could then evaluate his projections with regard to practicality and effectiveness in action. This was the meaning of Sartre's pronouncement about the revolutionary role of the intellectual with regard to social transformation: "revolutionary thinking is a *thinking within a situation*; it is the thinking of the oppressed in so far as they rebel together against oppression."[24]

This Sartrian conception of the revolutionary role of the middle-class intellectual in society evoked a moral ethos, in addition to its prescription of a methodology for formulating theory and guiding praxis. However much Sartre later regretted having published it, *Existentialism as a Humanism* enjoyed wide popularity at the time of its publication in 1947.[25] In this work he offered a concrete model of how the moral person ought to act. Foremost among the points treated is the need for the writer to project the image of moral rectitude in order to inspire public trust. The intellectual must be "obliged at every instance to perform exemplary acts."[26] After all, it is he who instructs the public and guides them in their own behavior. Accordingly, he takes upon himself the altruistic mission of furthering the welfare of others.

The intellectual is the individual who is most aware of his situation and that of others. His function is to provide the moral leadership and the intellectual basis that will result in the increased sense of community experienced by individuals and groups. His own freedom therefore manifests itself only by willing itself as an "indefinite movement through the freedom of others."[27] This pact of freedoms is an essential idea to Sartre's major premise that one person cannot be free unless all men are free. The intellectual is one who recognizes the inherent equality of all beings, regardless of ethnic origin or class differences. Sartre held that this attitude of generosity was the basis for the intellectual's solidarity with society's most exploited groups. Out of this line of reasoning he posited that the intellectual-worker tie served as the model for all possible human relationships.[28]

In *Literature and Existentialism* Sartre further developed this idea of the practical synthesis of self and other in the formation of the group. He proposed that the intellectual best exemplifies through his acts the ideal of collective responsibility. Through his generosity and solidarity with society's exploited groups, the intellectual successfully bridges the gap in his own experience between purely theoretical activity and effective social praxis.

Sartre's conceptualization of human freedom and the revolutionary role of the intellectual in society was intended as a philosophical challenge to Marxist orthodoxy, which, in contrast, had argued the primacy of productive forces in determining social and political change. Whereas traditional Marxists believed in the central role of the party as the instigator of society's transformation, Sartre and his fellow travelers defended the individual as the focus of activity. Whereas the Marxists emphasized the generally determined nature of social, political, and ideological phenomena vis-á-vis economic fact, Sartre's notion of a dialectical structure to society proposed that man both shaped and was shaped by the forces constituting his situation.

Sartre harshly criticized orthodox Marxists for their degrading image of a mankind that only passively responded to the overwhelming power of pre-existing productive forces. He implicitly criticized the largely sociological bent of the recent Marxist critical tradition when he urged an acceptance of the ideas of the young Marx and the ideas implicit in Hegel's conception of the dialectic, which can be read as an attempt to resituate man at the center of history. The existentialist thrust of Sartre's thought emphasized the intentional consciousness of man. The human being, according to this perspective, was entirely capable of formulating social objectives and then bringing them to fruition on the basis of a carefully planned project of action. Sartre's humanized vision of the social dialectic restored man to the center of the historical process.

The role of the intellectual and the writer in this new interpretation of the social dialectic was to encourage all men to accept a positive self-image of themselves as active and intentional beings with control over their respective situations. Merleau-Ponty, second to Sartre as ideological pontiff of this revival of Hegelian Marxism, and whose works were also admired by the young writers in Argentina, promoted to this end the object of the "profundization" of man understood as a project. As a consequence, he reproached the followers of Lenin for having ignored mankind's creative capacities in their conceptualization of a dialectic involving inert things and depersonalized social forces. In line with this human-centered notion of the dialectic, Merleau-Ponty held that human consciousness played a principle role in bringing about social change: "la révolution est le régime du déséquilibre créateur . . . il faut donc toujours une opposition à l'intéreur de la révolution."[29] Rozitchner would echo this view in the pages of *Contorno*, in his call for a moral revolution that would help guide Argentina in the months following the fall of Perón: "hay que formar también al hombre para poder solicitar de él algo más que la rendición, la sumisión incondicional que el peronismo solicitó y obtuvo."[30] Man, according to the existential Marxist point of view, was not an abstract being, but rather human; he was not merely a manipulated mass formed in relation to the conflict of classes, but rather a conscious presence who exercised a certain amount of control over objective forces and social processes. Sartre, Merleau-Ponty, and the *Contorno* thinkers defended an "open" Marxism which emphasized the potentiality of man in constituting his situation on the basis of active and intelligent participation.

Engagement Scrutinized

The attacks launched upon Sartre and Merleau-Ponty (as well as on their Argentine disciples) by the intellectuals of the organized Left are well documented elsewhere, and there is no need to enter into particulars here. Briefly, these attacks centered around four main issues (1) the existential Marxists' abandonment of the traditional dialectic of material or productive forces in favor of one that perceived the power of ideas or human subjectivity in effecting a transformation in the social infrastructure, (2) the existential Marxists' implicit denial of the Party as the revolutionary vanguard in favor of the morally-inspired intellectual, (3) their abandonment of the notion of class struggle in favor of an emphasis on intra-class collaboration, and (4) their substitution of the traditional goal of social or proletarian revolution for an emphasis on moral and ethical improvement. These four points, although outwardly resembling the agenda for a doctrinaire squabble among different factions, nevertheless help to clarify the enormous ideological distance that separated the *Contorno* group from the intellectuals of the traditional Left. Paradoxically, in a rare display of unity, their critics on the Left were joined by spokesmen from organized groups on the political Right in voicing several reservations about the Sartrian or Neo-Marxist program for social and cultural activism. Neither Sartre nor his Argentine disciples could turn a deaf ear to such unanimity in contradicting their deliberations.

Both the Left and the Right attacked Sartre and his fellow engagement advocates for their pretense of belonging to no social class and for the idea that they were admirably qualified to become the impartial judges and even leaders of society's development. The thinkers of the Left believed this type of thinking typical of those intellectuals who refused to recognize that they shared many of the same values and orientations as those held by the bourgeoisie; hence, it was no less than ideological nonsense to assert that intellectuals were the qualified leaders of a possible worker revolution.[31] This form of ideological voluntarism was an indication of the petit-bourgeois orientation that resisted proletarianization and of an intellectual reality that resisted application in practice. The critics of the Left, as well as centrist or establishment critics, also called attention to the pretension of the engaged writers, who believed they knew better than anyone else the optimum directions for society's advancement. Characteristic was Raymond Aron's observation that Sartre and his followers possessed a "Promethian *hybris*" and a "proud will" that hardly qualified them to think on behalf of all mankind.[32]

Today few would take issue with these detractors who criticized the "Neo-Marxists" for their pretense of being superior to the processes of history and of occupying a privileged role as cultural priests of the social revolution. It is of note, however, that in subsequent years Sartre, in addition to several of the *Contorno* writers, would realize the ineffective political consequences of the essentially idealistic orientation that they formerly embraced. Thus, they would come to recognize the validity of much of the orthodox Marxists' arguments against their positions. However, their agreement did not mean the total abandonment of their previous humanistic advocation.

Regardless of the shortcomings of the engagement doctrine—and there were many—it is still important to emphasize its lasting contributions. The defenders of engagement attempted to inject a Hegelianized notion of human subjectivity into a fossilized Marxist dogma that had emphasized almost exclusively the play of deterministic materialist forces. Herein lies the inherent incompatibility exising between Sartre and his *Contorno* followers, and the ideologues of the established parties of the Marxist Left. The existential Marxists believed that they enriched the existing ideological field as a result of their dialectical encounter with their situation. After discounting the excesses of this doctrine, one still recognizes their contribution of fertilizing the revolutionary promise of Marxism with their emphasis on man's freedom within the historical process. If they overvalued the possibilities for man's unlimited action and, as a consequence, the effectiveness of themselves and their writing as agents of social transformation, they nevertheless offered to their respective societies new and constructive options for the future. Héctor P. Agosti's criticism of the *Contorno* writers and other proponents of existential Marxism could also be taken as praise: their interaction resulted in a split of the political Left between what Lefebvre called "philosophical Marxists," who searched for truth and who had become converted into judges of the historical process, and "political Marxists," who had to go beyond or even adulterate the truth in order to be able to act effectively through their praxis.[33] If the activity of the *Contorno* writers had indeed resulted in such a division in the ideologocal and political landscape of the Argentine Left, then perhaps it was for the better. The *Contorno* writers were convinced that a movement of the Left could be effective only if it were guided by honest analysis and an appeal to human freedom.

3
Literary Criticism and Engagement

LITERATURE HAD A PRIMARY ROLE IN THE HUMANIZED SOCIAL REVOLUTION advocated by the proponents of *engagement*. Over and above the intentions or ideological persuasion of the writer, fictional narrative opened up for introspection and study the interior dimension of the human experience. In contrast with the written discourse of a sociological or political orientation, it explored man's subjective dimension and weighed the balance of motivation, values, and initiative with regard to the socio-historical situation. It was the ideal entry into man's historical presence in society—indeed, it captured "the true history of man," that is to say, man's presence as a thinking, conscious agent of change. Even at the hands of political conservatives, fictional literature confirmed the lesson of existentialist theorists that the central focus of history was individuals conscious of their values and ideals who were actively engaged in transforming their respective situations. Camus and Sartre, perhaps the two foremost proponents of post–World War II existentialism, came together in the belief that in narrative literature one found an admirable representation of the human condition in the different moments of man's development. As such, literature was the testimony par excellence of mankind's freedom.

Beyond these vague humanistic affirmations, however, Sartre's opinions about the role of narrative literature as a social force differed substantially from the ideas of Camus. Between about 1945 and 1955, he progressively came to believe that the intellectual, through his writing, could exercise a positive and formative force upon the minds of men and could therefore guide society in its development. The ideas associated with engagement spoke to the role of a "committed" literature, influencing the reader's ideas and hopefully inspiring him to action. As such, literature came to be evaluated on the basis of its effectiveness within the social setting. Even its aesthetic value was to be assessed primarily with regard to the moral message it imparted or its success in creating a sense of solidarity among readers and between the writer and the reading public. Literature, therefore, became relegated by Sartre and other engaged writers and critics to the status of a means in the larger struggle to redeem society or to move mankind onward in its social, political, and moral development.

After 1955 Sartre would largely reverse these opinions. He would then realize the relative uselessness of both art and moral exhortation for moving the individual or society. He would progressively abandon his faith in art as an instrument of social or historical action, although his belief in the humanistic message of art never came into question.[1] These later ideas must be taken into consideration in an overall assessment of the engagement movement. However, our purpose here is to return to Sartre's earlier advocation of the activist role of literature—and by extension, literary criticism—with society and to determine its impact upon his young followers in Argentina.

Throughout this whole period Camus, in contrast to Sartre, continually reaffirmed the artist's vocation as separate from, and in many ways superior to, that of the social activist. Camus never believed that too much could be achieved by transforming literature into an instrument of social militancy. He parted company with the followers of Sartre who would deny the specificity of art in favor of an apocalyptic ideology of social transformation whose basic premises he could not accept. In contrast to Sartre, who was a fervent proponent of revolutionary activity as a means for achieving social justice, Camus was an ontological pessimist in his belief that "Human insurrection, in its exalted and tragic forms, is only, and can only be, a prolonged protest against death, a violent accusation against the universal death penalty."[2] In spite of his profound skepticism about the redeeming qualities of social revolution, Camus never compromised his faith in man's noble and tragic nature, as his writing reveals.

However, the spirit of the time was decidedly on the side of Sartre. French intellectuals, by and large, responded to Sartre's call for them to enter into the social struggle and "commit" themselves, even though the existing political options might not be wholly satisfactory. In a similar manner, the idea of literary activism became highly fashionable. Literature, for the social militants, was widely perceived as an effective means of raising the consciousness of the working class through the instruction of their commonly held values, their situation of class exploitation, and the optimum means for organizing in order to improve their social lot. Many, if not the majority of writers held views that could be considered more "progressive" than those of the middle-of-the-road middle class and came to see literature as a moral force that could be used in instructing other members of their class about the advantages to be gained by supporting the working class in their pursuit of greater participation in all aspects of social life. Previously, literature had served as a defensive arm in the hands of the bourgeoisie for preserving its class hegemony.

Now, however, the theorists of engagement projected a new function as an instrument for promoting the historical ascent of the working class.

The veracity of the engagement theory rested upon three key assumptions: First, the petit-bourgeois writer, through his impartial study of social reality performed on the basis of Marxist categories, would recognize that society's future lay with the organization and promotion of a working class "revolution." Second, the intellectual would realize that his responsibility was to become himself involved in promoting that historical eventuality through his writing and other means at hand. And third, he would assimilate a "totalizing" perspective in both consciousness and writing that would lend greater objectivity to his evaluation of social forces and would also serve to convince the working class that he did indeed favor their interests. Clearly, engaged writing was most accessible for those intellectuals who already were favorably oriented toward the first two of these assumptions, namely, performing social analysis on the basis of class conflict and the assimilation of the Marxist ethos of utilizing one's knowledge for changing the world. Thus, the fundamental test of engaged writing for them lay in the third assumption, that the writer would assimilate a "totalizing" vision which would qualify him as a leader of worker militants.

The previous chapter briefly explained how the "synthetic" perspective of workers' subjective experiences serves to construct a group identity with supposedly "objective" status. This function therefore "totalizes" workers by reconciling their subjective and objective identities. It also "totalizes" society by linking petit-bourgeois writers to the working class. Fundamental to both aspects of this totalizing function is the Sartrian rendition of phenomenology, which came to be the philosophical core of existentialism.

Phenomenology

Sartre's phenomenological ontology was an attempt to develop a general theory of human experience that would orient human consciousness in relation to its potentiality for conceptualizing and acting upon external reality. As such, he attempted to reconcile the thought of both Husserl and Heidegger: in the former, he found a persuasive account of the ontology of pure consciousness; and in the latter, he found a convincing explanation for the role of consciousness in *situation*. Sartre took the two thinkers as complementary in their opposition. While he reproached Husserl for mistaking the method for the goal and for beginning an artificial ontology of the essence of pure consciousness,[3] he also reproached Heidegger for pretending to immediately reach the object in a sort of natural ontology of unreflective existence. Accordingly, Sartre contrasted and balanced the two thinkers in a totalizing perspective, giving due respect to the ambiguity of existence: he combined Husserl's existence of essences with Heidegger's essence of existence in the construction of his essentialist phenomenology. "His object is 'human reality,' man in situation. The method will define man as consciousness, center of intentions, and power of initiative, but only insofar as he is all of these things within his actual situation."[4]

Phenomenology, as a synthesis of the thought of both Husserl and Heidegger (and their philosophical predecessors), offered Sartre an ideal method for observing the world in and around himself and at the same time for highlighting his own emotional and sentimental response to that outside reality. It emphasized the sensory perception and affective experience of a person and thus contrasted with the positivistic study of persons or things considered as objective entities in and for themselves. Sartre viewed phenomenology as a new empiricism on account of its emphasis on the objective world, but one which was dependent upon experience and observation. While discovering new realities beyond the realm of what was strictly verifiable, it avoided idealism's shortcoming of isolating mental constructs from lived experience. It therefore established a middle ground between the radical materialism that characterized vulgar Marxist thought and liberal "spiritualism" that denied the importance of materiality and an entity's place within the world. It also established a middle ground between positivism and transcendentalism through its vision of the world and others from the viewpoint of the subject. As a consequence, phenomenology was an admirable methodological tool for discovering the relationships existing between men and linking men to their social and material surroundings.[5]

Sartre not only established the philosophical groundwork for engaged activity, but he also demonstrated, through his own critical writing, how these theories associated with phenomenology could be incorporated into a meaningful writing praxis. His *Saint Genet: Comedian and Martyr*, published in 1952, was the first work in which phenomenology formed the basis for literary criticism. This work set an important precedent for other writers—among them the young *Contorno* participants. Sartre's innovation in studying the work of Genet was "to trust his own eyes and view the work of art as an object in *his* world rather than himself as a potential object in the writer's world."[6] Although the traditional critical establishment was scandalized, Sartre won adherents for his exercise in new methodological doubt that asserted the subjective and contingent character of certain dimensions of experience.

A phenomenological criticism attracted activist intellectuals who sought in it a means of combatting their own isolation and regaining for themselves a meaningful place in the world. While continuing with their traditional function of analyzing society and culture as presented to them, they could also assert the importance of their own role as intellectuals in society. Sartre had provided a welcome justification for their dual pursuits as critics and individuals; he had provided a convenient and convincing marriage of both aesthetic and social objectives.

Theorists of the Left attacked the phenomenological thrust of engaged writing because it paid scant attention to what they held to be the sacred tenets of the materialistic dialectic and its supposedly revolutionary role in society. However, Sartre and his followers countered with the charge that traditional Marxism had already become irrelevant to the concerns of contemporary men in their quest for individual and social fulfillment; it had, in essence, excluded the subjective dimension of experience from its considerations. They retorted that phenomenology's contribution was to restore man to the world where he belonged, without sacrificing the goal of social transformation. After all, hadn't the phenomenology-based praxis of social involvement brought concerned intellectuals close to the world of suffering and need that they had formerly ignored?[7] A foremost objective of their writing was to reveal social abuses and to promote the means for eliminating them.

Sartre and his followers paid scant attention to the criticisms coming from the Marxist mainstream, that neither engagement nor phenomenology could adequately reconcile the enormous social differences separating the respective worlds of the petit-bourgeois writer and the proletarian masses. Indeed, Marxist dogma instructed about the resilience of values learned from early childhood and related to one's origins in a particular social class; regardless of the intellectual's commitment to "progressive" social and political goals, he could hardly hope to totally transcend the affective heritage of his initial class experience. The practitioners of engagement, however, were convinced existentialists. The voluntarism implicit in that body of thought countered the determinist thrust of mainstream Marxism by arguing that the writer, or any individual for that matter, was endowed with a freedom of action that enabled him to become whomever or whatever he set out to become. His acts revealed more than the events of his past in any evaluation of his usefulness to the proletarian cause; his *existence* took precedence over his *essence*. Granted, the intellectual and affective conversion to the workers' cause would not be easily accomplished, but the phenomenological approach to describing one's own subjective experience in relation to objective reality offered a means whereby one could continually reassess one's own progress in assimilating a desirable perspective.

It did not escape the *Contorno* writers that Sartre's discussion of engaged writing spoke more directly to the practice of the critic than to that of the fictional writer, even though the primary emphasis of *Literature and Existentialism* was on the writing of the latter. In that work, Sartre promised a deceptively facile solution for the perennial dilemma of the writers of the Left, whose two conflicting aims were the recognition of the specificity of literary discourse and the promotion of desirable social objectives through writing. Sartre offered something to all. For those writers or critics drawn to the literary aspects of writing, he went to great lengths to define his own brand of aesthetic theory—albeit a pragmatic and socially oriented aesthetics for the engaged writer. He posited that artistic pleasure was akin to the experience of prose writers or readers in capturing a sense of the totality of being when they engaged themselves completely in a given work; writers and individual readers exercised this freedom by communicating or understanding a truth about another individual or about their own situation. This pact of generosity was the key to the artistic or literary "joy" experienced by both authors and readers.[8]

Sartre also attempted to appeal to the ethically motivated writer or reader by defending both literary and critical discourse as forms of social praxis. Without falling into the socialist realists' trap of advocating the transformation of literature into sociology or political script, his somewhat dubious argument was that "words are action," and that the writer "knows that to reveal is to change and that one can reveal only by planning to change."[9] These words had an immense persuasive power over a young generation of writers who languished at the margin of society. Sartre offered a justification for their literary persuasion: their aesthetic constructions and philosophical deliberations did have importance with regard to the body politic. One did not have to abandon the labor of the intellectual in order to qualify as a social revolutionary. Indeed, Sartre's message was that engaged writing in itself constituted revolutionary praxis.

Culture and Politics

Early on, the *Contorno* writers formulated via the ideas of Sartre many of their theoretical goals and became aware of the objective limitations for their own participation in Argentina's cultural and political life. As previously mentioned, the mere selection of the word *contorno* as the name of their journal indicated their enthusiastic reception of the key Sartrian concept of *situation*. As with Sartre, any discussion of writing was related to their own commitment to action that would change society. For the *Contorno* writers, Sartre provided a justification for their own writing practice and instilled in them a new and higher appreciation for the role of producers of culture within the social collectivity.

The *Contorno* writers were particularly receptive to Sartre's idea that

Contorno

literature could assume a new and important role in the formation of values and perhaps in furthering social progress. Somewhat optimistically, Prieto, in *Borges y la nueva generación,* asserted that there existed "un nuevo tipo de lector y escritor," meaning that there was also a new type of literature "en la que el escritor debiera tomar partido por la *praxis* como acción en la historia y sobre la historia."[10] He followed Sartre in the suggestion that writing became historical action when the author was inspired by the circumstances that were particular to his own experience and when his writing expressed an appeal for human freedom. He pointed out that Sartre offered Argentine intellectuals a new appraisal of the *useful* function of literature that balanced out the other pole of the Horacian formula, the *sweet.* Without explaining in detail, Prieto wrote that he and his compatriots of *Contorno,* "con espíritu de seriedad," would focus on this useful aspect of literature by devoting their writing labors to the needs of the nation, while not losing sight of their primary object of study, which was the country's writers and their literature.[11]

Juan José Sebreli also embraced the Sartrian quest of a writing production that would respect the properties of the *belles lettres* and at the same time seek its own social relevance:

> Pese a lo que puedan llegar los teóricos del arte gratuito, la literatura es una función social, no puede existir más que por y para otro. Nadie escribe para sí mismo, todo libro no es sino una respuesta a la pregunta del público siempre. El escritor sólo puede salvarse, salvando su situación o sea salvando a su público.[12]

Sebreli suggested that because a writer owed his existence to the reading public, his literary function ought to be devoted to their salvation and, consequently, his own. Literature, he went on to claim, could serve the public by demystifying reality, that is, by creating an "authentic language" that clarified rather than confused, that laid bare the structures of class society and the economic processes of capital accumulation and worker exploitation. As such, the demystification process that he proposed involved not only the content of literature, but also the social function of language in general. The committed writer, according to Sebreli, must forsake the language of gratuitous cleverness that engenders solipcism and closed-off dialogue. Instead, he must seek an expression that distinguishes and defines, that traces a line of demarcation between true and false ideas.

As a group, the *Contorno* writers recognized that Sartre, a few years earlier, had traversed almost exactly the same political, as well as ideological, terrain that now beckoned to them. They found in the ideas of engagement a middle ground between the writing practice of the liberal intelligentsia and that of the ideological Left. Similar to their French mentor's falling-out with the literature of the bourgeoisie, they found fault with the formalist persuasion of the Argentine liberals for having largely excluded history or for having mystified the ties of the text to social or lived reality. They attacked with equal force the sociological criticism and fiction of writers affiliated with the ideological Left, whose adhesion to a Stalinized "social realism," although motivated by the best of intentions, nevertheless led to a denial of the specificity of literary discourse. The error of the liberal writers was that their emphasis on individual creativity led them, in large measure, to ignore society. The error of the traditional Marxists was that their emphasis on the social factors acting upon or determining literary production led them to minimize the role of the writer in composing, and the reader in comprehending, a given text.

The *Contorno* critics therefore demanded from the writers of their country a fiction that explored the dimensions of the human experience with regard to concrete and tangible problems of living in society. It would be incorrect to say that they merely emphasized the treatment of social and political issues in the fiction of the nation's writers. These were important, of course. However, a literature emphasizing ideological issues to the exclusion of other matters—as was the case with several writers of the ideological Left—ran the risk of simplifying difficult questions all out of sensible proportion. Instead, what the *Contorno* writers sought was a literature flavored by the rich odor of humanity that helped to reveal the complex questions confronting true-to-life beings. David Viñas exhorted the writer to create a personally rendered novelistic world in which man would be portrayed in the act of impregnating with humanity his total surroundings:

> Con otras palabras: dejar de hacer una literatura de cosas (mates, caballos, o ponchos o esquinas y melenas cuadradas que, al fin de cuentas, es lo mismo), prescindiendo de ellas u otorgándoles su verdadero valor porque no son sino ayudas, ingredientes o excusas, para pasar a hacer una literatura de hombres, pero de hombres que no estén sometidos a fuerzas inefables o a determinismos orgánicos o psíquicos, o geográficos o clasísticos, sino de hombres que se vayan haciendo a sí mismos y a su contorno, utilizándose a sí mismos y a todo lo que nos rodea. Sin complaciente optimismo ni plañidero pesimismo. Sin creer en 'destinos gloriosos' ni en 'pecados originales.' Sin nacionalismos carismáticos. . . . Una literatura de hombres, en fin, dispuestos a conjugar su libertad para obtener su cultura.[13]

Similarly lacking in Argentina was a critical tradition that addressed what was specific to literature—its conception, its formal attributes, the "pleasure" it gave the reader—while also taking into account the social factors acting upon both creators and consumers of art. Stated in another way, the *Contorno* writers found in engagement a satisfactory methodology of inquiry that accepted the specificity of art as a mode of self and social discovery and at the same time situated its formal analysis within the framework of social and productive forces. In short, it advocated a criticism that considered the text in relation to its multiple contexts and it held the writer to be one more "producer"—albeit a producer of cultural discourse—in society.

Parricidal Criticism

The *Contorno* writers met with wide approval among the youth of the country for taking the older writers of the country to task on account of the latters' presumed inauthenticity and their legacy of formal experimentation at the expense of responsibility and seriousness in the face of society's problems. How did all this transfer into an effective practice as literary critics? Again, the *Contorno* writers encountered in Sartrian engagement a convenient guide for channeling their intellectual energies into a socially oriented writing practice. They shared Sartre's predominantly ethical concerns with regard to writing. They understood the radical message of Sartre with regard to engaged literature: "although literature is one thing and morality a quite different one, at the heart of the aesthetic imperative we discern the moral imperative."[14] The "artistic imperative," they realized, was integrally related to their ideological or "ethical" commitment, since both could be realized through a proper orientation and interaction with the world. Jitrik provided a penetrating description of the integral relationship existing between artistic and social objectives:

> Porque no es un compromiso sino consigo mismo es por lo que resulta difícil. Exige una devoción sin límites, exagerada, porque hay que sacrificarle todo lo que se posee, aun aquellas materias tan parecidas a lo artístico como las ideas y los sentimientos y de los que dificilmente nos despojamos. Cada obra viene a ser una desnudez total y nueva del artista frente al mundo, una actitud que pide un repliegue íntimo luego del cual emerge todo macerado y resumido, yendo a participar de esa descripción elemental que es una obra de arte. Esta estética primaria, esta actitud elemental, ha sido rarísimas veces superada en nuestra literatura, también por el sentimiento o el temor que han tenido nuestros escritores de ser suburbanos de la cultura, es decir de no sentirse con derechos ni fuerzas para creer que sus objetos literarios pudieran aspirar a una universalidad.[15]

Jitrik suggested that what was generally accepted by other groups in his country as an artistic commitment was actually an escape from a more profound type of engagement. Great literature, he believed, involved not merely the skilled arrangement of words and the clever organization of concepts. Instead, it involved first and foremost a way of confronting the world, which, through technique, could then be rendered into text. To give one example, the *Contorno* writers were in agreement that writers such as Mallea and Borges had demonstrated more than adequately their mastery of words and procedures: they were doctors of technique. But their writing lacked vital substance, a result of their own lack of interaction with the reality in which they lived.

Prieto and others called attention to the "seriousness" of their own group, an attitude that contrasted with the fanciful escape into dreams, playful intrigues, and conceptual labyrinths that they believed typified the writing of the *Sur* group. Time and again the *Contorno* writers emphasized the self-sacrifice that their own brand of writing entailed. This literary asceticism was undoubtedly related, at least in part, to the defensiveness that Argentine writers have historically felt in front of a national reading public which disdained the writing of their native sons, as Prieto explained in *Sociología del público argentino*.[16] Jitrik would later identify as another source of this "seriousness" the frustration experienced as a result of the inevitable conflict existing between the reactionary social groups constituting the country's socioeconomic and cultural establishments and those writers who attempted to combat social injustices.[17] A passage from David Viñas's 1962 novel, *Dar la cara*—already referred to in Chapter One—summarizes eloquently the ostracism confronting many young Argentine writers:

> Los que pensaban demasiado, esos eran judíos . . . los que vacilaban pero terminaban en contra de los que pegaban y de los que humillaban, también eran judíos, asquerosos judíos. Los que no se conformaban con lo que le habían enseñado los viejos o en la escuela, y los que tampoco se quedaban tranquilos con lo que habían descubierto, eran judíos, judíos de alma. *Váyanse*. Los que sentían los ojos calientes cuando defendían lo que creían válido eran judíos; los que discutían enrojeciendo y dando manotazos en el aire, también eran judíos, judíos piojosos. *Judío ándate*. *Váyanse judíos*. Y los que no se quedaban en paz definiendo para siempre fulano es tal cosa o no tenemos salvación. Como dudar: judíos, que se fueran, judíos. "Sí, sí." Y los pobres imbéciles que creían que los hombres no estaban destinados a ser una mugre, judíos, judíos, aunque dijeran que no. Judíos.[18]

Viñas's novelistic character expresses well the *Contorno* group sentiment that if a writer confronted social injustice on a daily basis, then the only authentic stance possible was disconformity with that situation. His writing had to be an agent for change; it had to be directed against the forces perpetuating those injustices. This was especially so during Argentina's current crisis, when the hegemony of the oligarchy had eroded and when new social groups demanded their legitimate share of social wealth and power. Because the responsibility of the engaged writer was to defend the previously excluded groups, he was treated by the oligarchy as a Jew of the spirit. That was the price of his involvement. Only the superficially involved writer believed that the struggle would be brief or that significant rewards would be forthcoming in short order. Those who were attuned to the reality of social and political conflict, however, were aware that struggle on behalf of a just cause was its own reward and that one's involvement in that struggle needed no justification.

The *Contorno* writers knew that only by schooling themselves in social, political, and economic theory could they effectively denounce the prevailing injustices in society and criticize the groups and social forces that impeded progress. This commitment to furthering their own understanding was, in fact, an essential link in what Jitrik meant by the term *comunicar:*

> El hombre tiene una medida, un poder, una posibilidad, y es esa medida, ese poder, esa posibilidad lo que hay que describir, lo que hay que denunciar, pero tratando de no engalanar el alma, de no trocarla en algo tan inmutable como infalible, no, de no desprenderla de la ceguera que la une a las cosas tangibles e inexcusables de la realidad, ya que en las dificultades de esa realidad está el verdadero juego humano, para mentirla o para trascenderla.[19]

One writes because one has something to say, so it is obvious that at least a superficial intention of communication is inherent in the choice of becoming a writer. Jitrik, however, wished to distinguish between those who wrote in order to confuse and those who did so in order to elucidate the character of social associations and man's relationship to the environment.

Again, the *Contorno* writers found in the writers associated with the journal *Sur* the extreme examples of how a sensed superiority led to the production of a writing devoided of the stuff of reality. They found it ironic that the stated objective of *Sur* was its pursuit of the South American reality. Its founders had declared that *Sur* was "una revista americana por su origen, por su tono, por sus preocupaciones esenciales."[20] Yet, in spite of the journal's pretense of dealing with South America's situation, the overwhelming majority of its pages included Spanish translations of German philosophy, French and Anglo-American prose and poetry. Victoria Ocampo, the long-standing editor and inspirational force for *Sur,* had stated that the journal's founding in 1931 was motivated by her "strange love for America." She and other principal collaborators had stated that one of their most important missions as intellectuals was the diffusion of European culture in Latin America.[21] However, this patronizing "colonial" function, according to *Contorno* writer Oscar Masotta, was more an indication of the *Sur* supporters' disdain for Latin American culture than of any "strange" affection. Masotta was repelled by *Sur's* distasteful practice of deferring to European cultural standards, even when considering the literature which was clearly Argentine in topic or inspiration.[22]

The elitism of the *Sur* group was obvious, but there was another type of authorial distancing that the *Contorno* writers found just as distasteful. This occurred in the writing of many well-intentioned petit-bourgeois writers who nevertheless remained separated from the less fortunate social groups they pretended to favor. An example was Benito Lynch, whose writings singled out the underclass rural proletariat in the early decades of the twentieth century. Lynch, in spite of his sympathies for the gaucho and his vague support for social justice, never overcame the pervasive paternalism that his sensed superiority fostered:

> Lynch menoscaba el resultado novelístico de la ubicación y descripción del gaucho sedentario, al juzgar con ese aparente afán moralizante de escritor-noble-que-está-a-favor-de-los-desválidos-y-de-los-pobres-pero-orgullosos-gauchos-de-nuestra-patria-joven-grande, y al sumar elementos que desbaratan el juego narrativo.[23]

Lynch's genteel orientation was undoubtedly related to his lack of interest in the social and economic conditions that influenced the gaucho's behavior. In essence, the writer's moralizing attitude provided scapegoats for his own failure to become involved in the reality he pretended to describe.

In the opinion of the *Contorno* participants, the *Sur* writers and Lynch harbored the pretense of discovering and then communicating through their writing the reality of their society and their nation. However, they had largely failed in this enterprise on account of their own ideology of class superiority and their inflated self-perception as "gifted writers." Consequently, their writing served only to reinforce among a limited reading public the same distorted perceptions that nurtured its production. For the *Contorno* members, this writer-reader relationship, as it had come to exist among the cultured elite of the country, was little more than a game of mutual affirmation. Literature had ceased to provide a cutting edge against reality. It had ceased to perform a vital critical function with regard to the status quo. Rozitchner explained the entirely different function of a committed writing practice:

> La función del novelista será tal vez la de arrancarnos al espejismo de una realidad demasiado cercana, la de volvernos a un mundo de raíces primigenias, despertar a nuestra sensibilidad el apetito de posibles que la misma realidad contiene como una promesa exigible, descubrir en el mundo la inherencia personal a esa realidad que se descubre para cada uno de nosotros como la materia cálida en la que buscaremos moldear la consistencia de nuestros anhelos.[24]

The committed writer or critic, he explained, ought to focus on the simple acts of living or on the concrete relationships of men, but with the intention of penetrating beyond superficial appearances and presenting a more profound level of interaction. This process of comprehension through writing was not to be confused with a spiritualization of the concrete or its obfuscation in tricky abstractions. At times the writing advocated by Rozitchner would lead to the world of the prohibited and the taboo; at times it would lead to what was sordid or disdainful; it oftentimes would require the author to reveal his own values or aspects of his internal world, a practice that would not receive complacent applause from traditional elitist circles. His willingness to combine an active knowledge of his circumstances with an acceptance of his own subjectivity would allow him to internalize the outer reality and understand it profoundly. His writing, nurtured by that interaction of his being with that reality, would engage the sensitivity of the reader and might possibly incite and guide the latter's action in society.

Literary Engagement in Perspective

The national cultural dialogue during the latter years of Peronism was as charged as that occurring in the political arena. The young *Contorno* writers became protagonists in the conflictual atmosphere with their "serious" attacks upon the intellectuals from almost all other ideological tendencies. It was to be expected that their opponents responded in kind. However, the critical responses to their ideas and intentions were not altogether unwelcome. They knew that their many weaknesses would become clarified through the expected critical interchange. Indeed, they knew that the attacks of others constituted their brazen mirror. If accepted constructively, those attacks could guide them in the continual reassessment of their own perspectives. After all, their detractors, as well as themselves, participated in the same *situation*.

Several important issues were raised by writers who challenged *Contorno*'s enchantment with engagement criteria and the latter's nagging dissatisfaction with Argentina's recent literary past. The suggestion was made that the *Contorno* writers, in spite of their attacks on other writers for supposedly ignoring the specificity of the Argentine situation in the creation of a largely "Europeanized" literature, were themselves perhaps as intellectually "dependent" on account of nearly total assimilation of postwar French engagement ideas and ethos. Some detractors accused the *Contorno* writers of imposing upon their country's culture an extraneous critical canon that could not capture whatever might be particular or unique in that expression.[25] Another critic voiced a similar complaint, that their alteration between "elogios y palos" demonstrated that the young *Contorno* critics lacked a coherent hermeneutics for considering the nation's literary tradition.[26] These detractors pointed to a major shortcoming of the *Contorno* group's critical venture, its foundation upon a single, and perhaps narrow, philosophical interpretation of man's existence (that is, the existentialist idea that man was free to determine his destiny) and an equally narrow interpretation of the function of literature (that is, the promotion of man's exercise of that freedom). Herein lay a paradox of that critical venture: did not another writer with an idea different from the Sartrian view of mankind's freedom and responsibility have the same *freedom* to depict social reality according to his own criteria? The *Contorno* writers did come to realize that their precise interpretation of man's relationship to his situation and literature's function in society was not only the weakness of their enterprise, but perhaps also its greatest strength.[27]

On the one hand, the weakness of the *Contorno* writers' critical perspective becomes obvious when one inspects their comments about the type of fiction that fell entirely outside the bounds of a "committed" criterion. It is obvious that they were oblivious to the formal or artistic accomplishments of writers such as Borges, Mujica Láinez, and Larreta. In general, they considered literary technique a negative factor when it confused the reader's comprehension of history and worked against his advancement of consciousness. They therefore criticized the literature of verbal virtuosity for imprisoning both writers and readers in a formal web that repressed meaning beyond the literary text.[28] Generally, they were aware that their engaged criteria hardly served to highlight the values of a type of writing wholly different from what they advocated, but this problem hardly bothered them: "*La gloria* no nos dice sencillamente nada," Ismael Viñas and Noé Jitrik wrote in a short study of Larreta's historical novel.[29] This narrow conception of the "literariness" of fiction was most obvious in Adolfo Prieto's book-length study of the poetry and prose of Borges.[30] In short, Prieto's energies were largely misdirected because he did not realize that his own criteria of evaluation were largely extraneous to the preoccupations, and therefore the literary production, of the country's liberal writers.

On the other hand, this limited critical focus became a strength when they applied it to the work of other writers—perhaps the majority—who shared many if not all of the ideas inherent in their engaged focus. Jitrik, who brought to the *Contorno* group perhaps the broadest background in literary theory, wrote that "novelar es abarcar el género literario más cercano a la vida, una especial relación con la realidad, donde son seres humanos quienes cohabitan los intereses del autor; es el redescubrimiento de todas las cosas y no receta alusiva, donde se sobreentiende el desarrollo."[31] It stood to reason, then, that the critic could expect and even demand a minimum of human presence within the novelist's fictional world. Their criticism praised the author's personal involvement in his or her world of fiction. Highly regarded were those works which captured the writer's anguish in the form of the suffering experienced by fictional characters. The *Contorno* writers accepted their self-assigned mission of restoring a human or social focus to the cultural dialogue that had long been dominated by an elite of Europeanized aesthetes. This was the reason for their deliberate choice in the first stage of their critical mission, which witnessed the publication of the first four issues of their journal and ended more or less with the fall of Perón. Their choice was to consider the literary heritage of their country from an involved perspective. However, it is difficult to talk of a group approach to fictional literature after 1955, since national literature and culture would never again be the journal's primary focus.

The *Contorno* writers' phenomenological synthesis of subjective and objective observations, although heavy-handed in its application, had at least three objectives. First, by analyzing Argentina's literary heritage, they attempted to familiarize themselves with the past and present ideological currents that, taken as a whole, constituted the limits of their perception of the world. Through the study of fictional literature, which they enriched by readings in the social sciences, they investigated how specific individuals, and more specifically writers and protagonists from their own class, in different moments in the nation's history, had confronted their respective situations. Existentialists and at the same time Marxists, the *Contorno* writers sought in fiction that blend of subjective and social or objective tendencies which they understood as constituting the fundamental dialectic of mankind's history. Similarly, they sought in literary texts a comprehension of authorial values and attitudes that would help them to situate both author and text with regard to social class and political issues. They perceived this enterprise as a means of better understanding their own reality. Literature, in short, was a crossroads where individuals confronted society and through which they dialogued with their *situation:* "Queremos conocerla. Asumirla," they stated in the introductory essay to their issue treating the Argentine novel. The mere activity of forming judgments about that expression was a necessary counterpart to the more important task of forming a clear understanding of the nation's past and therefore their own present.

A second function of the *Contorno* attempt at a totalizing criticism of their country's literary tradition was to challenge the authority of the country's older writers and, at the same time, to demystify the premises of official thought that was encountered in both literary and political circles. Their mission was to document how the existing political groupings and movements inadequately represented the social and intellectual forces of the country. In a similar fashion, they keenly felt the need to demonstrate the class-bound nature of cultural and literary expression. If the writings of the older liberal intellectuals generally failed to treat the lived experience of Argentina's population, then the reasons for that exclusion had to be set forth.

A third explanation behind the *Contorno* writers' totalizing criticism was that it provided them with the theoretical basis necessary to *superar*, or venture beyond, their present circumstances. This meant that they, as writers, and more broadly as petit-bourgeois intellectuals, had to study in depth the objectives, performance, and results of other writers from their own historical tradition, in order to learn from the latter's mistakes and shortcomings. The *Contorno* writers realized that this type of criticism was but a prelude to other forms of social interaction: "Es parte del intento de comprender nuestra realidad, de efectuar una valoración de lo que aquí se ha hecho, y de ver a través de lo hecho. Aun no siendo la crítica la exclusiva ocupación de todos nostotros, nos asomamos a la literatura como a un testimonio."[32] Neither the literature they studied nor the criticism they wrote were ends in themselves, they stated. Both were preparatory experiences for future social praxis. Their attempt at achieving a dialectical focus through the subjective encounter with tradition had the ultimate goal of making fiction and criticism serve the individual and perhaps also the social collectivity. That was the only justification possible for art and other forms of cultural expression.

Literature and Society

The *Contorno* writers' initial confusion with regard to their political orientation was necessarily related to their decision to focus on literature and to exclude direct social or political anyalysis, as their entrance into comprehending their society. This literary orientation for social analysis was seen by their critics of the Left-Portantiero, Ramos, Agosti—as an indication of the group's ideological mystification and alienation. Indeed, the change in thematic emphasis in the *Contorno* double issue 7/8 of July 1956 indicated that several of the young writers were probably in agreement. But during the entire first period of their journal between 1953 and 1955, there was an apparent consensus that the group's "pasión de actuar, de actuar con la vida"—in the words of Ismael Viñas[33]—would be best fulfilled by restricting their critical energies to the engaged analysis of the country's literary heritage. Their own brand of "fidelity to the spirit," that was accomplished through "rebelliousness," "denounce-ment," and "seriousness," would go beyond the shortcomings of pre-vious writers and would therefore avoid the latters' "treason of the spirit." As discussed in earlier chapters, these vague phrases set the tone and provided the direction for the engaged criticism that characterized the first four issues of their journal.

Another possible reason for the *Contorno* writers' direct avoidance of social and political questions in the issues preceding the fall of Perón was their fear of retribution on the part of the regime in power. Their articles demonstrate their skill in cloaking criticisms in what were to all appear-ances innocuous literary discussions. The contemporary reader can sense the writers' frustrated or misplaced energy upon observing how their analyses often strayed beyond literary questions and touched upon issues related to class and society. The discussion about a writer of the past quickly blended into a discussion of how their own generation of young writers were inserted existentially into the national situation. León Rozitchner eloquently described the sense of *mauvaise foi* (a Sartrian term for the semiconscious mediation that neutralizes one's guilt) experienced by several of them:

> ¿Acaso no sabemos que nuestra tranquilidad actual es el precio de nuestra marginalidad, de nuestra inoperancia e ineficacia, del miedo que se hace narraciones y cosas faltas de interés, que no se refieren claramente a nuestros problemas ni siquiera en el orden subjetivo en el cual el escritor se complace en permanecer, porque lo interesante conduce al peligro? ¿Acaso no vivimos soslayando el peligro por medio de una *ineficacia buscada*, por la huida en lo general, y en la creación de mitos que esbozan para la mala fe de una salvación futura?[34]

He suggested that the writers of the country—especially the older writ-ers of the liberal establishment, such as Mallea—were impeded in their desire to discuss issues relevant to society and consequently sought a *refuge* in literary creation. Uruguayan critic Rodríguez Monegal sug-gested that up to the fall of Perón the *Contorno* writers, in their attacks upon the prestigious writers of the previous generation, had found a similar escape from the agonizing ambiguities they experienced on the social and political levels.[35] However, one can argue in partial defense of the *Contorno* writers that their so-called refuge stimulated an investigation of the broader contexts into which issues relative to literature, writers, and culture were necessarily inserted. Their early focus on the larger realities—they labeled this the "totality"—of literary creation and culture anticipated the last two *Contorno* double issues, in which they would treat directly, rather than obliquely, the most urgent social and political questions of their time.

The social and political message of their literary criticism did not go unnoticed. From across the estuary, Rodríguez Monegal called attention to the *Contorno* writers' rebelliousness vis-á-vis the more established writers of the country and their "apocalyptical" tendency to tear down the work of others without offering a positive substitute of their own.[36] The Uruguayan critic suggested that this was a cheap imitation of the French writers such as Merleau-Ponty, Camus, Sartre, and others who, during the Nazi occupation and then continuing into the 1940s, denounced relative ills while ignoring concrete problems. His observation about the *Contorno* writers' misplaced priorities was well taken: if they wished to examine the history and structure of the present sociopolitical impasse, then their indirect treatment of those issues was simply not enough. Indeed, they were mistaken even in the belief that their contextual study of national literary culture was an adequate means for comprehending national problems. The critics of the ideological Left went yet a step further: *Contorno*'s criticism rarely led to the consideration of issues other than those related to their own social class; the *Contorno* writers were mistaken in their belief that a familiarity with the literature and concerns of Argentina's writers, who were in their majority from the privileged or upper middle-class sectors of society, would adequately prepare them for understanding the experiences and needs of the proletariat. Similarly, a familiarity with literary culture hardly qualified them as students of the country's social, political, and economic dependency.

Although Rodríguez Monegal was essentially correct in his criticism of the *Contorno* writers' misplaced priorities, he was wrong in alleging that they merely imported the French existentialists' critical methodology and imitated their Promethean ethos. There is no doubt but that the *Contorno* writers had read with devoted admiration the available writings from the French existentialist school and that traces of the latter sparked their own criticism. But also important was the remarkable similarity between their situation and that faced by the French writers a decade before, which explains how the latter's ideas became so easily assimilated to the Argentine context, as previous chapters have demonstrated in detail. Both the *Contorno* writers and their French mentors confronted their respective societies in periods of rapid change: the old social elites were in crisis. the working class, newly ascendant, was hardly repre-

sented in political structures. the highly charged ideological environment and the sense of impending chaos left few people unaffected.
Given these similarities in objective situations, it is understandable that
the *Contorno* writers should find attractive solutions to their own problems in the engagement theories of the French literary Left.

In their editorial entitled "Terrorismo y complicidad," which headed
the double issue 5/6 of September 1955, the *Contorno* writers had no
need to refer to the straw issue of imported ideologies in confronting
indirectly the charge of an inappropriate "apocalyptical" thrust to their
own critical writings. Unfortunately, their focus was consistent with that
of previous numbers—in fact, it would remain unchanged until double
issue 7/8 at least—with regard to the issue of mistaken priorities; they
repeated their intention of studying "las letras—que reflejan el estado
del país. . . ." But they also provided an eloquent and persuasive justification for their own practice of critical negation: in political as well as in
literary circles there reigned a general complacency and lack of willingness to listen to or reason with opposing factions:

> Grupo, generación o facción, alabanzas y ataques se distribuyen
> según la posición de quien tenga la palabra. Nadie parece esperar
> opiniones de buena fe. Cada grupo posee sus santones, sus dioses y
> sus demonios. Las opiniones sobre el pasado se usan para avalar o
> atacar el presente; las opiniones sobre el presente son parte de la
> guerra particular, que cada uno obra en su beneficio. (1)

In that environment of closed doors and admitted lies, where
spokesmen refused to call things by their name or subject themselves to
self-criticism, intercommunication was all but impossible. All the more
reason, *Contorno* therefore argued, to "enfrentar la realidad," to review
and confront facts, values, works, and writers. All the more reason to
promote a climate of dialogue and polemic. Their critical project was
much more than "adolescent terrorism," because it had the goal of
helping to construct an intellectual environment more conducive to
resolving the grave social and political problems confronting the country.

In the two and a half years separating *Contorno* 1 from *Contorno* 5/6, the
main discernible difference in the young writers' attitude and critical
focus was the growing realization that their original lack of orientation
with regard to the larger issues of their time—as the article by I. Viñas
article in their first issue fervently stated—had no easy resolution. At
first, their uncertainty was portrayed as characteristic of youths reaching
maturity in a period of temporary social and political crisis. Their editorial introducing the 1955 issue, however, suggested the possibility that
moral truths, stable political positions, and ideological certainties were

now a thing of the past. They came to realize that their radical mission as intellectuals was to immerse themselves in an experience of continual and unceasing apprenticeship.

It is not so much the case that the *Contorno* writers came to maturity rejecting their heritage; more correct is the notion that their class and their society had disinherited them. By the end of the Peronist decade they had come to interpret their intellectual mission as that of transforming chaos into cosmos. Having been denied the assistance of mentors and guides, they had to rely upon their own resources in the struggle to create a new language that would restore coherence to their situation. Surely this solitary task nurtured their inner strength. Peronism was their test by fire. By its end they would communicate in their own writings a confidence in their interpretation of events that, in the opinion of many readers, was uncharacteristic given their relative youth.

After Perón's fall they would reflect that their uncertainty during these early years—of neither favoring Peronism nor opposing it—had caused untold anguish and frustration. But they also realized that that uncertainty served as a springboard for study and inner growth. Their ambiguity would become a source of pride: they had neither discredited themselves in the support of a corrupt pseudorevolution nor joined hands with the groups of social and political reaction in order to bring the *justicialista* regime down. Their neutrality, they would contend, was their foremost qualification as arbitrators between conflicting social and political groups. That middle position provided them with a unique perspective for analyzing the events of the previous decade and elevated them to a position of social and political leadership. Their task was now to steer the nation out of the political impasse in the turbulent years following Perón's fall.

4
From Perón to Frondizi

THE PERIOD COMMENCING WITH THE FALL OF PERÓN IN SEPTEMBER OF 1955
and ending in 1958 with the election of Arturo Frondizi as Argentina's
president can be considered the second of three distinct periods in the
trajectory of *Contorno* with regard to cultural and political issues. The so-
called "Revolución Libertadora" initiated a new period of uncertainty in
Argentina's national life. Across the nation, there was a nearly unanimous sentiment—the significant exception was in the ranks of organized labor—about only one issue: Perón had to go. But the different
social groups and political factions were in severe disagreement about
the worth of the many changes wrought upon the country in the previous ten years of *justicialista* leadership. Similarly, opinion was sorely
divided about Argentina's political future: One widely held position—
supported by the Hispanic nationalists, the cattle-exporting bourgeois,
and after 1958 the Popular Radicals (UCRP) and a sector of the Socialist
party—sought a strong-handed military rule in order to undo recent
working-class gains in salary and organization and return the country to
its liberal nationalist or conservative tradition.[1] A second popularly accepted option, one that angrily contested the first, sought a speedy
return to democratic practices and the integration of the Peronist working class into political life. Among those supporting this option were
several urban intellectual groups, organized labor, and after 1957 the
leftist, or intransigent faction of the Radical Party (UCRI). These latter
groups tended to accept what was generally associated with Peronism—
state initiative in industry, anti-imperialism, working-class organization—as essential forces in Argentine life that antedated the dictator and
would also survive him. By 1958 this latter option, which was favored by
the *Contorno* group, had gained broad support, a factor that largely
accounted for the election of Frondizi as president of the nation.

The waning years of Peronism witnessed the transition in the lives of
the majority of the *Contorno* members from students to professionals.
Ismael Viñas had already been active for several years as a lawyer, giving
special attention to labor issues. Prieto, after graduating from the Facultad de Letras in Buenos Aires, accepted a position in the National

University of Córdoba. Alcalde, after instructing in a private secondary school for several years, taught Greek and Latin in the Facultad de Filosofía at the Universidad del Litoral in Rosario, while sumultaneously serving as secretary for José Luis Romero's prestigious journal, *Imagi Mundi*. Halperín Donghi, after receiving his degree in 1954, followed Alcalde to the Universidad Nacional del Litoral in Rosario where, until 1958, he taught history. Jitrik, having returned to Buenos Aires in 1955 after several months of study at the Sorbonne in Paris, became active in political issues (he served as prosecretary of the National Senate from 1958 to 1961), while simultaneously publishing a flurry of books and articles on Argentine literature and writers. And lastly, David Viñas, while instructing in the Universidad Nacional in Rosario for two years, was already winning national acclaim as a novelist.[2]

With the fall of Perón came the government-sponsored intervention in the University of Buenos Aires, headed by José Luis Romero, in which several *Contorno* writers played prominent roles: Ismael Viñas was Romero's special assistant, while Noé Jitrik and Ramón Alcalde performed other important functions. This operation, which one participant has characterized as "francamente revolucionaria,"[3] attempted to accomplish what Perón had never dared: to cut the university's links with the traditional oligarchy of the city and province and to open its doors to previously excluded groups. One of its major accomplishments, unfortunately short-lived, was the revision of *concursos* (public examination of a professor's qualifications) in order to eliminate unqualified or dishonest instructors whose presence on university faculties was due to political or personal connections.[4] Another change was the implementation of night classes and a university extension program in order that workers and public employees, and not merely the sons and daughters of the financially able families, might better be able to take advantage of the publicly funded resources of the institution. A third area of action was the revitalization of curricular offerings, which had as its aim the implementation of courses treating the current social and economic structures of the country.

The university intervention under Romero was the *Contorno* writers' first taste of effective political action. Their enthusiasm for direct involvement grew as they saw how their criteria for national transformation became successfully transformed into social fact.[5] But why stop there, when the whole nation was ripe for change?

A New Political Option

The few years leading up to the "Revolución Libertadora" witnessed significant changes in the ideas of the *Contorno* writers. As the mystifications perpetuated by Perón faded in the face of the regime's declining economic fortune and growing social and political opposition, the young writers slowly overcame many of the ambiguities in the theoretical terrain that had previously been such a source of discomfort and forged what they believed to be a more coherent understanding of the national situation. Before, their uncertainty with regard to political options had contributed to their inactivity; now, armed with what they held to be a clairvoyant perspective of events, they launched themselves fervently into political activity.

More lucidly than most other interpreters of the national situation at the time, they realized that Peronism had owed its political ascension to, among other reasons, the efficient response it offered to the new economic and social situation of the country. Perón had demonstrated his understanding of the nation's need for new spheres of industrial economic development. Similarly, he comprehended the urgent necessity of guiding the activity of the country's recently swollen ranks of urban workers and incorporating that new presence into the existing political structures. The *Contorno* writers realized that Peronist industrial and worker policies would not disappear overnight, even when the leader of the Peronist coalition had been deposed, since they had been implemented as a logical and necessary response to the new and largely unalterable realities of the country. For this reason, the *Contorno* writers were convinced that any viable government in the near future would have to function with the support of the 2.2 million organized workers that had been the mainstay of Perón's coalition.

To their way of thinking, the ideal solution to this problem would involve the reconciliation of worker, industrial, and middle-class interests. During his early years, Perón had achieved the successful collaboration of workers and industrialists, along with leaders from the military and the Church, but had never attracted large numbers of the middle class to his movement. This, in essence, was to the *Contorno* way of thinking one of regime's greatest weaknesses and the crucial point in its instability: Perón's insensitivity to middle-class concerns and, correspondingly, the lack of middle-class support for his program.[6] They asked themselves: Was it possible to reconstruct a semblance of the Peronist coalition without Perón? Would it be possible to win the support of the middle class and simultaneously eliminate the corruption, demagoguery, and authoritarian tactics that had characterized Perón's leadership? This goal appeared particularly elusive given the determined resistance that many groups of the middle class—for example, the Radicals, Socialists, and liberal intellectuals—had always maintained with regard to working-class participation in government during the Peronato.

This political position, which had evolved in the minds of the *Contorno* writers as a result of painful soul searching and careful analysis, distanced them from almost all of the existing political factions in the country. It was, however, their honest attempt to reconcile in theory the inescapable social realities of the country. They wanted, in a sense, "to save Peronism from Peronism," as critic Ernesto Goldar acidly pointed out.[7] But the *Contorno* group went one step further than previous Peronist defenders by utilizing Marxist categories in their politico-economic analysis and in their promotion of a national transformation similar to what Marxist groups called the democratic "bourgeois revolution" on the periphery. However, it must be pointed out that the *Contorno* writers never seriously considered an alliance with the organized political groups of the Marxist left—in fact, their hostility to the Communist and Socialist parties remained unchanged. Clearly, they were attempting to define a totally new position in the nation's political landscape. For this reason, they undoubtedly left many observers perplexed on account of their call for middle-class leadership of a new multi-class coalition, a position that no middle-class political party or group had heretofore envisioned or sanctioned. The *Contorno* intellectuals, true to their promise, were proposing new and untested solutions in order to aid the country in a moment of impasse. Their detractors called them naive initiates who theorized political options without seriously considering the fundamental problem of a lack of organized constituencies or interest groups that would lend support to such options. Clearly, they ran the risk of all precursors who faced marginalization because their ideas were too advanced, given the realities of their situation. Were their ideas impractical, or were they merely the fruit of wishful thinking?

The axis of the *Contorno* proposal was the renovation and revitalization of the now defunct populist or multi-class coalition. They admired the genius of Perón, who a decade earlier had realized that an alignment of workers and industrialists was essential in his pursuit of national economic development and his goal of ending his country's humiliating relationship of "reciprocal interdependence" with Great Britain.[8] The *Contorno* thinkers shared this ambition of economic independence and recognized the continuing need of establishing a unity of national groups in order to thwart the advance of foreign economic interests in their country.

In retrospect, it is obvious that the *Contorno* writers responded to a widespread sentiment throughout Latin America: Nationalistic thinkers and planners in several countries hoped to build upon the relative prosperity enjoyed in the region during the "import substitution" industrialization period of the war years,[9] in order to achieve significant economic independence in relatively short order. The unique conversion of social, economic, and political factors favorable to these objectives culminated in the emergence of populist regimes in several countries. The MNR in Bolivia, Goulart's Brazil, and Mexico's PRI, in addition to Peronism in Argentina, are the foremost examples.

In addition to their sensitivity to pan-Latin American tendencies, the *Contorno* writers' enthusiasm for multi-class politics also had a source in the philosophical ideas of European existentialism. They were aware of the political debates in postwar France and viewed with interest how the Popular Front's successful resistance to fascicm there had contributed to the current enthusiasm for a multi-class alliance of the "New Left."[10] No, the attractions of populist politics had not died in France with the end of the Resistance struggle. Nor had populism in Argentina been rent asunder with the collapse of the Peronist coalition some months before. For the *Contorno* writers, it was to be expected that the intellectual climate of the period would lead them to seek a reestablishment of the multi-class alliance that had brought the country so many favorable changes, but had also left unfulfilled so many promises.

The *Contorno* writers' advocacy of populist politics, their rhetoric of rebellion and revolution, and their recognition of the need for significant structural changes in Argentina reveal their agreement with certain basic aspects of Peronism, but in one area they displayed a fundamental difference: the central role they ascribed to the middle class, and especially to the intellectual middle class, in guiding society's desired transformation. As with their promotion of a multi-class alliance and the country's economic independence, their program of middle-class leadership corresponded in large measure to the prevalent ideas of the time. First of all, one can discern in their writing the lingering traces of the conservative liberal thought that characterized the articulated mission— but not the practice—of the older writers of the country. Like those writers who constituted the nucleus of *Sur* and *La nación*, the *Contorno* writers aspired to the status of what Ortega y Gasset had defined as "concerned intellectuals," that is, those aware of themselves *and their situation*, who would reconstitute a "creative elite" to guide the society as a whole. A second articulation of this same idea of intellectual leadership came from national historians who interpreted the events of the twentieth century as a testimony to the progressive and necessary ascension of the middle classes into the leadership positions of the country. These thinkers believed that the time was now ripe for extending and transcending the University Reform of 1918 and Irigoyen's aborted middle-class revolution in the nation's politics during the 1920s. A third articulation of middle-class leadership came from social science researchers such as North American John J. Johnson and later Argentine Gino Germani, who wrote that the middle sectors have historically depicted themselves as the social force capable of carrying the country forward in its growth and material progress.[11] (This perspective would culminate in the "developmentalist" social and economic programs of Frondizi.) Yet a forth intellectual current that converged with the others in the *Contorno* writer's support for the middle classes—but especially the middle-class intellectuals' leadership—was the conglomerate of ideas associated with existentialism and fueled by the personal example of Jean-Paul Sartre, as discussed in chapter 2. Briefly summarized here, these ideas spoke of overcoming the traditional intelligentsia's separateness and 'extra-materialidad," that in many cases led to its harmful divorce from society, by endowing it with a positive social role. Concerned intellectuals, according to Adolfo Prieto, were those who were most capable of rendering "un examen totalizador del proceso;"[12] therefore, they were the logical arbitrators of conflicting class and group interests and the legitimate interpreters of the will of the nation as a whole.

In summary, there were two principles guiding the *Contorno* writers' projected entrance into political activity: First, they would promote a multi-class coalition uniting labor, industry, and the middle class, with the goals of achieving labor and industrial reforms and greater economic independence for the country. Second, they would promote a government and a society led by the middle classes, in which the intellectuals would have the dual responsibilities of instructing society in the desirable options for change and arbitrating differences between social and political factions.

Analysis led to political action. If no credible political force existed within the country's spectrum of parties that supported the *Contorno* prescription for an intellectual-led multi-class alliance, then one would have to be created.[13] The hope was that if they themselves took the initiative in demonstrating the need for such a movement, then other middle-class groups would also realize the benefits in participating. Their movement would reconstitute the Peronist coalition between workers and industry, but this time it would be guided by middle-class intellectuals and not by an undependable charismatic leader. Without detailed and specific suggestions, they advocated a radicalization of the *justicialista* promises of social and economic equality through what Perón never attempted: a serious change in social, political, and economic structures.[14]

Peronism Re-evaluted

The *Contorno* double issue 7/8 published in July 1956 treating Peronism must be read in the light of the writers' political objectives of creating this multi-party electoral alliance. As they saw it, there were two major obstacles standing in the way of forming that alliance: the middle class's instinctive opposition to the working-class participation and the latter's justified suspicions about participating in another bourgeoisie-led alliance, especially after the deceptions suffered at the hands of Perón. How could the *Contorno* writers best convince the fence-straddling groups of both the working and middle classes that such an alliance was in their mutual interest? Interpreting their role as the intermediaries who were essential for bringing the two classes together, they opted for a writing style with personalized and informal tone. They would convince with their command of the facts and their solid analysis of events; but they would also strive to win the trust of all parties through their down-to-earth bearing, their sincerity, and disinterest.

Central to their strategy was the countering of mainstream middle-class hostility with a critical, but essentially positive, portrait of the working class's role in the events of the previous decade. Osiris Troiani had this in mind when he drew a distinction between Peronism's progressive *ideology* with regard to the worker and its otherwise negative performace:

> El peronismo . . . implantó la política sobre nuevas bases: defensa de los intereses populares y de la comunidad nacional. Los otros no defendían sino cierta idea abstracta del hombre, abstracta y trasnochada. Esa ideología era, moral e intelectualmente, superior a la del liberalismo.[15]

Liberalism, with its abstract promises of political freedom and the development of mankind's potentialities, had never advocated improvements in the working class's standard of living nor their broadened participation in the political process. Peronism, at the very least, promised these changes. However, Troiani did not hesitate to point out that while Perón at times signaled the beginning of Argentina's much-needed social revolution, he in fact did a great deal to impede its development. Perón, at the very least, possessed a vague desire for changes that, in the face of the impossibility of their realization, led him to a politics based on demogoguery and lies: "Nosotros nos habíamos sustraído a la marea pestilente con el recurso del desprecio. Por la simple razón de que ese hombre mentía—mentía porque denunciaba un estado de cosas que él no podía ni quería corregir. . . ."[16]

I. Viñas, more harsh in his judgment, saw Perón as a master manipulator of public sentiment in the interest of reaction. Perón, he wrote, inherited a potentially revolutionary social situation that he disarmed by converting social discontent into cathartic, but in the end, inconsequential, dramatics:

El peronismo tuvo una virtud: supo captar el sentido revolucionario activo que tenía lo que de por sí era síntoma de una revolución: llevado a símbolo. . . . [A]l teatralizarse y transformarse de síntoma en símbolo, perdió eficacia, se convirtió en mera descarga emocional, en gesto de rebeldía, tal como los accesos de violencia más o menos dirigidos y las manifestaciones y concentraciones frenéticas, agotadoras: el hombre que ha gritado, aguantado de pie y caminado en marchas interminables, se vacía para los actos revolucionarios. El mito llevado a objectivo en sí mismo desvía de otros objectivos. Perón encauzó una eventual revolución y la transformó en una gran pieza teatral, casi farsa, casi tragedia dionisíaca.[17]

Through his revolutionary theatrics, Perón neutralized the possibilities of positive action and left his rebellious following in a political void. In this analysis, Viñas distinguished between the master of deceit (Perón) and the popular classes. The former manipulated the latter to his own ends, and the workers, whom Viñas called "la parte sincera" of Peronism, were left with only unfulfilled promises.

Rozitchner's essay in the same *Contorno* issue struck hardest at the deposed *justicialista* leader, but at the same time offered a sympathetically critical perspective of the working class. Perón, implied Rozitchner, was the astute agent of the bourgeois oligarchy whose dictatorial role served to impede proletarian advancement and to neutralize through political action the profound demographic and social changes recently affecting the country. As such, Perón's revolutionary rhetoric merely deflected attention from his programs, which fell far short of their stated intentions. One may dispute the correctness of Rozitchner's assertion that the proletariat was the only group that satisfied itself with mere illusions and did not experience net material gains during the decade of Peronist *justicialismo* (Perón did encourage proletarian militancy early in his administration, and the derivative benefits to the working class were, in fact, substantial).[18] Few, however, would dispute Rozitchner's claim that Peronism was a phenomenon of cultural misery. This was especially so for the working class, he argued, since, from beginning to end, their expectations and actions were manipulated by "El Gran Utilizador." Echoing the ideas of Franz Fanon, he wrote that since the workers never had to struggle for the benefits so eagerly granted from above, they never overcame their traditional passivity and never achieved a solidarity of class:

No hubo obstáculos por superar: eran superados por decreto; no hubo unidad por realizar: la unidad se obtenía en la afirmación automática; no hubo sueldos que reclamar: los aumentos se decretaban desde arriba; no hubo superación cultural: fue un desborde

de las mismas pasiones que se complacían en la satisfacción in-
stantánea, sin futuro.[19]

In sum, Peronism substituted social revolution with the mere illusion of
revolution. Rozitchner implied that profound social change was still
imminent and inescapable, but that it would not come about without
significant struggle; indeed, he instructed that sacrifices and suffering
on the part of many people was the inevitable price of successful change.
Peronism, because of its unfulfilled promises, was at best a test case from
which the progressive middle-class intellectuals, as well as the nation's
workers, would extract bitter lessons of the past in order to forge a
coherent plan of political action for the future.

The most impassioned justification of Peronism by any *Contorno* writer
was presented in a frank personal testimony by Juan José Sebreli—views
that he has only recently seen fit to recant.[20] Paradoxically, he defended
the movement by affirming what Peronism's detractors had argued all
along, namely that resentment was its guiding principle and motivating
force: "¡Cómo no iban a aferrarse a su resentimiento estos parias, si era lo
único que los dignificaba en un mundo de injusticias y opresión!"[21] He
accepted the argument of those who saw in Peronism the undermining
of the country's moral structure, but he eloquently pointed out the
positive aspects of that demolition:

> Masas y juventudes fueron el elemento dominante de la Nueva
> Argentina. Ambas con un sentido de la provocación casi surrealista,
> se consagraron alegremente al exitante deporte de socavar los ci-
> mientos de la Vieja Argentina, es decir, el mundo de los viejos y las
> aristocracias. Un destino burlón y vengativo encontró en la más
> osada de las partiquinas el instrumento para humillar a la más
> orgullosa de las oligarquías.[22]

Instead of emphasizing the tragic aspects of Peronism's revolutionary
charade, he called attention to the fact that the majority of the population
enjoyed material abundance and contentment: almost everyone was
"out to have a good time." This lack of solemnity was precisely what set
Peronism apart from the much-compared fascist experiences in Western
Europe. Peronism, Sebreli argued, combined the most uncontrolled
form of liberty with despotism. Then—in words reminiscent of the
deliberations of M. Bakhtin—the dialectical assertion: "Pero la diversión
es diversificación, esto es, cambio. La otra cara de la fiesta permanente
es la declaración permanente de la revolución."[23] While others denounced the alienating nature of Perón's tactics with regard to the working class, Sebreli argued that it was possible to free an individual from
one alienation only by delivering him to another. In short, Perón's

demagoguery and lies, however distasteful for the advocates of pure revolutions, did succeed in convincing a population of dominated consciences in a situation for which rational arguments were of no avail. Perón's worthy message, conveyed through unworthy means, was that the proletariat had a legitimate claim to political power, that years of exploitation justified their increased share of the nation's wealth.

The opinions of the *Contorno* writers might have diverged with regard to details, but they were united in the conviction that Peronism was but a prelude to the social and political revolution that was to come. While other groups mused upon the desolation of the previous decade, they carefully measured the steps leading to an optimistic future. There were differences with regard to their degree of conviction concerning the possibility of achieving profound social change through the reinstitution of a multi-class political coalition; but, as a group, they demonstrated their eagerness to assume the responsibilities inherent in their self-declared role of society's intellectual leaders.

A Program of Cultural Activism

At that moment the *Contorno* writers' general agreement on political objectives was due as much to idealistic optimism and the vagueness of their specific proposals, as it was to a deliberated reckoning of actual possibilities for action. They were criticized for their presumption in assuming a leadership role with regard to a situation for which they had almost no experience. Nevertheless, they forged ahead, armed only with what they believed to be an adequate solution to their country's political impasse. As writers and intellectuals, they were aware that culture was their appropriate sphere of action. Given their diverse fields of inquiry (history, literature, law, psychology, sociology, etc.) it is to be expected that their views would differ with regard to the proper or possible relationship of cultural activity to political governance or socio-economic production. Consequently, it is also to be expected that they would propose differing roles for themselves, as producers of culture, in bringing about their desired electoral coalition.

At one extreme was Sebreli, who professed perhaps the most materialistic or deterministic of philosophical orientations among the *Contorno* group. He was soberly aware of the limitations inherent in any political action: that a political leader, no matter how "powerful" or persuasive, cannot simply initiate fundamental changes and make those changes endure if they contradicted the underlying social and economic forces. As an example, Sebreli wrote that "Perón no inventó el peronismo, por el contrario, puede decirse que ese conjunto de condiciones políticas, económicas y sociales que es el peronismo lo inventó a Perón, encontró en él una forma de expresión y un nombre, que podría haber sido cualquier otro."[24] Rather than believe that Perón invented his *justicialista* program out of mere ideological conviction and then implemented it through sheer force of persuasion, one could better understand that his programs came about as an urgent response to pre-existing conditions. Implicit was the suggestion that a continuation of Perón's most constructive programs, now that Perón himself was absent, would be possible only if the objective conditions of the country allowed. Sebreli emphasized the difficulties involved in stablizing a worker–middle-class alliance due to the immense differences separating their respective interests and the historical legacy of conflict and suspicion. Although the *Contorno* group's writing mission could not hope to dramatically alter this situation, he nevertheless believed that it could help somewhat in convincing others of the necessity of the reforms they advocated.

León Rozitchner, more specifically than the other *Contorno* contributors, examined the Peronist experience from the perspective of working-class values and cultural production. According to his analysis, a potential revolution was derailed because Perón masterfully filled the ideological void of proletarian culture. Previously, the working class hardly manifested a collective memory and its written history was non-existent. Related was its lack of firm cultural values and coherent directions for its militancy. Consequently, it readily fell victim to the regime's propaganda. The psychologically dependent workers quickly lost whatever sense of personal or group goals that they might have possessed and complacently accepted the material gains offered them. Without a developed class consciousness, the workers were likely victims for Perón's self-serving justifications of his contradictory, and in the end deficient, *justicialista* program. Largely on account of their acquired habit of passively accepting their situation, the workers were hard pressed to internalize the maxim that activity and initiative were essential for constructing a strong cultural base, which, in its turn, would be their most formidable arm in the struggle for individual improvement and class advancement.

This perceptive analysis unfortunately did not provide Rozitchner with concrete suggestions for the *Contorno* writers' cultural activism. His principal recommendation was that the group establish links of communication between workers and middle-class intellectuals and take advantage of the few opportunities that the situation offered for collaboration: "Tal vez nuestra labor consista en inseminar este mundo cultural para que de alguna manera brote, lanzar a la vida un sentido que la realidad nos descubre en un momento de privilegio como el presente. . . ."[25] Without mentioning how this was to be accomplished over and beyond rhetorical gesutres of good will, he stressed the need for both middle-class intellectuals and workers to establish an intra-class dialogue in order to rise above the isolation in which they found themselves.

Sebreli and Rozitchner inherently recognized the troubling disequilibrium existing between their group's ambitious political goals and the rather limited "cultural" means at their disposal for realizing them. But there was another troubling issue: the problems inherent in passing from theorization to practice. The nucleus of the group came together with the realization that their culturalist orientation need not be abandoned, even when their entrance into the realm of political action was inevitable. David Viñas most appropriately captured this new spirit: "No se podía permanecer al margen alardeando de pureza impoluta—de necesidad de conservarla, digo—o de una total y lúcida comprensión de lo que occurría. Era necesario otra cosa. Hundirse, incrustarse en lo que estaba ocurriendo, aun a riesgo, claro está, de no conservar ni tanta lucidez ni tanta pulcritud."[26] He realized that when analysis finally led into action, they must be humble enough to recognize the imperfect and transitory nature of that analysis. Indeed, they would have to accept the fact that pure and absolute theories inevitably faded in importance in front of the constantly evolving reality.

Slowly, a dramatic change was taking place in the consciousness of the *Contorno* writers. Previously they had been content to observe from the sidelines and criticize or guide through their writing. Previously, they had spoken to social and political issues through the medium of the literary text or the cultural essay. Now they were talking of the possibility—no, the necessity—of direct political action. This dramatic change in *Contorno* orientation was the primary cause of the group's producing the first *Cuaderno* in July 1957, that is, slightly more than a year after their issue on Peronism. Undoubtedly, the rapidly developing political situation of the country contributed to the diminished emphasis given to cultural or literary topics by the group's most politically oriented members—Ismael Viñas, Ramón Alcalde, and, to a lesser degree, León Rozitchner. Viñas was quite explicit with regard to the group's new direction: "Hemos llegado al convencimiento de que las cosas más urgentes, por lo menos se resuelven en el plano político. Y que todas, de un modo o de otro, se resuelven *también* en el plano político."[27] Viñas, through dedicated legal work over the previous few years, had won the confidence of several union leaders, principally in the meat-freezing industry. He had become convinced of his group's previous ineffectiveness, precisely because their ideological "demolition" of the older

generation of writers had not, and could not, become transferred into
concrete political acts. Theory, he came to believe, could only free itself
of mystifications when it passed into action:

> Tenemos, o creemos tener la evidencia de que los grupitos intelec-
> tuales no pueden pasar en el plano político de insistir en la forma-
> ción de peñas de teóricos de café, en las que se pueden decir cosas
> muy ingeniosas o muy hábiles, y si se quiere las más ruidosas, por
> lo mismo que son gratuitas. Era imprescindible entrar en un movi-
> miento político efectivo y real, no levantar entelequias.[28]

"Totality" and Political Analysis

It is one thing to identify a problem, and it is quite another to theorize
a solution; it is a step of yet increasing complexity to apply that theoretical solution in practice. In Sartre's idea of *situation* the *Contorno*
writers found their first approximation to the conflicting demands involved in realizing their totalization of individual and social goals with
regard to writing. Sartrian engagement began with the understanding
that in order for the writer to generate the type of ideas that reveal the
world and effectively act upon it, he himself must be a participant in the
affairs of society. The engaged writer, therefore, had to abandon the
essentially mistaken idea that he must strive for as "objective" a point of
view as possible; on the contrary, the *Contorno* writers learned from
Sartre that the writer spoke authentically only when he was conscious of
the perspective that he brought to the critical function.[29] The *Contorno*
members therefore accepted as a given that they participated in a situation that included themselves as well as their surroundings. To describe
their society, they knew that their words must inevitably describe themselves, and vice versa. David Viñas therefore emphasized the necessity
for the new writer to know his own character and to attempt to realize a
totalized vision without "el divorcio entre su subjetividad y su contorno."[30] When one's personal vision was formed through involvement
within his objective situation, then his criticism could be an effective
agent of change. Praxis was impossible if one was oblivious to, or
isolated from, the social forces around him.

From the start, the concept of "totality" commanded a central position
in the *Contorno* writers' praxis. First, they sought in the reconciliation of
existentialism and Marxism a marriage of personal salvation with social
transformation. Second, the ideas of Sartrian engagement (that itself was
forged through the unity of phenomenological and materialist perspectives) conveniently guided their passage from theoretical to political
activity. And third, their study of texts—albeit literary ones—necessarily
led to the study of contexts; their study of Argentina's literary past

inevitably led them to project a group identity for themselves and a plan of action for the present.

Their political orientation at this time also called for a totalization of the active forces in society: the constitution of a worker-middle-class electoral alliance. They realized that their own destiny as middle-class intellectuals was integrally and intimately related to the destiny of Argentina's workers. Out of this conviction came their commitment to promote a dialogue with the organized proletariat that hopefully would grow into a working relationship in the social and political arenas. They were resolved to break out of the tradition of indifference or sophisticated snobbery that until then had typified the intelligentsia's treatment of workers. They would attempt to understand the world of the workers because they understood that the workers' world was inevitably related to their own. Out of this realization grew their commitment to seek the common bonds uniting themselves, the producers of culture, to the workers, who were producers of goods and services. The *Contorno* writers were disposed to seek the areas of possible dialogue where the intellectual sons and daughters of the petite bourgeoisie could break bread with the newly franchised workers. Their mission was to create a literary and critical language that would speak to the two social classes and would therefore work toward the emergence of common political objectives and interests.

The paradigmatic examples of an absence of a "totalized" relationship to society were the writers associated with the journal *Sur*, who considered themselves above the concerns of the masses. Osiris Troiani wrote:

> Si algo nos distinguía de nuestros mayores, y aun de los camaradas que se incorporaban sin esfuerzo a la vida literaria, era la idea de que nuestra evolución intelectual debía asimilarse intimamente a la de nuestro país. Su destino era el nuestro. la humanidad iba a alguna parte, la historia tenía un sentido, y por lo tanto, también lo tenía mi existencia. Todo lo individual, salvo ese tributo a la circunstancia, tenía algo de escandaloso, de obsceno.[31]

Whereas the *Sur* writers considered themselves to be uninvolved in the country's present impasse and free of blame for its recent conflicts, the *Contorno* writers were determined to understand their own ideological and historical links with Argentina's past and present. Once Perón had been toppled, it was not enough to forget the past and proceed on. No. Peronism was *their* past, it was part of them. Rodolfo Mario Pandolfi wrote with a vigorous tone:

> Podemos aplaudir o escupir a Perón: lo mismo da. Perón es nuestra sombra, nuestro pasado inmediato, *nuestro tiempo*. Es la dimensión

del *hecho argentino* que no podemos rechazar, es la dimensión incorporada para siempre a nuestra exigencia nacional.

El peronismo, pues nos está dado: es necesario desentrañarlo, es necesario desentrañar las motivaciones que informaron durante una década la conducta de gran parte de la clase trabajadora. Si queremos hoy edificar una comunidad argentina en la democracia, debemos encontrar el lenguaje que posibilite nuestra comunicación con las multitudes que creyeron en Perón, que rescataron a Perón el 17 de octubre, y que siguieron a Perón durante diez años.[32]

The *Contorno* writers had their areas of contention with the populist leader and the proletarian labor bosses, but that did not give them the license to denounce or ignore what was displeasing and then congratulate themselves for what they considered to be their clairvoyant perspective of events. Instead, they realized that their radical task was to comprehend the nature of those events as if they themselves were participants, and not to project the possibility of themselves attaining a neutral, removed perspective.

The *Contorno* double issue treating Peronism illustrated especially well this "totalizing" intention of understanding events from the perspective of the participants. Pandolfi, Prieto, and Rozitchner's provocative articles attempted to penetrate into the proletarian experience—that is, from what they depicted as the perspective of the working class.[33] This involved a type of analysis that integrated the information learned from official histories with data of a more subjective nature: intricate motives, psychological tensions and class-bound preferences, habits, and orientations. History and sociology, the core disciplines of the traditional intellectual establishment, could only partially reveal what the *Contorno* writers hoped to discuss in these articles. They sought a meeting ground between the data provided by a scientifically verifiable historical materialism and the less accessible information related to one's subjective experience. A hostile reader might characterize this type of writing as presumptuous; a more favorably inclined reader would see it as an act of generosity. The *Contorno* writers were entirely aware of the potential liabilities, but also the potential benefits, of such an exposition.

A precondition for attempting this synthetic or totalizing type of analysis was the writers' awareness of how their values and the writing medium acted to influence their own mode of perceiving the experience of others. Only by coming to grips with their own values could they attempt to conceptualize the experience of others. This operation was a prerequisite to effective political action, as the editorial committee of *Contorno* understood clearly:

Queremos conocer [la realidad]. Asumirla. Trabajar con ella, no con verdades de confección. La mera actividad judicial—algo ridículo por sí, y posiblemente reprochable a quienes hasta ahora poco hemos hecho—es sólo una tarea secundaria, un sub-producto; pero una tarea imprescindible para lograr ver claro, y paralela a toda otra. . . . Porque sentimos la necesidad de asumirla y, si podemos, contribuir a superarla, creemos que la primera obligación es decir lo que pensamos con franqueza.[34]

They had to speak frankly about their own values and objectives before they could begin to dialogue with the working class and other groups of the country's middle class. Then, that self-recognition would serve as a starting point for their observations about the behavior or motiations of others. The failure to undergo this Socratic experience was equivalent to assuming a dishonest posture in front of their reality. They needed to break out of the restrictive subjectivity that defined their class and to avoid the pitfall of projecting their own values upon extraneous beings. Only then could they "asumir la realidad," that is, form through their dialectical relationship with that reality a more functional orientation than that inherited from their class of origin.

This dialectical confrontation with their own reality was not what many would consider an acceptable basis upon which to establish a critical writing practice. But traditional procedures and formal presentations smacked of bureaucratic insensitivity for these youthful writers. Their passionate desire to become involved could not tolerate a faceless linguistic front. They would write as individuals, and the opinions expressed would be their own. They were the active agents who, through their writing, would act upon society.

In the same issue devoted to disentangling the enigmas of Peronism, Juan José Sebreli offered another perspective of the means for understanding social and political events from the inside: the testimony. He, more than any other *Contorno* participant, acknowledged the Peronist phenomenon, and even its ugly demise, as an overall positive experience in the development of the country. Peronism, he wrote in words reminiscent of Pandolfi in the quote above, "es nuestro lote."[35] He explained that he had to fathom the enigma of Peronism in order to find out who he himself was. It was impossible, therefore, to discuss the Peronist phenomenon without talking about himself. Fatally intertwined were subject and object, the observer and the observed. Sebreli was entirely aware of the shortcomings of traditional descriptions for historical events: "En descripciones que los demás hacen de nuestra propia vida, tal vez podamos conocernos, pero nunca reconocernos. Le faltará ese calor de intimidad que la hace intransferible." These words embodied the Sartrian idea of the *otreadad*, that one must recognize and know oneself as a subject of history in order to escape the prison of alienation. This applied equally to the writer, who must not fall into the temptation of describing the activity of others from a passive and uninvolved perspective. Instead,

> creo que no basta con ver la verdad—tarea que puede realizar cualquiera de esos historiadores bien informados e imparciales, sino que es necesario verla desde el punto de vista, único e intransferible, que ocupamos en la sociedad, en el mundo. Lo contrario es colocarse fuera de lugar, es decir, caer en la utopía. Por eso creo que también mi limitado punto de vista es imprescindible en el conjunto, y por eso, prescindiendo de estadísticas y de documentos que podrían rectificar y corregir mi óptica, prefiero basarme sólo en las experiencias singulares y concretas en que he tomado contacto con el peronismo.[36]

The limitation of this brand of hermeneutics is that it can show only one side of reality, even though it is accomplished with utter honesty. Sebreli pointed out the paradoxical result of his search for a totalized relationship with reality: the need to resign himself to never being able to capture the absolute truth of any issue. When applied to Peronism, this meant that the "historiographical impartiality" of a removed observer such as himself would never triumph over the political passion of those directly involved.[37]

Rozitchner, in his article, proposed a form of "totalizing" writing as a means for exploring Peronism from the point of view of the proletariat. He believed that he was better able to do this than the writers of the traditional intellectual elite, whom he criticized for trying to portray political events

> a partir de consideraciones simplemente personales, como una extensión hacia la generalidad de ese mundo redondo y perfecto en el cual permanecen, de aquellos que sitúan sus contradicciones, cuando las sienten, ante la transcendencia absoluta y como misterio de lo supremamente incomprensible.[38]

Furthermore, he believed himself more qualified than even the proletarian intellectuals for analyzing working-class experience, because the latter were "encerrados en la restringida subjetividad que delimita la clase, que torna comprensible sólo lo que nos es afín y ajeno lo que nos es extraño." Although he did not achieve this detached perspective completely and consistently—as discussed below—his ideas nevertheless contributed to the group's exploration of the means for comprehending the proletarian experience from the perspective of the middle-class intellectual.

Osiris Troiani, like Rozitchner, tried to come to grips with the conscious thought of the middle class for his own generation, that of 1940—

"una generación ausente," as he labeled it—in order to comprehend more fully the Peronist phenomenon. His momentarily heightened consciousness led him to a substantial self-criticism:

> Los que pretenden el nombre de generación del 40 hicieron media docena de poemas elegíacos. No han renovado nada, ni siquiera la técnica literaria. . . . Nosotros no quisimos enmerdarnos con la fronda intelectual, y hemos terminado por enmerdarnos de nosotros mismos.[39]

Ismael Viñas, in his turn, provided a similarly personal overview of the Peronist decade. His major concern was his own generation who for ten years had been attracted by the promises of Peronism, in spite of the movement's reactionary tendencies. His fear was that early enthusiasm followed by disappointment usually led people to a "complejo de culpa que les distorciona el pasado inmediato y los puede llevar a las actitudes más irracionales."[40] Because Argentinians of all walks of life had lived the last decade with each convinced that he had the most adequate solution, there resulted a continual misunderstanding between individuals and groups. Viñas's solution to this problem was for all to adopt a certain sense of relativity. Through his article he hoped to demonstrate, in both manner of presentation and message, that an effort at comprehension would facilitate communication, especially between the workers and the middle classes.

David Viñas urged his cohorts to accept in even more intense form an intermingling of their destinies with the objects of their writing analyses. For him, the academic understanding of social forces and its subsequent expression through literature was only the first step toward social involvement. He urged his generation to go one step further and give themselves over to their situation in the totality of their personal and social dimensions. Only then was it possible for writers to "*escribir y vivir como culpables. Sin ventajas, porque los otros son todos. . . . Los otros somos nosotros mismos. De ahí que no se puede escribir de cualquier cosa, sina de esto, de todo esto. . . .*"[41] Viñas, perhaps more than any of the other *Contorno* writers at the time, realized that a passion rooted in suffering drove the inquiring mind to comprehend the world as a self-activated unity of coherent parts. That comprehension taught that he, no more nor less than others, played a role in the inevitable *devenir* of history, that he, in his turn, must attempt through his acts, to transform frozen images of the past into meaningful tools for the present. One was "guilty" because one was necessarily involved in one's situation; one therefore had a personal obligation for its welfare, especially in times of crisis.

According to Viñas, the intellectual did not lack causes for "guilt" since he, more than others, had at his disposition the necessary information for understanding the contradictions between his privileged socioeconomic position and the human misery resulting from the nation's underdeveloped productive capacities and skewed distribution of wealth. Another cause of anguish was the recognition of the anachronistic character of the country's cultural and intellectual traditions in comparison to those of Europe. Previous generations of writers and thinkers had developed sophisticated psychological mechanisms for avoiding the recognition of this guilt. These mechanisms had, in time, become incorporated into a complacent lifestyle with reinforcing sets of attitudes and values. The *Contorno* writers, upon studying the life and thought patterns of the country's previous generations of writers, became quite familiar with a number of these stratagems. What better explanation existed for the "desarraigo" or "soledad" of the intellectual—those qualities interpreted by hundreds of writers over the last century and a half as characteristic of Argentine cultural life—than the ability or lack of desire to confront the blatant contradictions in their lives? The liberal writers of the *Martinfierrista* generation (Borges, Mallea, etc.) had, over time, developed their own responses to basically the same problem: the mental apartheid they concocted in order to separate the life of the spirit from that of the body, *la Argentina invisible* from *la Argentina visible*, "la mentalidad universalista" as opposed to "la mentalidad aluvial,"[42] in short, civilization versus barbarism. Rodolfo Kusch explained that the *Sur* writers' defensiveness was a result of "una cultura basada en un ethos de supresión."[43] This intellectual *mauvaise foi* created in those intellectuals a sentiment of nirvana which in turn reinforced the tendency to perceive their reality in false or distorted terms. *Mauvaise foi* was only possible when one refused to confront one's ideas with the reality they pretended to interpret, when one's reflections bore little relevance to one's situation.

The *Contorno* writers realized that the *Sur* group's self-imposed isolation was directly related to the latter's sterile abstract meditations. They therefore realized that an accurate comprehension of their own situation could not be divorced from their own participation in that situation. "Assuming" one's reality meant accepting responsibility for its problems. Kusch wrote: "El tiempo habrá de ajustar nuestro anacronismo—o del país, si persistimos—para obligarnos a reconocer dolorosamente nuestra barbarie, aun con el riesgo de ser 'invisibles' para el Occidente."[44] This choice involved some possible trade-offs: the partial sacrifice of one's active participation in the most advanced dialogues taking place in the West for involvement in the enterprise of constructing basic cultural institutions in one's own country; the praise of the elite for service to the masses; the economic protection of the oligarchy for social and political struggle alongside the workers; alienated but complacent silence for social involvement.

Viñas's idea about "writing with guilt" had another interpretation that pertained to the situation of the *Contorno* writers as petit-bourgeois intellectuals. Several of them realized that their social mission was to unite in solidarity with the less fortunate classes and struggle for the transformation of society. But inherent in this gesture of solidarity was a fundamental contradiction: by joining hands with the insurgent pro-letarian masses, they would be organizing in opposition to their own mother class. The involvement depicted by Viñas was therefore more than social and political struggle: it was confrontation with their own reactionary values, which were a legacy of their privileged social origins. His novel, *Dar la cara*, depicted the typical trajectory of progressive petit-bourgeois intellectuals in Argentina's past: "que eran muy revolu-cionarios cuando estaban en segundo o en tercer año de la facultad, pero que cuando se trató de ubicarse y quedarse se convirtieron. . . ." The "niños huelguistas" of one day would be the "viejos conservadores" of the next.[45] One protection against the sell-out of one's previously pro-gressive values was the practice of self-criticism. For the petit-bourgeois writer, this was a struggle akin to the religious quest for perfection: social tension served as the motivating force for self-improvement and action.

Taken together, all of these articles constituting the *Contorno* issue dedicated to the analysis of Argentine society during el Peronato demon-strate the group's collective goal of cultivating a critical passion that would lead to a broader understanding of their situation. Passion, in this sense, meant embracing their reality as concrete subjects and speaking from that perspective without any pretense of omniscience. Engaged criticism could only be produced by one in touch with his own values who was motivated to go forth and encounter other human presences in the world. Critical observation could not be separated from interaction. The *Contorno* writers' conception of a "visión totalizante" meant pre-cisely this: the mutual recognition between two or more subjectivities, and the internalization of an event through participation. It was the recognition of the intricate dialectic between the subject and the object, it was the passage from observation to involvement.

The Frondizi Alliance

At that moment, the *Contorno* writers began to realize the benefits that could be gained through collaboration with the newly constituted Unión Cívica Radical Intransigente (UCRI), led by fellow university intellectual Arturo Frondizi, whose spokesmen articulated, at least initially, its commitment to a nationalist program of the Left and the active participation of the popular classes in national life. Frondizi promised to reunite the populist coalition and thus salvage the more positive aspects of Peronism under more enlightened leadership. They found in his "antiintelectualismo intelectual y su populismo profesional"[46] a possible resolution to their personal contradictions and the fulfillment of the multi-class alliance that they envisioned. Their eventual declaration of support for the UCRI in the elections of 1958 came about as the result of long and serious deliberations, and not without significant dissent or reservations.

But there were obvious dangers in allying themselves to the Frondizi movement: all politicians to a certain degree are Machiavellian in the exercise of power, as I. Viñas reminded the *Cuaderno* reader,[47] and there was no reason to believe that Frondizi would be any exception. Similarly, Rozitchner warned about the dangers in confiding in a mercurial politician who, when later installed in office, many times reneges on his campaign promises.[48] These premonitions would turn out to be prophetic.

In the early months of 1958 the *Contorno* participants came to the conclusion that Frondizismo offered the best of all possible options for realizing their own objectives, and especially in light of the military junta's prohibition of Peronist party participation in the coming elections. Although they hardly welcomed the inevitable struggle against reactionary interests within the Radical party, they looked forward to the opportunity of collaborating with the worker leadership there represented. There were risks for their involvement: their own energy and good will might be co-opted; working class interests promoted during the campaign might be abandoned later. They viewed Frondizi's decision to seek the support of the Catholic church hierarchy, in violation of previous assurances, as an obvious warning of what might happen later to other aspects of the coalition's program: "Nos inquieta profundamente la significancia material de esta cohesión espiritual que se anhela, las relaciones concretas que el imperialismo mantiene con la Iglesia . . .," wrote Rozitchner.[49] From early on they were attuned to the dangers of promoting an alliance that could go astray. They also realized that participation in the Frondizi accord promised no easy and immediate fulfillment for their long-range social and political goals.

The *Contorno* writers were encouraged by the general responsiveness of many different sectors of the middle class to the UCRI's proposed alliance with the Peronist party and its apparent support for working-class participation in the future government. Political spokesmen of the Left and student leaders of FUBA, all of whom only a few years before had attacked Peronism, were now promoting a united front linking students, leftists, and workers. In 1957 the term "izquierda nacional" became incorporated into the political vocabulary of the country in response to the broadly based sentiment for revolutionary change under a multi-class governmental coalition.[50] In general, these developments coincided with a blossoming of Marxist thought throughout broad sectors of the middle class and a favorable reappraisal of Peronism—two issues which fueled the hopes of the *Contorno* writers in their projections of imminent social and political triumphs. They noted the general spirit of optimism and the widespread feeling that significant changes in the country were at hand; they believed that they could be instrumental in bringing these changes about.[51]

They were also encouraged by the possibility of exercising direct influence in the formulation of UCRI policies. A few of the *Contorno* writers served as members of advisory task forces that reported directly to the Radical party's presidential candidate; there was the possibility that this type of input and influence would continue even after Frondizi's successful election. They therefore decided to venture beyond the safe theoretical confines of the intellectual's world and enter, with defenses ready, into the perilous political arena.

What was to be their new program of action in the light of the changed situation of the country and their newly assumed position in support of the UCRI? Their first objective was to make their influence felt upon Frondizi and the evolving UCRI governance program. In mid-1957 I. Viñas, Rozitchner, and Alcalde, integrating a group affiliated with the UCRI, presented the party's presidential candidate with a declaration manifesting their disagreement with several points of his program. With a similar end the group brought into publication *Contorno cuadernos*—as mentioned previously—whose two issues (July 1957 and February 1958) criticized, respectively, the UCRI's alliance with the Catholic church and that party's pre-election overtures to the institutions of international finance.

Alcalde detailed a plan for applying continual pressure on the government in an article printed in the first issue of *Contorno cuadernos*.[52] He identified as top priority the group's continued promotion of class consciousness among the nation's workers. For this task they were aptly qualified, given their sensitivity to cultural issues and their ability to link these to more specifically social and political objectives. In this they could remedy and surpass the deficient cultural activity of the writers of the organized Left who, although articulating a clearly defined program for the country's transformation, did so in a language hardly accessible to the workers and flavored with paternalistic overtones. The *Contorno* writers, unlike the "aristocratic" Socialist and self-righteous Communist party militants, held the conviction that the masses had the capacity to

comprehend and the right to participate in deciding the fundamental
socioeconomic issues confronting the country as a whole.

In regard to how the *Contorno* writers would further the *concientización*
process among the popular classes through political and social action,
Alcalde admitted: "La Izquierda no debe forzar el estado de conciencia
colectivo queriendo llevar a la prática todas las consecuencias teóricas de
sus posiciones filosóficas, sino que debe limitarse a crear las condiciones
materiales que irán haciendo evolucionar la conciencia de clase."[53] In the
first instance, this was a call for flexibility in the group's political program. He urged, for example, that the Left accommodate to the religious
sentiment of the broad sector of the masses without minimizing, however, its opposition to the Church's official influence in a future UCRI
government. In the second instance, he restated the idea articulated by
Sebreli and Halperín, that only a significant change in material conditions could make possible an evolution in popular consciousness. Like
them, Alcalde was aware of the inherent limitations of any cultural
program which was not accompanied by modifications in the economic,
social, and political orders.

Yet another urgent area of action, in the light of Frondizi's need to
capture middle-class as well as worker votes in order to assure a victory
in the coming elections, was the *Contorno* need to promote the concilia-
tion of class interests. Rozitchner had written earlier:

> Nosotros creemos, y esa es muestra tarea actual, que existe otra
> posibilidad [a la violencia entre clases], es decir, . . . conciliar los
> diversos aspectos de la lucha de clases sin renunciamientos ni
> tergiversaciones, en una creciente integración de las masas traba-
> jadoras argentinas dentro de esa verdad que sólo su fuerza y su
> conciencia tornarán posible.[54]

It is to be expected that this goal of ameliorating interclass tensions
would be severely criticized by thinkers schooled in traditional Marxism,
who accepted as an inalterable reality the conflict of interests separating
social classes. In short order, the *Contorno* writers would be accused by
the more radicalized elements on Argentina's political scene for having
played naively into the hands of an oppressive bourgeoisie. It would be
easy to criticize the *Contorno* writers for this attempt at promoting intra-
class harmony, in the light of Frondizi's—and therefore their own—
failure. But, as explained above, they were writing at the end of a decade
of populist successes across the South American continent that had
resulted from the support of a large sector of the population who
believed in the promise of intra-class coalitions. In short, the ideological
climate at the time was conducive to the *Contorno* writers' optimism
about forming such an electoral alliance and executing through demo-

cratic channels a profound restructuring of their society. A generous observer would view the *Contorno* writers as poker players who staked an odds-even bet, and lost.

The Perón-to-Frondizi Period in Perspective

The *Contorno* writers were subjected to a critical assault on the part of their contemporaries, which in its turn motivated their own unsparing self-criticism. The first of several theoretical shortcomings of their thought during this period, as pointed out in an article appearing in the *Gaceta literaria* of May 1956, was the group's apparent obsession with themselves and their own present and future importance.[55] Another critic attacked the *Contorno* writers for a similar reason, that the strong subjectivity in their writing made their political program "más sentimental que conceptual, bastante indefinido."[56] These critics correctly pointed out that the *Contorno* writers often generalized from their individual experiences, a factor that contributed to distorted analysis. This is seen clearly in their introduction to the issue devoted to Peronism:

> el grupo de *Contorno*, como la mayor parte de los hombres que tiene ahora entre veinticinco y treinta y cinco años de edad, se frustró en cuanto padeció, porque no le era dado actuar, un momento ambiguo tironeado por fuerzas ambiguas y apentencias que sólo en la acción podían clarificarse y precisarse.[57]

Their detractors quickly pointed out that the *Contorno* writers were presumptuous to assume that the majority of the country's youth were tormented by the same indecision as they. Obviously, the Peronist workers falling within this age group were not inactive. And if the workers had suffered in their political participation, then in all probability their frustration hardly resembled the anxieties experienced by the *Contorno* writers. Their critics were largely correct: in spite of the *Contorno* writers' desire to achieve objectivity and comprehension in their analyses, they still fell at times into a narrow subjectivity.

Their infatuation with the method of analysis that combined subjective evaluation and objective perception led to Adolfo Prieto's belief—overoptimistic, without doubt—in his group's "orgullo de desengaño."[58] Ismael Viñas and Rozitchner expressed a variant of the same idea in their respective articles, that a fortuitous series of events had generously laid bare the usually veiled structures of their society and that they, almost alone among the informed analysts of the present crisis, had been able to take advantage of that momentary clarity on account of their relatively unclouded perception which was due to their identity as petit-bourgeois intellectuals—that is, their situation as intermediaries between social classes.[59] But the newly found confidence of the young writers was a dual-edged sword: while it provided them with the confidence to venture into uncharted areas, it also blinded them to certain hazards. In the case of the *Contorno* group, their sensed superiority prevented them from recognizing that their situation was similar to that of many progressive intellectuals in the West: their frustrations resulted at least in part from their ambiguous relationship to the other groups and classes in society.[60]

Pride also prohibited them from recognizing in their own thought many irrationalist tendencies which they shared with other writers of their own tradition. David Viñas lucidly wrote in 1959 about the perspective of his group during the period in question:

> El desencuentro con la realidad nos llevaba irreparablemente a todo tipo de explicaciones irracionalistas: misticismo, telurismo, racismo. Basta con leer a Solero, Massah, Murena o Kusch para advertir a lo que podríamos haber llegado todos nosotros. Basta recordar que preferíamos la idea a su encarnación.[61]

Viñas referred to Solero, Massah, and Kusch, who participated with *Contorno*'s early issues, but who, in addition to Murena, later broke with the nucleus of the group and rejected the goal of social relevance in favor of the irrationalist tradition of Martínez Estrada and Mallea. Viñas realized that notwithstanding his own disapproval at present, he and the other *Contorno* faithfuls had in the past felt the same temptation to perform subjective or theoretical deliberations, without taking into account the issue of relevance or applicability to the sociopolitical reality.

Examples of their own fall into abstract or subjective analysis can be found in several of the essays included in the *Contorno* issue treating Peronism. The young writers assumed that they were going beyond a "bourgeois" perspective in their search for new solutions, but all too often they employed ahistorical categories as a basis for their judgments which were reminiscent of Mallea's nostalgia or the anti-modern anarchism of Martínez Estrada. Rozitchner, in the article on proletarian and bourgeois experiences during the previous decade, for example, lashed out at the individuals and classes that used Peronism as a springboard for their own advancement.[62] He cast the blame for Peronism's failure on this commercial "emputecimiento"—or whoring—in the public and private sectors, while totally failing to mention the new corporate role of the state and the unprecedented powers wielded by the authoritarian leader, two factors that had obviously resulted from changing historical circumstances and not a decline in Argentine social values.

Ismael Viñas indirectly exonerated Rozitchner in the essay, "Miedos, complejos y malosentendidos," in which he attacked the tendency of certain sectors of the bourgeoisie to criticize Peronism with largely moralistic arguments. Those attacks were insincere "porque los intereses de esa burguesía están inexorablemente ligados al enriquecimiento individual, al sistema de la propiedad privada, y ésta, en última instancia, no significa sino el despojo de otros."[63] He pointed out that writers of the liberal establishment rarely protested the exploitative practices of factory owners which, unfortunately, even surpassed in impact the less favorable actions of the Peronist workers. Those critics complained, however, when corrupt labor leaders or political bosses benefited through similarly questionable practices. His purpose in writing was not to defend one group over the other, but rather to point out that what Rozitcher had called "emputecimiento" was characteristic not only of Peronism, but also of many societies, if not all, that operate within the capitalist system.

Another instance of a *Contorno* writer's reliance on moralist arguments rather than objective analysis, was Osiris Troiani's criticism of Peronist leaders for the lack of correspondence between their articulated programs and the practical accomplishments of the regime. In part, his articulation of these contradictions constituted an effective criticism of Peronist practices. Indeed, he himself had urged this type of response on the part of the opposition writers: "Una oposición eficaz debía moverse dentro de aquellos límites: sólo así era posible 'desbordar' al peronismo. Aventajarlo en vocación nacional y en empuje revolucionario. Denunciar su [sic] yerros diplomáticos y económicos. . . ."[64] But Troiani's exhortations lost much of their effect when they assumed a moralistic flavor. For example, he suggested that the lack of correspondence between Peronism's articulated policies and final results may well have resulted from the spread of a Spenglerian decadence: "la barbarie y la decadencia . . . Eran dos lesbianas; dentro de nosotros mismos, unidad en un monstruoso nudo de amor." Rather than attempt to explain the socioeconomic and political factors causing such contradictions, his analysis, like that of Rozitchner, yielded to indignation.

A more serious mystification, which was very much related to the *Contorno* writers' emphasis on generational clashes and moral shortcomings, was their failure to grant greater consideration to the role of socioeconomic and political factors in the disintegration of the Peronist social and electoral alliance.[65] For all their pretense at having achieved a "totalizing" view of Argentine society during this period, it is evident that they focused on their own group's insertion into an innerclass rivalry to the near exclusion of issues related to social and group conflict. This would explain the overdetermination of literary questions at the expense of politics in their early issues. Their critical zeal had first played itself out on the cultural level. True, in later issues they overcame that

shortcoming by emphasizing social and political matters. But their recent writing still manifested a serious theoretical disorientation, as manifested by the continued reluctance or theoretical inability to come to
grips with the principles of political economy or a Marxism-inspired
sociology. In their writing between 1956 and 1958, one looks in vain for
more than a passing mention of the country's still powerful agro-
oligarchy. Also absent from *Contorno* pages was any serious analysis of
the internal structures of Argentina's underdevelopment, that is to say,
the recent history of the country's agro-exporting sector, its relationship
to the industrial bourgeoisie and international capital, and its historical
resistance to the development of the country's industrial capacity and
the ascension of the middle class to political power. Similarly absent
from the pages of *Contorno* was any historical discussion of the role of the
country's armed forces in government and politics, especially in the so-
called Revolución libertadora against Perón in 1955. With the wisdom of
hindsight, the contemporary reader cannot help but observe that *Contorno* gave no indication whatsoever of the internal factions and vying
interests within the armed forces which would lead to the latter's "almost bloodless" overthrow of the Frondizi government in November
1958[66]—that is to say, less than six months after the country's return to
civil authority. This last event anticipated the military's outright seizure
of power in 1962 and their nearly continuous dominance of Argentine
politics from that year until January 1984.

Added to the *Contorno* writers' partial blindness with regard to the
roles of the industrial bourgeoisie, the agro-oligarchy, and the military in
Argentina's power equation was their inconsistent and at times demagogic usage of words such as "bourgeoisie" and "oligarchy," which
reveals a general lack of rigor in their sociopolitical analyses. The following sentences demonstrate the wide variance, and thus hardly rigorous
application, of the first of those terms by the different writers of the
group. Rozitchner begins by positing that "la burguesía civil" constituted
one of the three principal groups initially supporting Peronism (along
with the Church and the army), with many of its members later abandoning the movement and thus precipitating its fall.[67] However, two
pages later he discusses "los valores de la burguesía" as if the group
constituted a monolithic and integral force opposed to the proletariat
and possessing a distinct baggage of values (one wonders if the petite
bourgeoisie had a place in his scheme).[68] Similarly inconsistent was
Troiani's personified, Machiavellian "bourgeoisie," which was "pre-
visora" and "clarividente" in how it forced Perón against the Church and
then the army as a means of disarming the working-class revolution and
thus gaining another decade of tranquility.[69] Yet another application of
the term is found in Pandolfi's portrait of a monolithic capitalist sector,

which "en cuya estupidez," never realized that the dictator's conduct of the workers was in its interest and only reluctantly supported Perón's grandiose schemes for the nation's industrialization.[70] Yet a fourth interpretation was that of Ismael Viñas, who argued that in spite of their areas of mutual competition, the petite and high bourgeoisies converged with regard to material interests and "reverential" values and therefore became "accomplices" in bringing about the fall of Perón.[71]

The two *Contorno* analyses that best withstand rigorous scrutiny with regard to the politico-economic and social construction of Peronism were written by Sebreli and Halperín Donghi. Sebreli's rapidly drawn analysis highlighted the radical breech of interests separating the two principal arms of the capitalist class: the industrialists, with their nationalist aims, and the "oligarquía agropecuaria," with its dependency upon imperialist monopolies.[72] In a similar fashion, Halperín avoided using the confusing term "bourgeoisie" altogether. Instead, it was "un sector industrial" in rapid ascent during the 1940s which saw with alarm how reactionary political groups in the country received the wholehearted support of "grupos económicos tradicionalmente dominantes" in their attempt to defeat the government and thereby dismantle the fragile industrialization which had occurred during the Second World War.[73]

These diverse interpretations of the interests, values, and actions of the bourgeoisie during Peronism reveal at worse a superficial understanding of social and political forces on the part of several of the *Contorno* writers, and at best the absence of a unified and rigorous conceptualization of social reality for their group thought. In sum, the *Contorno* articles on the pre-Frondizi period were characterized by a general lack of consistency and at times a disturbing superficiality with regard to the use of sociological terminology. All of this was an indication of several of the writers' ambiguous comprehension of socioeconomic interests acting upon political forces. This lack of methodological rigor would inevitably contribute to their subsequent failure in political action, as discussed in the chapter that follows.[74]

It is easy to highlight the weaknesses of the *Contorno* project during the period beginning with the fall of Perón and closing with the election of Frondizi. However, perhaps outweighing, for the contemporary reader, these theoretical errors and abstract sociopolitcal conceptualizations are their demonstrated desire for involvement and their willingness to redress previous errors. In their own actions, they had attempted to avoid the shortcomings of the older liberal writers who assumed no risks when they criticized as uninvolved observers. Although their own attempt at fusing objective analysis with subjective testimony largely failed as a corrective for the shortcomings of the other writers, it was not a total failure. What still survived was their *disposition* for personal commitment, their realization that personal involvement in society was the prerequisite for their ideas to become relevant to actual experience. They stated in the editorial of the *Contorno* issue treating Peronism that they would write "desde adentro, como individuos que escriben mojados después de la lluvia, no como aquellos que se pretenden secos, intactos, y señores de todo el universo."[75] All of this was theoretical, of course, and could only be evaluated according to how it served as a guide for further activity.

The Explosion of the Frondizi Illusion
and the Demise of *Contorno*

FRONDIZI'S POLITICAL TURNABOUT IN HIS FIRST SIX MONTHS IN OFFICE
motivated the *Contorno* writers to produce the journal's last issue, a
combination of numbers nine and ten, in April of 1959. If the double
issue was conceived as an indictment of that administration's actions up
to the date, it can also be read by the present-day reader—imbued with
retrospective knowledge—as an eloquent *despedida*, or final good-bye, to
their writing public. Three essays constituted the total issue:
Rozitchner's "Un paso adelante, dos atrás" (pp. 1–15), I. Viñas's "Orden
y progreso" (pp. 15–75), and Halperín's "El espejo de la historia" (pp. 76–
81). The first two of these articles focused on the events and issues of the
Frondizi government, while the last one attempted to view the group's
recent experiences in the light of the historical past. Although this
double issue focused upon issues related to the social-scientific orientation of the three writers represented, the journal's direction by Prieto, D.
Viñas, Adelaida Gigli, I. Viñas, and Rozitchner meant that this orientation continued to reflect the ideas and sentiments of the *Contorno* nucleus.

Arturo Frondizi, the son of Italian immigrants, was a doctor of law and
a professor of economics. During the period of military rule from 1955 to
1958, he led the UPRI, or "Intransigent" wing of the Radical party, to
national prominence by denouncing the military's alliance with the agro-
oligarchy and foreign imperialism, and by pledging to protect the interests of workers and the middle class. In defense of economic nationalism, he had criticized Perón's contract with Standard Oil of
California for the exploitation of Patagonian reserves, just as he came to
oppose the laissez-faire economic principles followed by the juntas in
returning many state agencies to private hands and in reopening other
sectors of the national economy to foreign investment. The nation's
workers, increasingly dissatisfied with the military governments' dis-
memberment of social programs, cutback of wages, forceful takeover of
industrial unions, and imprisonment of labor leaders, were favorably

disposed to a government led by one such as Frondizi, especially in the light of the law prohibiting the Peronist party from participation in the elections slated for May 1957.

Frondizi, early displaying some of the opportunism that would later characterize his actions as president, assured his electoral victory by signing an agreement with the exiled leader of the *justicialista* movement: he received the assurance of two million votes in return for his promise, upon assuming the presidency, to legalize the Peronist party and to end governmental intervention in the CGT (General Confederation of Workers), which would make possible the resumption of worker-oriented governmental policies.[1]

Once in office, Frondizi's acts followed a path diametrically opposed to what he had promoted as a candidate. Confronted by an economic crisis, he immediately embarked upon a neo-liberal plan for national recovery. One of his first acts was to enter into a contract with Standard Oil, arguing that its terms safeguarded local interests by converting the nation into a net exporter of petroleum products. A second highly unpopular move which adversely affected the working class was the stabilization agreement with the International Monetary Fund in December 1958. This led the government to drop subsidies and price controls, restrict imports, and limit all wage hikes to corresponding increases in productivity. Then, the declaration of a national state of siege to suppress the labor strike of the state petroleum company effectively ended Frondizi's cordial relationship with the Peronist movement and the workers. Moreover, he betrayed the nationalist and anti-imperialist platform that had contributed to his election by signing contracts with eight foreign oil companies. The military, fearing Frondizi's realignment with the Peronist labor groups, forced a dismissal of his entire economic team and their replacement with others who would continue the policies aimed at freeing private and international business interests from state regulation and redistributing financial resources from consumers to entrepreneurs.[2] All of these actions were in direct contradiction to Frondizi's earlier campaign promises and dealt a death blow to the two principles which had united his shaky coalition: economic nationalism and the integration of the Peronists into the political system.

Needless to say, these events had a devastating effect upon the morale of the *Contorno* group. The title of David Viñas's 1959 essay expressed well the indignation that they immediately felt: they were "una generación traicionada."[3] Their honesty had been co-opted by political manipulators; their good will had proven ineffective in front of powerbrokers; their idealistic dreams of democratic social revolution had been crushed by unmovable economic interests. Rozitchner's essay in the *Contorno* issue of April 1959 repeated their denunciations of a corrupt political system in the same moralistic vein: the writers of his group were the victims of "el gran fraude nacional" that left them "decepcionados, desengañados y próximos al abandono y al nihilismo."[4]

Their first impulse was to blame others for their own ineffective actions, but in a second moment they realized that their own illusions and mystifications about the political game they had played contributed in no small way to the less than desirable consequences. "Ingenuidad o tración, el dilema paralítico es para muchos inconfesable," admitted Rozitchner. Whether it was more their own naïveté or the bad will of others, the result was nevertheless the same, and required the same preliminary action in response: a thorough study of the circumstances contributing to the Frondizi debacle and an equally frank examination of their own previous assessments and illusions which had led them into the pernicious electoral alliance. In spite of their past failures, and perhaps because of them, the young writers were now committed more than ever to continuing in the activist path that they had chosen. They realized that their own participation in the Frondizi affair was merely the reenactment of the chronic dilemma that had traditionally confronted progressive forces in their country: the incapacity of the Left for comprehending politico-economic and social forces in order to initiate effective action.

The articles by Ismael Viñas and Rozitchner were solid contributions to understanding the circumstances leading to the dramatic changes in policy on the part of the Frondizi administration and at the same time evidence of the significant strides that the young writers had made in channeling their indignation into constructive activity. The UPRI, they both realized, was constituted by several different groups whose competing and contradicting priorities were largely responsible for Frondizi's inconsistent advocations. Viñas detected a clash between two groups: those cabinet officials with union support, who believed that the party's ambitious plans for national industrialization could only occur as part of a larger economic, social, and political revolution; and an even more powerful sector of Frondizi supporters with business orientation, who desired a continuation of the country's industrial development through national as well as international investment, but without the state embarking on new reforms in the areas of labor legislation and social welfare.[5] Rozitchner, without going into nearly as much detail as Viñas, depicted a basic disequilibrium existing in the country between a progressive sector with access to political power through the voting box and a sector of more reactionary interests allied to the agro-bourgeoisie, which wielded disproportionate control over the rest of society in relation to their scant electoral representation. In front of these clashes of interests, Frondizi had tread a perilous measure: he was not a victimizer, instead he was "preso de una realidad." His manipulations—which the *Contorno* writers in no way pardoned or forgave—were therefore understood as the weak leader's response to his own inability to reconcile irreconcilable interests. Rozitchner wrote that it was Frondizi's bad fortune to have been forced to administer to powerful economic interests and, in doing so, sacrifice any moral or cultural objectives that he might have advocated.[6]

This analysis in itself contributed substantially to the process of radicalization that was occurring in the *Contorno* writers' ideas, and carried many of them one step nearer to a full acceptance of the traditional Marxist formulation concerning the central role of society's infrastructure—that is, the conglomerate of productive forces constituting its economic base—in influencing and at times determining not only the political configurations of that society, but also its culture. Viñas articulated this idea in a tentative fashion: "¿Es ilegítimo llegar a la conclusión de que no son los hombres que están en las funciones políticas quienes han concebido un plan y lo aplican? Todo autoriza a asegurar que no."[7] Indeed, the four million votes in favor of the UPRI's nationalistic, prolabor, and anti-imperialistic platform ended up wielding little influence in front of well-entrenched economic interests that were supported by the military. Rozitchner, with moralist tone, proposed that this power equation represented the most recent stage in the development of the society of material abundance, where dollars spoke louder than dreams, where crude materialist greed outweighed the pursuit of more altruistic goals.[8] Viñas, however, more soberly located the area of deception in their own thought: as typical intellectuals of the middle class, their analyses had failed to grant due importance to economic factors, which many times outweigh decisions made in the realm of politics:

> Hombres de clase media, tal vez estén pagando un pecado de presunción, típico de su clase por lo demás: el de creer que la política y la historia la hacen los dirigentes, capaces de iluminar y de dirigir el proceso, permutando su carácter privilegiado en lo económico por una situación de *dirigentes* en lo social y político.[9]

Even more disturbing for Viñas was the realization that many of the economic forces that had so brutally intervened in the political process had their focus of power beyond the frontiers of the country itself. This was the first instance in which a *Contorno* writer explicitly accepted the position of Argentina within a world capitalist economy as a point of departure for detailed analysis, and attempted to view the interplay of local economic, political, social, and cultural factors in relation to external forces:

Nosotros seguimos cumpliendo nuestro papel de país subordinado, integrado en forma de elemento dependiente dentro de un orbe que no sólo impone sus condiciones sino que va determinando nuestra estructura íntegra, en que lo económico y lo que se pretende separar como si fuera posible hacerlo al darle un rótulo: conciencia nacional, cultura, ideología, constituyen un todo inescindible. Las ideologías, y hasta las tácticas en que ellas se expresan en la acción, no son otra cosa que la manifestación de una trasformación en el orbe capitalista a la que nosotros nos adaptamos, aceptando el papel subordinado que se nos asigna. El actual gobierno no hace sino cumplir una etapa en el proceso que comenzó a ser cumplido por el peronismo, de la que fue un momento intermedio el gobierno militar, y cuyo origen se encuentra fuera de nuestras fronteras.[10]

Although many of these ideas had been anticipated in essays written by Alcalde, Masotta, and Sebreli,[11] Viñas firmly established here an essential point that would have to be taken into account in any future deliberation with regard to the middle-class intellectuals' intervention in the national political process: that Argentina's relationship to external interests had suffered a qualitative change. Historically, the country's agricultural and industrial development, in addition to its social structure, had been deformed by international interests. But, in recent decades, there occurred the convergence of several key factors: Argentina's greater dependence on international financial institutions, the international monopolies' expanded control of marketing and technology, the nation's significantly expanded economy that was structured in relation to broad consumer demand, and the advent of a mass communications network. All these meant that imperialism's new inroads into Argentina threatened to leave no aspect of national life unaffected: "Y esa deformación va a ser total, *totalitaria*, tal como son todos los procesos sociales. Nuestra estructura cultural en su integridad va a padecer ese proceso defamante."[12] These observations anticipated the fertile investigations by several of the *Contorno* writers in subsequent decades, detailing how society and culture on the periphery were affected by their financial, technological, and industrial subservience to the developed countries of the Northern Hemisphere.[13]

The Assault on Liberalism

The *Contorno* writers' acceptance of an interpretation for the Frondizi phenomenon that largely concorded with the traditional Marxist conception of the primacy of economic over social and political factors in the determination of society's hegemonic groups, went hand in hand with the radical assault they now launched against several ideas associated with economic and political liberalism. Indeed, their previous belief in the legitimacy of parliamentary democracy and the possibilities for democratically legislated social change had echoed the idealistic goals embraced by some of Argentina's greatest public figures—Moreno, Rivadavia, Sarmiento, Alberdi, Echeverría—whose own thought had its sources of inspiration in the liberal traditions of France and the United States. But, as Rozitchner pointed out, the Frondizi debacle made evident the powerlessness of rhetoric in the face of politico-economic facts, it demonstrated the limits to idealistic cultural programs for effecting the transformation of society.[14] Never before in the country's history had the contradictions of liberalism been so evident: the bourgeoisie, which benefited most from the rights of private property and laissez-faire economics—two central principles advocated by liberals everywhere— were the most flagrant violators of that doctrine's political legacy of democracy and parliamentary government.

The essay titled "El espejo de la historia" by Halperín Donghi, published in the same *Contorno* issue, continued with the critique of liberalism by analyzing the impact of the Generation of 1837 (Echeverría, Sarmiento, Alberdi) upon the sociopolitical situation of the time and by implicitly comparing the situation of that group with the writer-activists of *Contorno*. The Frondizi government's complicity with economically privileged groups, Halperín pointed out, had precedents in the 1837 movement that resulted in the consolidation of the national state centered in Buenos Aires (Halperín also indicated other possible precedents: Roca in 1890 and Justo in 1930). The writer-activists of 1837, like those of *Contorno*, demonstrated a fidelity to a "vocación iluminista," since they had placed little emphasis on knowledge gained from practical experience and had largely ignored factors relevant to the political economy of their situation.[15] The programs they proposed for the country's transformation were naturally affected by their scant identification with the interests of the country's popular classes. They mistakenly placed a priority on the development of a sound, doctrinaire theory, in accordance with idealistic principles. As a result, their intellectual labor later proved to be relatively ineffective on account of its "extrema libertad ideológica." Because of these shortcomings, the worthy goals embraced in youthful years later had to be compromised or abandoned after the fall of Rosas in 1852, since they were largely inapplicable to the circumstances which they presumed to describe.

On this basis, Halperín questioned the effectiveness of a political doctrine such as liberalism which was founded more on idealist principles than on a concrete understanding of the politico-economic and social forces at play: "Era excesivamente presuntuoso creer que esas fuerzas reales necesitasen para algo la adhesión de unos cuantos teorizadores políticos, y era todavía más presuntuoso creer que esos mismos teorizadores, puestos a gobernantes, podrían desviarles en el rumbo de su ciega marcha. . . [sic]."[16] While the other writers of *Contorno* did not share the degree of Halperín's pessimism with regard to the intellectual's scant power to effect social or political change, they nevertheless agreed with his assessment of the relative ineffectiveness of highly principled parliamentary and cultural programs, especially those based on the promises of political liberalism, for guiding or hastening society's transformation.

The Frondizi episode had been, they concluded, the enactment of an inconsequential political game in the face of a predetermined economic reality. It was the futile exercise of debate and vote according to the rhetoric of liberalism, which served in the last regard only to lend a façade of legitimacy to pre-existing economic privilege. According to Rozitchner, the charade exemplified the "autolimitación del liberalismo, la incongruencia entre sus principios y sus actos. . . ."[17] The clarification and detailed exposition of this realization would be the primary focus of subsequent essays by several *Contorno* participants.[18]

Re-evaluation of the Role of the Middle Class

The *Contorno* writers' rude awakening to these realities—the primacy of economic interests over political deliberations, the centralization of economic power outside of the frontiers of the country, and the bankruptcy of liberalism—inevitably led to a reassessment of their previous program for national renovation, and, in a related fashion, their own role for bringing about desired ends. Of central importance in this reformulation of strategy was their previous assessment that the middle class could be led into the role of arbitrator between bourgeois and proletarian interests, and consequently, core group for uniting a multi-class alliance.

Another issue reconsidered was the role that they themselves hoped to play with regard to the working class. Implicitly, they had previously striven to assume for themselves a leadership role with the objective of promoting a moral reform of the worker movement: idealistically, they had sought the deliverance of the masses out of infamy and the latter's transformation into a "better humanity." They had perceived the Peronist masses as a malleable group which was receptive to their enlightened leadership. Juan Carlos Portantiero compared the pretensions of the *Contorno* writers to those of the country's progressive middle class ever since the University Reform in 1917: common to all was the desire to become the leaders of a movement with the proletariat constituting their obedient and servile followers.[19] Ernesto Goldar, also critical of the *Contorno* endeavor, interpreted David Viñas's story, "El avión negro" (written in the post-Peronist period), as a projection of working class passivity: the workers, as depicted by Viñas, were accustomed to having solutions come from on high in the form of miracles; they were portrayed as having been inculcated with a respect for a social system characterized by "paternalismo dadivoso que les regalaba derechos y que los ha malcriado. . . ." The workers, then, were "inconscientes individuos que esperan la vuelta de Perón de la misma manera que esperan llover."[20] The Peronist masses, in the mind of Viñas and other *Contorno* writers, could be led by any capable and intelligent leader. If Perón had been able to lead them, then why not Frondizi? Indeed, the possibility must have entered the minds of the *Contorno* writers that they themselves could partially supplant Perón, at least with regard to cultural and perhaps social issues, and could therefore administer the process of worker *conducción* along new and constructive lines.

Under strong attack by critics such as Portantiero and Goldar, the *Contorno* writers, by 1959, were subjecting themselves to arduous self-criticism. Before, they had never seriously questioned the viability of a populist electoral coalition for bringing about a desired socio-economic transformation of the country. Their experience with Frondizism, however, confirmed their unspoken doubts about the willingness and perhaps ability of middle-class leaders to pursue revolutionary policies with the objective of supplanting the country's entrenched oligarchic interests. At issue was not only their need to adopt a more effective strategy for promoting social and political change; they also began to recognize the necessity of abandoning idealistic principles when confronted by the prospects of revolution involving society's lower classes. More than a century before, Echeverría, Sarmiento, and Alberdi, when faced with a similar situation, abandoned their revolutionary creed of republicanism, brotherhood, and liberty, and (over and above their differing responses) opted for the security of property and an authoritarian political order as a means of avoiding a potentially uncontrollable social clash. The *Contorno* participants now found a contemporary example of the same phenomenon: the unwillingness of the middle class to support even the moderate demands of the "unruly" workers, who continued in their obedience to Perón. The *Contorno* writers were familiar with the literature of the ideological left that somewhat schematically catalogued the middle class as a special arm of the bourgeoisie—indeed, the label of "petite bourgeoisie," a legacy of nineteenth-century Marxist thought, made this association clear. At the beginning of their writing militancy, the *Contorno* writers had argued that nothing linked them—neither class interests nor personal values—to the country's bourgeoisie. Instead, they had argued that because they were petit-bourgeois *intellectuals*, they were true social intermediaries: neither bourgeoisie nor proletariat, they shared characteristics and aspirations of both. Now, after their frustrated experience with Frondizi, they were more apt to listen to the criticism of one such as quasi-Marxist, Peronist supporter, and FORJA (Radical Orientation Forces of Argentine Youth) ideologue, J. J. Hernández Arregui. The latter described the insecurity of the middle class as a result of a clash between the values acquired in their humble origins and those that spoke to realized aspirations of increased social prestige and economic security.[21] He argued that the liberal ideals of middle-class thinkers served on most occasions as a rationalization for the social privilege that they enjoyed: even though the most progressive members of the middle-class intelligentsia would sincerely defend and promote those ideals, their pronouncements rarely, if ever, led to substantial changes. I. Viñas acknowledged his acceptance of this view of the essentially anti-revolutionary role of the middle class. He quoted the well-known passage from the writings of Antonio Gramsci that described how the progressive stance of many middle-class individuals often yielded few benefits for workers, but did result in extending the hegemony of the bourgeoisie over previously marginalized social groups.[22] This was because the progressive voices of the bourgeoisie or petite bourgeoisie only belatedly become aware of the seismic transformation of society and of their own class, which they, with their revolutionary rhetoric, naively promote or set in motion. Many—too many, according to Gramsci—therefore panic at the prospect of social disruption and "vuelven al rendil," that is, they abandon the revolution and opt instead for a defense of more conservative or traditional middle-class values.

A New Plan of Action

It was clear that the nucleus of writers still participating with *Contorno* at this stage—in particular, the Viñas brothers, Rozitchner, Gigli, Prieto, and Halperín—wished to avoid the course of involvement denounced by Gramsci. But the options for future activism were not clear. At least one thing was now obvious to both Rozitchner and I. Viñas: any possibility for revolutionary change lay only with the proletariat; they, as individuals and as a group, would no longer place their confidence in the ambiguous and unreliable middle class, and certainly not with the self-serving bourgeoisie. However, this realization, in itself, did not translate into a clear and concrete program of action for themselves. Rozitchner and I. Viñas also realized that the workers were hardly unanimous in their support for the substantial social changes that *Contorno* believed were imperative. The working class, in their view, had made significant strides toward attaining a self-conscious ideology, but they still had hardly advanced beyond the recognition that concerted action could win them piece-meal benefits within the bourgeoisie-dominated system. No, the proletariat was hardly ready to lead the country in social revolution.

Both Rozitchner and I. Viñas therefore spoke of the continued need for an ideologically advanced nucleus of middle-class intellectuals such as themselves to prepare the working class for its central role at some future moment. Was this the same prescription that they had offered some years before, but now cloaked with a more Marxist tone? Yes and no. Yes, in the sense that they, as the "izquierda consciente"—in the words of Viñas,[23] would still provide the leadership for proletarian militancy; their role as clerics and educators of the working class would remain substantially the same. But their role now and in the future would differ in several key respects. Now they spoke to the need for turning away from middle-class groups as the inspiration and nucleus for the social transformation they envisioned. The industrial bourgeoisie could no longer be counted on for its support. Now they proposed that the working class alone, regardless of whether it was supported or opposed by other social classes, would have to garner the necessary social and political support for bringing about desired changes. In this respect, the options now suggested by Rozitchner and I. Viñas broke paths with their previous prescription for social action.

Rozitchner offered a dramatic metaphorical description of how this new role for radicalized middle-class intellectuals was to come about. The first step was to achieve "la ruptura del cordón unbilical que nos ata todavía a la burguesía."[24] They had to create a distance between society's elite and themselves, and then first on the ideological level, in economic, political, and social terms. Rozitchner explained: "separarse de los mitos ideológicos de izquierda de la burguesía constituye tal vez el máximo esfuerzo en la tarea de esclarecimiento de la izquierda." Viñas's diction was equally metaphoric:

> La situación que vivimos nos empuja irresistiblemente hacia ese nuevo mundo, empuja hacia la muerte [de] las viejas estructuras. Nuestra tarea consiste en colaborar en ese parto, en apresurar a la historia, en evitar otras posibilidades temporarias que puede provocar el mundo viejo al tratar de sobrevivir.[25]

A second aspect of their newly projected leadership role involved their own position vis-à-vis the working class. One error of the past was the belief that they, as intellectuals, could lead from on high, that is, without being personally involved themselves. Previously, they had tried to legitimize their militancy by calling attention to their own altruistic objectives and the clear social analysis they offered. Now, they realized that these were not enough, that an effective leadership must now lead from *within*:

No nos engañemos: la izquierda objetivamente está en el proletariado, porque nuestra izquierda consciente es fundamental-
mente de clase media; y aun los grupos más conscientes del propio
proletariado, por su misma politización—que no es otra cosa que
culturización—son más presionados por el condicionamiento de la
sociedad global de lo que nos queremos confesar. Unos y otros
debemos tomar claro conocimiento de eso, animarnos a reconocerlo
para poder superarlo: matar al *hombre viejo* que todos llevamos
dentro, suicidarnos para renacer de veras.[26]

Viñas wrote that any progressive intellectuals who hoped to offer leadership from within the proletarian movement had to assimilate themselves to that movement. Intellectuals would have to overcome
reactionary bourgeois tendencies in their own thought and motivations—a process Viñas likened to a figurative suicide—in order to think
and act, and then hopefully lead the masses in the enterprise of national
transformation.

The three writers represented in the final *Contorno* issue only treated
the principal issues, but hardly defined a specific course of action for
purging the bourgeois orientations from their own thought and for
entering into an effective relationship with the working-class movement.
However, each did provide a few general admonitions for guiding their
future activity. All three—Rozitchner, I. Viñas, and Halperín Donghi—
were in agreement that the entire process would be arduous, complex,
and contradictory. All suggested that the process would take years and
perhaps decades, not just months. Rozitchner was particularly critical of
himself and his group for their previous optimism and their naive hopes
for instantaneous, and in effect, magical, solutions:

Creímos en el pasaje instantáneo inmediato, a partir de esas elec-
ciones formuladas en el voto que nos habrían de transportar de
golpe a una Arcadia soñada donde ni el imperialismo ni los militares
ni la prensa traficada ni otras tantas muchas cosas existirían: que-
rímos una solución mágica que compensara nuestra ineficacia, que
convirtiera nuestros sueños en realidad.[27]

I. Viñas, in his turn, emphasized the need to steer away from pat
solutions cloaked in abstract ideological terms or dressed up as apocalyptic prophesies. Instead, they had a constant need to adjust their
perspective to the realities at hand and to re-evaluate their situation and
the possible avenues for effective action.

Viñas returned once again to the danger of advocating idealistic or
overly ambitious goals in the face of a large intractable social reality: that
practice would lead to an inevitable separation between theory and
practice, with the end result being their condemnation to inaction. He

spoke to the need for humility in recognizing that an individual or group could come to possess only a partial understanding of the complex and multifaceted social reality. It was necessary to avoid the arrogance that typified the spokesmen of the ideological Left, which arose from the latters' belief that they alone possessed the "correct" diagnosis for society's ills. In order to combat the same brand of dogmatism within their own thought, Viñas signaled a necessary "liberación del mito *culturalista*" and the need to guard in one's own thought against "las formas positivistas del iluminismo local, disfraz del conservadorismo aristocratizante."[28] Halperín's reflections took a similar direction. To be a revolutionary in theory, he paradoxically stated, was to renounce all revolutionary pretension.[29] Worse yet, nothing betrayed the real revolution more effectively than the image of a false revolution.

All three writers were in solid agreement about a related matter: the need for social activists to be personally involved in the social process in order to protect themselves against the sterile and potentially counterproductive enterprise of abstract theorization. Political activity would provide intellectuals with concrete data for the continual reformulation of objectives and tactics and would help them avoid the temptation of tracing an image of possible goals or actions which outstripped the potentialities for actual change. Furthermore, an intermingling with workers would help intellectuals to educate themselves about their concrete needs and aspirations; it would help to establish their leadership—if the potential for leadership was present—among working-class associates. Continual organizing activity would also work against the pernicious tendencies for the politically more advanced elements in any movement to separate themselves from those they presumably led, and would help them to rise above the old and essentially counterproductive "aristocratic image" of the intelligentsia as the endowed and enlightened leaders of passive masses. Rozitchner articulated this goal eloquently:

> debemos quedar a un paso, pero sólo a uno, de esta realidad política que está pasando a los hechos. Debemos quedar unidos a la realidad no en la infinita lejanía de la imaginación consoladora, sino sólo a un paso de distancia en el tiempo. Los valores que proyectamos deben comenzar a transformar la realidad a partir de este mismo presente.[30]

Rozitchner was aware that intimate contact with the social reality in which one lived was only a means toward an end. It served in the necessary task of combatting one's own complacency; it was the path by which accurate theorization of the struggle was possible. Also, it was indispensable for transforming their theories into efficient and effective strategies of action. This whole process had only one certification, however: the degree to which one's interaction truly contributed to the modification of his situation.

An Inner Transformation

Rozitchner, better than Viñas and Halperín, articulated the theoretical and affective bridges that united the diverse concerns of the *Contorno* group over the previous decade. In seven years and through ten issues, their focus had passed from engaged literary criticsm to political theorization, and now to political activism. The theoretical bridge uniting these stages was the awareness that they as individuals were intimately related to their situation, that their personal salvation was inextricably linked to the salvation of society. Rozitchner could not call his essay complete without adding a highly personal "Epílogo para decepcionados" in which he reaffirmed these links and related them to the social and political factors that still impeded their personal search:

> Porque, en síntesis, hemos querido decir esto: nuestra intimidad, lo que tenemos de absoluto y de excepción, eso que vamos afanosamente a cultivar en el aislamiento, no puede cultivarse ni recuperarse en el aislamiento. O nos recuperamos todos juntos, o no lo hace nadie, pues las categorías de la intimidad, en la sociedad actual, están inficionadas por las categorías de lo económico y lo político. . . .
> Lo cual quiere decir: sólo en la actividad exterior, sólo en la relación con los demás hombres y sus luchas, sólo en la objectividad podremos recuperar ese absoluto que en la soledad se consuela con la ficción. Sólo en la exterioridad podemos recuperar nuestra intimidad.[31]

Deception with the political process, he stated, could easily lead one to abandon the social struggle and withdraw to the limited security offered by one's inner world. However, this choice was founded on the mistaken idea that the self could exist in isolation from society. Rozitchner suggested that harmony, inner peace, and conflict-free action—any quality that the defeated social activist desperately sought—could only be achieved or recuperated in and through social interaction. He reaffirmed the Sartrian message that had occupied such an important dimension a decade before in their formation as writers and intellectuals: Either we recover together, or not at all, because one's intimate values and motivations are inevitably influenced by the larger society; the categories of the intimate self, even the most secret and imprecise apsects of one's affective being, are shared with others who co-inhabit our situation.

"¿Palabras y palabras?" Rozitchner interrogated himself. He provided a concrete example of what resulted when an activist experienced a separation between intimate and public identities. The traditional revolutionaries of the Left had utterly lacked effectiveness in their actions, Rozitchner suggested, because they preferred to convert the social struggle into an abstract theoretical construct that only remotely related to their own lives. The visionaries of the Left avoided personal involvement in the revolution; they were like the prophet who becomes a martyr only to his own prophesies: "Ellos postergan su personalidad revolucionaria proyectándola hacia el futuro, y por ahora sólo claman por su advenimiento mágico en el liso y llano plano de la política declamatoria."[32] Small wonder that their words, although rigorously systematic and doctrinally pure, were still almost worthless as a guide for organizational activity. Rozitchner therefore warned against the temptation of converting political activity into mere imaginative symbolism in the hope of appeasing one's own conscience. One way of avoiding this conformist trap was to strive for a totalizing comprehension of one's situation in order to view the contradictions of one's intimate life as they related to the objective conditions in which one lived. Proceeding one step further, Rozitchner suggested (in words reminiscent of David Viñas's earlier admonition of "asir furiosamente nuestra media") that the concerned middle-class intellectual who strove for effective social and political involvement must view his own person in relation to the totality of his situation. This meant that he must internalize the social risk experienced as an activist and make it an integral part of his personality and life. If this operation were successful, then one's subjective life would be joined to the social struggle. Consequently, one's struggle to achieve the transformation of society would parallel the struggle to transform one's personality. This identification of personal and social concerns, Rozitchner warned, was not merely a pretentious means of calling attention to oneself; it was the only way one could concretize in a comprehensive fashion the sense of reality that one's situation presented.

Ismael Viñas discussed the same need of uniting the personal crusade with the revolutionary quest, but placed more emphasis on the beneficial results for the social struggle and less on the philosophical or moral benefits for the person involved. His discussion revolved around a subject that, since *Contorno's* auspicious beginnings, had been a constant topic of discussion: the preoccupation with his own group in relation to the social whole. Unchanged was the recognition that he and other *Contorno* writers could only realize themselves as individuals through effective intellectual and organizational activity. Now, the issue was to go beyond a model of social leadership from on high and, instead, forge the necessary social links to lead successfully from within. But the group was not yet ready for assuming that responsibility: they first had to face up to the fact that as members of the middle class they had assimilated the myths of their class which were difficult to distinguish from social fact. This meant that their successful incorporation into the worker movement involved far more than the renunciation of economic privilege: they also had to strive constantly to recognize how those myths acted upon their own motivations at every turn and affected their values and orientations. Therefore, it was necessary to realize how the revolutionary goals and objectives arrived at through intellectual conviction and rational deliberation would be opposed by their most intimate and spontaneous tendencies. For that reason, he called upon his group to undergo a type of suicide (as quoted above) in order to kill the old being that all of them carried within, so that they could be politically "born anew." This process would not be easy; it would involve continual self-criticism and redefinition of priorities. It would involve a continual reassessment of the distance separating their conscious orientations from their most intimate values.

The Frondizi debacle was a measure of the *Contorno* writers' own political naïveté. Frondizi had failed to keep pre-election promises to the middle-class intellectuals and to the Peronist working class on account of the intense pressures placed upon him by the economic interests of the country that stood to lose in the event of a significant social transformation. The *Contorno* members had greatly underestimated the resistance that innovation in Argentina's social and political systems would provoke. They had believed in the facile solutions of the ballot box and the effectiveness of political maneuvers: "todo se resuelve en el plano político," Ismael Viñas had suggested a year or so before the Frondizi election. Now they knew that Viñas's diagnosis had been far too simplistic. They realized that any change whatever would only come about slowly and be accompanied by enormous sacrifices. This realization would usher in a whole new set of techniques for advancing the mass consciousness; it would accompany a new set of principles for guiding the social and political behavior of many of them in subsequent decades.

6
Conclusion

THE PUBLICATION OF *CONTORNO* BETWEEN 1953 AND 1959 COINCIDED WITH events of enormous importance for Argentina as a whole. Today it is commonly accepted that the journal offered perhaps the most coherent and thoughtful orientation of any existing organ of expression for evaluating Argentina's recent past and projecting a program for future action in the political, social, and cultural spheres. The participating writers' strength was their awareness of what seems today to be an obvious fact, that in order for any social or political program to be effective, it must speak to the dramatic changes in their country's recent past.

Indeed, the changes within the country were significant. Before the Peronist decade, the working class had been largely unorganized, lacking in class consciousness, and marginalized in its social and political participation. After Peronism, the proletariat was organized and militant and had come to constitute perhaps the largest electoral and political force in the country. Before the Peronist decade, there had existed a modest industrialization capacity in the coastal areas of the nation; after Peronism, Argentina was one of the two industrial giants of the continent, producing for national consumption and exportation all types of consumer goods, while having achieved significant advances in many basic industries, such as energy, steel, and transportation. Before the Peronist decade, the national government had performed a moderating function among the private interests of the country; at the end of that decade, the state directly controlled the greater part of the nation's petroleum and aviation industries, communications, public transportation, and banking systems; it also directed the international commercialization of a large percentage of the nation's stock and agricultural products.

In retrospect, it is also apparent today that the Peronist decade in Argentina, which coincided with the period immediately following World War II, constituted a turning point for social and economic conditions that were continental as well as national in scope. In general, it was a period of accelerated economic expansion, population growth, and urbanization. On the positive side, the newly industrialized sectors of the domestic economy that had been financed largely through foreign capital investment, now produced for a broad national market the consumer goods (autos, televisions, refrigerators, etc.) which previously had been available only to the region's economic and social elite. A negative consequence of this modernization was the progressive loss of control for local industries throughout Latin America in favor of multinational trusts and cartels. This accompanied Latin America's increased productive, financial, and technological dependency. Local political systems became more susceptible to the pressures wielded by international agencies or foreign governments. In truth, the economic, political, and ideological configurations in most Latin American countries had been radically altered.

Another change affecting the different Latin American societies was the dramatic increase in numbers of the middle class that played an expanded role in society and politics. This especially affected the lives and ambitions of the *Contorno* youths, given the fact that all of them hailed from the middle class. In Argentina, perhaps more so than in other Latin American societies, the middle class already exercised considerable influence in government, and its priorities for professional and industrial advancement now pressured for significant modifications in the nation's economic organization. Since the depression years of the 1930s, national analysts had pointed to the imperative of modifying the latifundia-based land-tenure system that had, until then, sustained the nation's agro-oligarchy. They pointed out with increasing frequency how that relatively small privileged group of land owners and cattle exporters exercised a disproportionate influence over the country's politics and culture. For decades, theorists had argued that it was the middle class's destiny to usurp the agro-oligarchy's position of authority. Perón's push toward industrialization confirmed the fact that the middle class now existed in sufficient numbers and with sufficient managerial skills to predominate in all spheres of national life.

Also significant was the new concentration in Argentina's cities of workers who hailed from the interior provinces. Drawn to new employment opportunities in the country's expanding industrial infrastructure, these "cabecitas negras"—as the white, urban population of the cities commonly referred to them—abandoned their economically depressed and geographically isolated rural settings and sought a new life in the city. Many of them initially experienced the scorn of the Europeanized urban population on account of their antiquated customs and rural or "gaucho" culture. But this new worker population progressively adapted to city life. By the 1940s, they were beginning to recognize that the sheer

magnitude of their numbers and their important role in the new industrial sector entitled them to a greater degree of participation in local
governmental structures than what they had previously exercised.

The contribution of the *Contorno* writers was their attempt to accommodate these important demographic, social, and economic transformations within successful strategies for intellectual involvement. From its
first issue, it was evident to all that *Contorno* successfully captured a
spirit of rebelliousness and frustration that characterized the attitudes of
a broad sector of the nation's youth. Although their early critics, and
even some of the *Contorno* participants themselves, associated these
young intellectuals with a national Generation of 1945 or 1950,[1] later
writers have tended to call attention to how their orientations anticipated
the period of literary and critical writing that was only beginning to
emerge when Perón fell in 1955.[2] The remarks of Juan Carlos Portantiero
about the *Contorno* group and other young intellectuals during this
period are important in this regard: "Yo creo que en los últimos años de
Perón, y más específicamente cuando Perón cae (que son años de revelo
intelectual, donde se produce este proceso en el ensayo y la novela), este
proceso de aparición de nuevas gentes está marcado por una reflexión
crítica muy profunda, que el intelectual se hace sobre todo el pasado
argentino."[3]

Many of the *Contorno* writers' formative experiences that were related
to the national situation also correlated with trends which were both
hemispheric and international in scope. For example, Peronist populism
(understood here as the social and electoral coalition of industrialists and
workers) and Frondizi's promise to achieve a similar alliance had their
parallels in Brazil, Bolivia, Chile, and other countries. The *Contorno*
writers' enthusiasm for and then disillusionment with populism were
experiences shared by young intellectuals throughout Latin America.[4]

This was a period of ideological *abertura* for intellectuals throughout
Latin America. Nassar, Nehru, Perón, and other leaders had popularized the term "Third World" in reference to the less-developed countries of the world that did not participate directly in the Cold War
between the two superpowers. During the years of *Contorno* publication,
however, the term also came to be applied in the ideological realm: a
"Third World" intellectual was one who searched for a middle ground
between the philosophies of liberalism and Stalinist Marxism. On the
one hand, the *Contorno* writers—who were in this respect representative
of their generation of Latin American intellectuals—had been raised in
the liberal tradition and accepted as their own many of that creed's
highest values. Nevertheless, they took upon themselves a critique of
liberalism, especially as to how that philosophy functioned as the ideological justification in Argentina for oppressive and elitist practices. On

the other hand, they found in existentialism and phenomenology the philosophical avenues for avoiding the dogmatic implications of traditional Marxism's historical or materialistic determinism and at the same time retaining Marxism's revolutionary thrust. Out of these two branches of thought—the critique of liberalism and the unfreezing of Marxist-Leninist thought—emerged what is known today as the Neo-Marxist school.

It has been argued that the *Contorno* writers therefore belong to a continental grouping on the basis of broad historical and social factors that influenced not only their intellectual formation, but also the manner in which they perceived their situation.[5] The devastating power of the atomic bomb, the social and political turbulence throughout Africa, Asia, and Latin America, the scientific technification of production, the massification of man in labor, living, and leisure, were some of the broad experiences that had both direct and indirect effects on their ideas.[6] One result was the feeling shared among young intellectuals throughout the hemisphere of a general sense of separateness from the actual state of things, as if the sum total of their cultural inheritance from previous generations amounted to little more than a dead weight that had to be removed in order to implement their own renovating project for the future. Angel Rama indicates that the primary intellectual attribute of this *promoción* of Latin American writers and intellectuals is their

> disconformidad con un estado de cosas que han heredado como un peso muerto, mucho más que cualquier proyecto renovador de futuro, que algunos no avizorarán y que otros no encontrararán nunca. Pero coinciden en la insatisfacción, en el reproche, en la diagnosis certera de la enfermedad, lo que nos proveerá de una abundante narrativa sobre la decadencia y la decrepitud que a veces se objectivara en el análisis de los órdenes sociales. . . .[7]

These individuals coincided in the dissatisfaction, and at times anger, with which they diagnosed the diseases of their respective societies. Refuge or flight from these problems would have been possible. However, this generation, in general, possessed an "amor a América, salud sanguinea, coraje, trascendencia, hambre de humana creación, calidez y fervor"—according to another observer[8]—that guided their response in more constructive channels. Their commitment was direct and unwaivering. Other Latin Americans belonging to this hemispheric generation are Fidel Castro, Edmundo Desnoes, Roberto Fernández Retamar, Carlos Fuentes, Gabriel García Márquez, Ernesto "Che" Guevara, Gustavo Gutiérrez, Mario Vargas Llosa, Camilo Torres, and others. Most were born between 1925 and 1935; they have excelled in such diverse fields as literature, government, religion, and education.

Characteristic of this postwar generation was a Third World consciousness. Uniting the *Contorno* writers to the young generation of
writers and intellectuals across Latin America was their sensitivity to
their countries' marginal, even subservient, position vis-à-vis the developed nations of the North. They perceived that the cold war, which
pitted against each other the two most powerful countries of the Northern Hemisphere, caused a continued disregard and at times aggravation
of poor countries' problems. Their formative years paralleled a growing
awareness on the part of many people that neither the capitalist nor the
socialist powers of the industrialized Northern Hemisphere wholeheartedly sought an amelioration of the underdeveloped world's endemic
problems of malnutrition and low productivity. This hemispheric generation therefore came together in its opposition to imperialism and internal colonialism, those two forces that continued to impede Latin
America's development. This explains in part their commitment to the
principles of human rights and economic justice, two issues that, in the
past, had constituted the platform for many Latin American middle-class
movements. This new group, however, unconditionally demanded
Third World economic, political, and cultural sovereignty.

This Third World protest was characterized not only by its content, but
also by the form in which it was carried out. The principal figures
constituting this hemispheric generation did not content themselves
with moral indignation, as had the Arielist Generation of 1900, but
sought instead an active response. An obstacle to their involvement was
the lack of a conceptual framework for understanding the problems
besetting their societies. These activists therefore tended to reject easy
solutions or pat ideological explanations; their hallmark was rather the
continual search for appropriate avenues for action that took into account the dynamic, evolving social reality. Their particular task was the
continual reassessment of their situation in order to embody their
awareness in effective praxis.

A Tradition of Activist Writing

Throughout the life of their journal, the *Contorno* writers teetered
ambiguously between two potential roles. In some moments, their mission had the appearance of a generational renovation, through which
their language of social relevance and personal involvement would substitute for older forms of expression: they were the rebellious youth
whose ambition was to supplant the older writers of their class as the
country's ritual priests of the written tradition. In other moments, however, their protest seemed to promise a radical redefinition of the intellectual's function in society. As such, they would lead the progressive

middle class into a new alliance with the workers, in the hope of realizing dramatic transformations in the nation's economic, social, and political institutions.

They were aware that their objectives of social militancy tied them to other intellectual movements in Argentina's past. They, as well as the writers of 1837, 1900, and 1922, came of age in a moment of social crisis, when the hegemony of predominant groups of the country was under challenge. All of the leftist movements in the past had attempted to open new avenues of communication with significant groups that had recently acquired a degree of social importance. The writers of 1837—Alberdi, Echeverría, Sarmiento—sought in the newly ascendant commercial and professional classes of the cities a mainstay for the progressive order they envisioned. The Generation of 1900—Lugones, Ugarte, Sánchez, Payró, Carriego, Almafuerte—responded to the rapid increase in urban population and the corresponding rise in social turbulence in Buenos Aires at the turn of the century: the group they courted and instructed was the growing middle class. A quarter of a century later, the Boedo group (named after the street where the offices of the journal *Claridad* were located)—Arlt, Mariani, González Tuñón, Yunque, Barletta, Amorim, and Castelnuovo—was the brother to radicalism in politics, because both were nourished by the middle class, now organized and for the first time exercising political power. In their own moment, the *Contorno* writers responded to the entrance of the working class as an organized force on the nation's social and political scenes. Common to all of these movements was the intellectuals' shared mission of serving their respective societies as cultural and social intermediaries: while hailing from the outer circles of the country's elite, they strove to assist more marginal social groups in their respective struggles for social ascendance. A common goal was the broadening of the social and cultural dialogue in order to integrate the newly emerging groups into the social totality.

Similarities continue with regard to ideological orientation. The principal leaders of the four leftist literary movements were intellectuals, meaning that they had in common a disposition toward ideas and book learning. Although the knowledge they possessed about their respective societies was based on estimable powers of observation and intimate familiarity with the existing written sources of information, they still lacked—in the majority of cases—a practical knowledge of their respective realities that was based on direct and personal interaction with different social groups. Added to their "culturalist" orientation was their fascination with the ideas currently enjoying popularity in European intellectual circles. Romanticism and *socialismo*—that is, the pre-positivistic or "eclectic" ideas deriving mainly from the writings of Saint-

Simon—fueled the early activism of the 1837 thinkers; anarchism and socialism inspired the 1900 generation; bolshevik socialist principles and Marxism provided the social panaceas for the Boedo writers; and the existentialist variant of Marxism, as defined primarily through the writings of Sartre, Camus, and Merleau-Ponty, provided the ideological framework for the *Contorno* writers' militancy. By the time of their journal's last issue in 1959, the *Contorno* writers realized that they, like their leftist literary predecessors, had harbored a belief in the superiority of their own conceptual framework which many times obstructed their perception of factors relevant to the political economy of their situation. Uniting *Contorno* to the previous movements of intellectual militancy was the inherent weakness of the "cultural priest" role that they depicted for themselves: their militancy was founded on a sense of their own superiority, which was necessarily accompanied by a subtle disdain for those whom they pretended to lead.

The *Contorno* writers were familiar with some of the shortcomings of previous intellectual militants. Although the group as a whole never succeeded in overcoming many similar shortcomings during the life of their journal, they did attempt to do so, as is evident in the changing focus for their writing militancy throughout its different stages. Similarly, they were at times entirely aware of the possible dangers that awaited them, given the options chosen for their participation. For example, they had foreseen the possibility of Frondizi not abiding by his campaign promises once elected. When those fears were finally realized, the group clearly understood how their previous illusions had fallen into the well-worn pattern of the other idealistic and militant intellectuals who had preceded them in their country's tradition.

Also evident was the growing humility with which they viewed their own ability to understand the fluid national situation. At the fall of Perón, they had been convinced that the ideological mystifications veiling the social and political mechanisms of the country had suddenly lifted and that their group—almost alone—was therefore privileged to a perspective of that reality which no other group enjoyed. But by 1959 they had come to realize that their previously "clarivoyant" vision of things had been clouded by one principal factor: a confusion with regard to their own position vis-à-vis other social groups. Before, their supposed privileged view of reality had been a cause for enthusiasm; now, their more sober awakening was accompanied by an anguished awareness of their limited power to effect change and even to diagnose society's options. Their new realization was that their critics of seven years back had been entirely correct in describing the *Contorno* writers as impetuous upstarts without a well-seasoned theoretical framework for their militancy. Before, the *Contorno* writers had denied their ties to tradition; now, they were forced to accept the fact that their actions and ideas had conformed in large part to the patterns established by the intellectual militants of the past. The parallels were too obvious and could not be ignored. Their decision now was to accept those similarities as a social fact in order to confront them more effectively.

Beyond Engagement

The theories and practices associated with engagement provided a meaningful orientation for the *Contorno* writers throughout the period of their journal's publication. They were explicitly embraced during the period of literary criticism, from 1953 to 1956; they underlay many of the young writers' ideas with regard to an intellectual leadership of the working class throughout the post-Peronist period and up through the close of the journal in 1959. Engagement, in short, had fueled the *Contorno* writers' ambitions for involvement in society. It had provided an initial ideological framework for their vague desires to establish a dialogue with the working class; it had also inspired their objective of the proletariat's integration into national life under the benign tutorship of progressive middle-class intellectuals.

Seen in retrospect, the ideas associated with engagement conveniently offered a theoretical solution for a number of the young writers' most vexing dilemmas. First of all, by promising to make their intellectual endeavors more relevant to society's urgent problems, engagement would help them overcome the sense of powerlessness they previously felt with regard to society. Second, it promised an end to the writer's traditional isolation by providing a bridge of communication between themselves and the working class. Third, it projected the means whereby their writing would become converted into effective political action; through their engaged writing, they themselves would be transformed from social marginals into protagonists. In general, the *Contorno* writers were captivated by engagement's promise of heightening the social role of previously undervalued superstructural concerns—rational persuasion, subjective motivations, literature, writing, and, in general, culture.

Not all of these promises of engagement held equal sway over any two of the *Contorno* participants at any one time; it is even possible that at least a few of the young writers never became unduly influenced by any one of them. In general, however, these preconceptions of a new social power wielded by the intellectual through his writing guided the group in its initial writing experiences. By and large, these unrealistic expectations became contributing factors in the *Contorno* members' shift in focus from literary to social and political concerns, beginning with their journal's fifth issue in 1956.

Early on, the *Contorno* writers had been taken to task for the unrealizable promises of political action that they associated with an engaged intellectual practice, and the inflated social importance that they bestowed upon their own role as activist-intellectuals. By the time of their final disillusionment with Frondizi—which coincided with the last issue of their journal—they themselves hardly needed to be convinced of the questionable theoretical basis of their previous program for intellectual activism. Their disappointment with Frondizi, however, resulted in a dramatic reorientation, but certainly not the end, of their ambitions for social involvement. In short, engagement was the ideological plan that had momentarily systematized and defined, but never contained or limited, the original motivations that attracted the *Contorno* writers to it in the first place.

Indeed, at no moment during the trajectory of their writing militancy had they fallen into self-righteousness or an uncritical acceptance of either engagement or Frondizism. On the contrary, constant in their thought was the awareness of the gap that existed between their stated political or cultural goals and the possibilities for realizing them. Also evident throughout was an emotional tension due to the contradictions they knew to exist between what they wished to achieve and their actual achievement. As they stated in their issue treating Peronism: "nos sentimos incómodos dentro de nuestra piel."[9] That discomfort lends itself to various interpretations, but for the most part it was a positive force. David Viñas suggested that they, as individuals and as a group, must "escribir y vivir como culpables." He was aware that discomfort fostered a continual doubting of one's own premises. It led one to constantly test hypotheses in concrete situations. To their credit, the writers of *Contorno* never fell into dogmatisms; they knew that no one theory or body of knowledge was completely adequate as a guide for action, and that only through an unceasing process of self-criticism could their analyses avoid falling into abstractions. They understood their disequilibrium as a precondition for change.

Engagement, they came to realize, was only a stage in their ideological development. It had to be surpassed both in theory and practice because the means it provided were not adequate for achieving the ends it proposed. In order to proceed beyond engagement, they had to be conscious of its limitations; they had to confront the class-oriented values that had led them to that set of theories in the first place. By the closure of their journal, they realized the need to gravitate toward new, and hopefully more effective, solutions.

Contorno's Legacy for the 1980s

The social and political crisis that launched the *Contorno* writers into activity and motivated thousands of young readers to eagerly follow the ideas expressed in the successive issues of their journal has not yet been resolved. In the last century Argentina has experienced a breath-taking modernization, which has dramatically changed the face of the nation: the country boasts of its beautiful cities, a formidable export trade, a broad consumer market, and a national culture that, to the superficial glance, breathes cosmopolitanism and universality. But those aspects of modernization are also marred by symptoms of a truncated, or dependent, development. By the Great Depression in the 1930s, it became universally recognized that the country's veneer of modernism no longer hid its deeply rooted problems. Inequality and exploitation were not the exception, but the rule. In effect, an agrarian and cattle-producing oligarchy still controlled the country's economy and still wielded a disproportionate share of social and political power. In spite of its spectacular modernization, Argentina still possessed a colonial economy: exports consisting primarily of foodstuffs and raw materials paid for imports of manufactured and capital goods. In addition, Argentina was energy dependent and its commerce and banking activities were almost entirely controlled by international interests.

The popularity of Perón was due in large part to the widespread indignation felt about these endemic national problems. Notwithstanding the *justicialista* leader's shortcomings, he initiated a governmental program that promised the country's emergence from the throes of dependency. He drew upon the patriotic sentiments of the country's industrialists and workers, in addition to the support of Church and military leaders, in order to work harmoniously on behalf of national development. During several years this populist coalition provided broad popular support for the implementation of the admirable objectives that he articulated.

In the first moment, it was the *Contorno* writers' object to continue struggling for the goals that Perón had first promised, then failed to deliver. Their intention was to do so largely through a similar coalition, uniting workers and industrialists, but now including significant sectors of the middle class. Even though their goals of social justice and national economic independence remained largely unchanged throughout the period of their journal's publication, the political means they proposed for achieving those goals underwent continual revision. By the end of that period, they had belatedly abandoned their hope for widespread middle-class support in a democratic political revolution. Soberly, they came to the realization that the oligarchy's social, economic, and political power would have to be curtailed. This would come about only if the working class, allied to the militant sectors of the middle class, could exercise the power of the state in order to undo two centuries of dependency and lead the nation into uncharted revolutionary waters.

All of that is past history. The outcome of the *Contorno* dream is well known: Frondizi's promises; his subsequent abandonment of the working-class program; the 1962 military coup; the succession of ineffective civilian regimes and authoritarian military juntas; the interclass war of the 1970s; the unparalleled brutality of military bosses during the horrendous "dirty war"; the monstrous mismanagement and corruption of the country's economic resources; and the tragically absurd unleashing of chauvinistic fury in the Malvinas debacle. In short, the promise of social transformation has been thwarted time and again. Although much has changed, Argentina's problems have only become more acute. One could argue that for thirty years the forces of reaction have done everything short of dismembering the country in order that its dependency and stagnation not be overcome. The crisis of decades is not yet at its end. Thirty years ago the young intellectual writers of *Contorno* pointed to a way out of that impasse; the impasse remains, and their call for a resolution to the country's crisis still resounds.

But now a third of a century has passed since they, as young idealistic activists, advocated a revolution of the Left led by militant workers and class-conscious intellectuals. They could argue today that a broad-based coalition similar to what they envisioned three decades ago still offers the best hope for leading the country into reforms that would guarantee the viability of its institutional structures for the uncertain future. One could argue that the country's heartening attempts in recent years to return to democratic and constitutional governance is but the first step in that direction. However, it goes without saying that there remains at least one foreboding parallel, one silent participant that could strike at any moment in order to split asunder any hopes of change: a desperate and discredited military establishment, supported by ruthless right-wing civilian *gorilas*, that threatens to return to power and reestablish a brutal authoritarian control over the country.

Is the *Contorno* prescription of a newly revived populist coalition uniting proletariat and middle class a historically dated option? Recent history in the Southern Cone seems to demonstrate the inadequacy of nationalist populism, even in spite of widespread anti-imperialist sentiments among the population.[10] It is too early to judge whether the process of internationalization of the Argentine economy in the last three decades is irreversible; it is too early to judge whether the control exercised in New York, Washington, and London over vital aspects of Argentine national life is indeed in a state of crisis at present. *Contorno's* call for national transformation has now been joined by a multitude of other voices that also seek viable solutions for the country's seemingly unfathomable ills.

The *Contorno* writers' articulation of the crisis experienced by their society will remain memorable: "Rebeldía, rechazo, desconcierto" are the words initiating their first issue which summarize their frustrations and vague sense of commitment to struggle on behalf of the country. At that time, they humbly admitted their lack of a firm sense of direction: "Tenemous nuestra propia retórica juvenil. No estamos seguros de nuestra verdad." This was the recurring message in each subsequent *Contorno* issue: their willingness to study the issues, their passion for becoming involved. Present-day readers still recognize the positive value of the *Contorno* writers' impassioned search for a resolution to their country's crisis. Because their journalistic activism occurred during a fluid moment of Argentine political history, their ideas and programs were bound to be superseded with the passing of time. The *Contorno* writers' primary strengths, then, were the constancy of their struggle and their flexibility in adapting to changing circumstances.

Their personalized conception of the writing task has many precedents, and so does their self-conception as cultural activists.[11] Critics have rightfully assailed them for what was at times an overly subjective orientation in studying their situation and in projecting their own mission within society. Like other concerned writers in this century, they attempted to incorporate the stuff of lived experience into literature, to heighten the role of culture within society. In addition, they attempted to combine their subjective needs with their critical quest. They chose to live the crisis of their country "romantically": personal involvement was a key to the political solution that they advocated.

Writing, for them, was born of a profound inner need: first and foremost they were writers. But what was special about their sensitivity was the need to fuse their destiny as individuals with that of their society. Through their writing, they strove to assume an integral role in the historical process. As literary generations come and go, the mythos under which the *Contorno* writers operated will be bombasted and praised, criticized and embraced. Their literary ethos will never be accepted by all writers. But that ethos, in its general form, in its general *contorno*, will survive as a worthy example for how one group of writers sought to expand their influence beyond the narrow confines of the intellectual community and launch a social and political revolution from the pages of their journal.

Notes

Chapter 1. Introduction

1. Studies treating the writer's or intellectual's relationship to the middle class in the developing society are: António Cândido, "Literatura y subdesarrollo," in *América latina en su literatura*, ed. César Fernández Moreno (Madrid: Siglo Veintiuno, 1971), pp. 335–53; Frantz Fanon, *The Wretched of the Earth*, trans. Constance Farrington, Preface by Jean-Paul Sartre (New York: Grove, 1963); Susantha Goonatilake, *Crippled Minds: An Exploration into Colonial Culture* (Delhi: Vikas Publishing House, 1982); John J. Johnson, *Political Change in Latin America: The Emergence of the Middle Sectors* (Stanford: Stanford University Press, 1958); José Guilherme Merquior, "Situación del escritor," in *América latina en su literatura*, ed. Fernández Moreno, ibid., pp. 372–88; Fernando Morán, *Novela y semidesarrollo (una interpretación de la novela hispanoamericana y española)* (Madrid: Taurus, 1971); and Adolfo Prieto, *Literatura y subdesarrollo: notas para un análisis de la litertura argentina (Rosario: Biblioteca, 1968)*.

2. Leonardo Senkman, *La identidad judía en la literatura argentina* (Buenos Aires: Pardes, S.R.L., 1983), calls attention to how the novels by David Viñas treat issues relevant to Judaism. In *Un dios cotidiano* (1956) a young Jewish boy is the object of "morbosa curiosidad" on the part of his classmates, who delight in their attempts to humiliate him. In *Dar la cara* (1962) protagonist Bernardo Carmán—according to Senkman—"vive su judeidad como el índice personal y familiar de una condición que no le preocupa. Lo vive como un data más de su origen. . . ."

3. Studies by the *Contorno* writers on the topic of Judaism are: León Rozitchner, *Ser judío* (Buenos Aires: Editorial de la Flor, 1967); Juan José Sebreli, *La cuestión judía en la Argentina* (Buenos Aires: Tiempo Contemporáneo, 1968); Ismael Viñas, "Claves, del antisemitismo en la Argentina" (in Hebrew), *Dispersión y Unidad* 81/82 (Jerusalem, 1977); "Judíos en la Argentina" (in Hebrew), *Dispersión y Unidad* 83/84 (1977)—reprinted in English in *Forum* 3 (1977); and "Los judíos y la sociedad argentina—un análisis clasista," *Controversia* 83/84 (Buenos Aires, 1983).

4. For bibliographical and biographical information on the *Contorno* participants, see Adolfo Prieto, *Diccionario básico de literatura argentina* (Buenos Aires: Centro Editor de América Latina, 1968); Pedro Orgambide and Roberto Yahni, *Enciclopedia de la literatura argentina* (Buenos Aires: Sudamericana, 1970); David Viñas et al., *Contorno: una selección*, ed. and prologue by Carlos Mangone and Jorge Warley (Buenos Aires: Centro Editor de América Latina, 1983), pp. 169–72; and *Quién es quién en la Argentina*, 9th ed. (Buenos Aires: Quién es Quién, 1969).

5. Ismael Viñas, in a letter to the author dated 21 January 1985, affirms that Susana Fiorito published several articles in *Marcha* (Montevideo), in addition to serving as Secretaria de Redacción for *Política*. She published a book, *Comisiones obreras en España*, and directed the publications of the Sitra-Sitram Workers

Union throughout its period of activity. She, according to Viñas, was the only one of the journal's nucleus who "engaged Sebreli in argument."

6. Carlos Mangone and Jorge Warley, "Prólogo," to D. Viñas et. al., *Contorno: una selección*, p. iii.

7. Juan José Sebreli, "El joven Mosotta," *Arte nova* 5 (1980).

8. "Peronismo. . . . ¿y lo otro?" (reputed to be written by David Viñas) is the title of the lead editorial for *Contorno*'s combined 5/6 issue of 1956, which is a source for the ideas expressed in this paragraph.

9. Ismael Viñas, "La generación argentina de 1945," *Comentario* 5, no. 18 (1958): 38.

10. This paragraph is based largely upon the information provided by Tulio Halperín Donghi, "José Luis Romero y su lugar in la historiografía argentina," in José Luis Romero, *Las ideologías de la cultura nacional y otros ensayos*, ed. Luis Alberto Romero (Buenos Aires: Centro Editor de América Latina, 1982), 187–236; and Juan José Hernández Arregui, *La formación de la conciencia nacional (1930–1960)*, 2d ed. enlarged (Buenos Aires: Hachea, 1970), pp. 471–75.

11. Halperín Donghi, "José Luis Romero," p. 193.

12. Ernesto Goldar, *El peronismo en la literatura argentina* (Buenos Aires: Freeland, 1971), p. 29, reaches this conclusion on the basis of a critical reading of David Viñas's short stories.

13. This is the reading of Viñas's short stories offered by Halperín Donghi, "José Luis Romero," p. 193.

14. Ismael Viñas, "La traición de los hombres honestos," *Contorno* 1 (1953): 2.

15. Aristocratic nationalism is the ideology of the Argentine landowners, sometimes called the "agro-oligarchy," who never coalesced into a specific political grouping or party. The vague beliefs associated with this ideology are (1) Argentina's golden age was in the indefinite past when upper-class landowners offered a benign social leadership and when the country was not yet threatened by problems stemming from immigration, industrialization, and the participation of the masses in public life, (2) laissez-faire economic doctrines (its supporters are the heirs to 19th century liberalism), but—paradoxically—the need for the state to support agro-interests during and after the Great Depression of the 1930s, (3) opposition to any form of state-supported worker protection or rights, (4) exaltation of the Fatherland, (5) pro-military in the affairs of the state (especially during the "infamous decade" of the 1930s). Its principal spokesmen have been Leopoldo Lugones in the 1920s, novelist Gustavo Martínez Zuviria (Hugo Wast), and revisionist historians José María Rosa, Jr., Carlos Ibarguren, Julio and Rodolfo Irazusta.

16. With quasi-Marxist, anti-imperialist and worker-oriented beliefs, the progressive nationalists (called "integral" or "leftist" nationalists by some writers) constituted one of the mainstays of Perón's *justicialista* movement in the 1940s and 1950s. Alejandro Bunge provided an early economic analysis for this movement that underlined the need for significant reforms in the productive system of the country, and Leopoldo Lugones provided an impassioned political expression for the movement in *La gran Argentina* (1930). Some beliefs associated with progressive nationalism are (1) anti-liberal economics, meaning the need for state in governing agro-production and commercialization and in promoting industrialization in order to achieve economic independence from imperialism, (2) authoritarian practices in the political structures of society modeled after Mussolini's corporativism, (3) fear of political disorder and social chaos, and thus the need to incorporate the masses into the political and social mainstream in order to control them most effectively, and (4) Catholicism as the national

religion. Some well-known supporters are: Fuerza de Orientación Radical de la Joven Argentina (FORJA) militants Arturo Jauretche, Raúl Scalabrini Ortiz, and later Juan José Hernández Arregui; novelists Manuel Gálvez and Leopoldo Marechal; essayists Marcelo Sánchez Sorondo, Mario Amadeo, Juan Carlos Goyeneche, and Cosme Beccar Varela.

17. Among the parties of the organized Left were the Socialists, the Communists, and the Trotskyists. The Socialist party was one of the earliest and most prestigous in the hemisphere. In recent years, its reformist bent has reflected the interests of its principal constituency: teachers, small businessmen, artisans, and skilled workers. They were decidedly liberal with regard to economic policies, disavowed the class struggle, and refused to admit the negative effects of imperialism upon the country's productive infrastructure. In contrast, the Communist party followed orthodox, "vulgar" Marxist tendencies and was largely obedient to the decisions and lines of analysis that emanated from its international center. Its spokesmen believed that (1) Argentina's bourgeois revolution had occurred early in the present century, (2) the country was now ripe for a socialist revolution led by the proletariat, with the participation of the campesinos, (3) Peronism was a localized form of fascism that consequently held back proletarian advancement. In general, the Communist Party had few established links with the working-class movement throughout the Peronist decade. Foremost among the Communist spokesmen were Rodolfo Puiggros and Aníbal Ponce. The Trotskyist groups, small and militant, generally discounted the importance of struggles or clashes between different social groups or classes within Argentina; they harbored the unrealistic idea of creating a workers' party that would seize power and forcefully impose a revolutionary program upon the country. A vocal advocate of these beliefs was Jorge Abelardo Ramos.

18. The term "liberal" had a clear and unambiguous application in Argentine social and political thought only up through the first half of the previous century: Moreno, Rivadavia, Echeverría, and the young Sarmiento all defended laissez-faire economic policies, political republicanism, constitutional government, and a broadened social participation that stopped short of egalitarian democracy. By mid-century, however, liberalism came to be identified with the belief system of the rural cattle producers and the newly emerging agro-oligarchy of the country with links to British imperialism; while favoring laissez-faire economics, they were decidedly anti-liberal in their support for political authoritarianism and Buenos Aires predominance in the affairs of the state. From 1880 to about 1930 the liberals were considered cultural heroes for having steered the country into general prosperity and a high standard of living. After that last year, with the advent of the Great Depression, liberals were universally scorned for having promoted economic inequality, social privilege, electoral exclusivism, and fraud. Laissez-faire economics came to be associated with support for the agro-oligarchy, latifundia, and anti-industrial policies. During the Peronist decade, liberals were generally those opposing the *justicialista* regime's corporatist policies, restrictions on free trade, and promotion of the working class. In general, liberalism in recent decades has been associated with these orientations (1) anti-working-class, (2) anti-military, (3) anti-Catholic, and (4) anti-corporatist. Its principal cultural organs were the journal *Sur* and the daily newspaper *La nación*. Liberal literary writers have included Borges, Bioy Casares, Caillet-Bois, Mujica Láinez, S. Ocampo, V. Ocampo, F. Romero, E. Mallea, and S. Bullrich.

19. For a treatment of the ideological and political groups active during and

immediately following the first Peronist decade, see sec. 1 of my dissertation, "The Argentine Generation of 1955: Politics, the Essay, and Literary Criticism" (Ph.D. diss., University of Michigan, 1977).

20. I. Viñas, "Traición de los hombres honestos," p. 2.

21. I. Viñas, "Generación argentina de 1945," p. 38.

22. Prieto, *Literatura y subdesarrollo*, p. 186.

23. This is the thesis of John J. Johnson, *Political Change in Latin America: The Emergence of the Middle Sectors* (Stanford: Stanford University Press, 1958). Prieto, *Literatura y subdesarrollo*, presents the thesis that "underdevelopment" in its cultural form is characteristic primarily of the middle sectors, and manifests itself particularly well in the writings of Arlt, Martínez Estrada, Gálvez, and other writers of petit-bourgeois extraction.

24. See pt. 2 of my dissertation, "The Argentine Generation of 1955," for a detailed treatment of the *Contorno* group's "parricidal" criticism of their *maestros*.

25. David Viñas, "Una generación traicionada," appeared in two issues of *Marcha*: 22, no. 992 (1959): 12–15, 20; and no. 993 (1960): 22–33. Here I quote from p. 12.

26. Emir Rodríguez Monegal, "El juicio de los parricidas: la nueva generación argentina y sus maestros," *Marcha*, 30 December 1955 to 10 February 1956; reprinted as *El juicio de los parricidas: la nueva generación argentina y sus maestros* (Buenos Aires: Deucalión, 1956). In this work Rodríguez Monegal studies several other writer-critics in addition to those participating with *Contorno*, for example, H. A. Murena and Jorge Abelardo Ramos.

27. David Viñas, "La historia excluída: ubicación de Martínez Estrada," *Contorno* 4 (1954): 16.

Chapter 2. Engagement and the Responsibility of the Intellectual in Society

1. I. Viñas, "Generación argentina de 1945," pp. 35–36.

2. Francis Jeanson, a close associate of Sartre in the late forties and early fifties, published "Albert Camus ou l'âme revoltée," the unfavorable review of *The Rebel* in the May 1952 issue of *Les Temps Modernes* (in addition to several other important essays criticizing Camus's world view), which triggered the split between Sartre and Camus. See Robert V. Stone, "Translator's Introduction," *Sarte and the Problem of Morality*, by Francis Jeanson, trans. Robert V. Stone (Bloomington: Indiana University Press, 1980), pp. xvi–xix, for a good critical perspective of the dispute.

3. Albert Camus, *The Rebel*, trans. Anthony Bower (New York: Vintage Press, 1957), p. 303. Camus's *L'Homme révolté* was originally published in Paris by Gallimard in 1951.

4. Peter Royle, *The Sartre-Camus Controversy: A Literary and Philosophical Critique* (Ottowa: University of Ottowa Press, 1982).

5. Jean-Paul Sartre, *Anti-Semite and Jew*, trans. George J. Becker (New York: Schocken Books, 1948), p. 89.

6. Sartre, *Anti-Semite*, p. 69.

7. See Thomas R. Flynn, *Sartre and Marxist Existentialism: The Test Case of Collective Responsibility* (Chicago: University of Chicago Press, 1984), pp. 54–64.

8. Adolfo Prieto, *Borges y la nueva generación* (Buenos Aires: Editorial Letras Universitarias, 1954), p. 87.

9. D. Viñas, "Historia excluída," p. 16.

10. Sarte wrote that in his youth his generation was drawn to both Marxism and existentialism: "We were convinced *at one and the same time* that historical materialism furnished the only valid interpretation of history, and that existentialism remained the only concrete approach to reality." Jean-Paul Sartre, *Search for a Method*, trans. Hazel Barnes (New York: Random House, 1963), p. 21.

11. Noé Jitrik, "Los comunistas (Manauta, Barletta, Yunque, Varela)," *Contorno* 5/6 (1955): 51.

12. David Viñas, "Arlt y los comunistas," *Contorno* 2 (1954).

13. I have explored the contributions of the *Contorno* writers to the conceptualization of cultural dependency in the chapter entitled "The Argentine Generation of 1955 and the Problematic of Cultural Dependency," in "Argentine Generation," pp. 435–82.

14. Jean-Paul Sartre, "Materialism and Revolution," in *Literary and Political Essays*, trans. Annette Michelson (New York: Collier Books, 1965), p. 227.

15. Jean-Paul Sarte, *Qu'est-ce que la Littérature?* (1947) was originally translated as *What is Literature?*, but subsequent editions have borne the title *Literature & Existentialism*. My edition was translated by Bernard Frechtman (New York: Citadel, 1962).

16. Useful works treating the philosophical roots of engagement are: Arthur Hirch, *The French Left* (Montreal: Black Rose Books, 1982), that analyzes the ideological and political context of the engagement movement in postwar France; Edward N. Lee and Maurice Mandelbaum, eds., *Phenomenology and Existentialism* (Baltimore: Johns Hopkins Press, 1967); and George Novak, ed., *Existentialism Versus Marxism: Conflicting Views on Humanism* (New York: Delta Press, 1966).

17. Jean-Paul Sartre, *Being and Nothingness*, trans. Hazel E. Barnes (New York: Washington Square Press, 1969), p. 627.

18. Sartre, *Being and Nothingness*, p. 629.

19. Sartre, *Being and Nothingness*, p. 663.

20. Wilfred Desan, *The Marxism of Jean-Paul Sartre* (Glouster, Mass.: Peter Smith, 1974), pp. 86–87.

21. Jean-Paul Sartre, David Rousset, and Gérard Rosenthal, *Entretiens sur la politique* (Paris: Gallimard, 1949), pp. 36–41.

22. Jean-Paul Sartre, *Critique de la raison dialectique*, vol. 1 (Paris: Gallimard, 1960), p. 174, my translation.

23. Sartre, *Literature & Existentialism*, p. 114.

24. Sartre, "Materialism and Revolution," p. 227.

25. Jeanson, *Sartre and the Problem of Morality*, p. 22.

26. Jean-Paul Sartre, *Existentialism and Humanism*, trans. Philip Mairet (London: Methuen, 1948), p. 293.

27. Flynn, *Sartre*, p. 39, quotes Simone de Beauvoire.

28. Flynn, *Sartre*, pp. 33–43, provides a critique of this reasoning.

29. Maurice Merleau-Ponty, *Les Aventures de la dialectique* (Paris: Gallimard, 1956), p. 277.

30. León Rozitchner, "Experiencia proletaria y experiencia burguesa," *Contorno* 7/8 (1956): 8.

31. Ernesto Giudici, "Neocapitalismo," in Guidici et al., *¿Qué es la izquierda?*, p. 19.

32. Quoted by Victor Brombert, "Raymond Aron and the French Intellectuals," *Yale French Studies* 16 (1955–56): 23.

33. Agosti, "La 'crisis' del marxismo," p. 55.

Chapter 3. Literary Criticism and Engagement

1. Royle, *The Sartre-Camus Controversy*, pp. 89–92.

2. Albert, *Camus The Rebel: An Essay on Man in Revolt* (New York: Alfred A. Knopf, 1957), p. 100.

3. Thomas W. Busch, "Sartre's Use of the Reduction: *Being and Nothingness* Reconsidered," in Hugh J. Silverman and Frederick A. Elliston, eds., *Jean-Paul Sartre: Contemporary Approaches to His Philosophy* (Pittsburgh: Duquesne University, 1980), pp. 17–29, confusedly views in Husserl a "deep humanism" comparable to that of Sartre, in the former's depiction of a "free, self-determining being . . . and free in regard to his capacities for rationally shaping himself and his surrounding world" (p. 29). Actually, this view of man actively shaping his existence becomes prevalent in the thought of Husserl only beginning with his *Crisis of European Sciences*, published in 1954. The earlier works of Husserl that influenced Sartre hardly depicted this movement to the human in his situation. Rather, as Sartre states in *Being and Nothingness*, p. 119, Husserl "shut himself up inside the *cogito* . . ."

4. Jeanson, *Sartre and the Problem of Morality*, p. 82. This modified version of the 1947 classic is still unsurpassed in its interpretation of Sartrian thought. Also helpful is Joseph P. Fell III, *Emotion in the Thought of Sartre* (New York and London: Columbia University Press, 1965).

5. Desan, *Marxism*, pp. 1–8.

6. René Girard, "Existentialism and Criticism," *Yale French Studies* 16 (1955–1956): 51.

7. Jean-Paul Sartre, *The Transcendence of the Ego* vol. 6, trans. Forrest Williams and Robert Kirkpatrick (New York: Farrar, Straus and Giroux, 1957) p. 105.

8. Sartre, *Literature & Existentialism*, pp. 49–61.

9. Sartre, *Literature*, pp. 23–24.

10. Prieto, *Borges y la nueva generación*, p. 20. A few years later, Prieto indicated the importance that Sartre had on his ideas in his book on Borges: "Hoy, siendo contemporáneo de las brillantes reflexiones que Sartre dedicó al problema (de la utilidad de la literatura), remito al curioso a su obra *¿Qué es la literatura?* antes que repertirlo y repetirlo mal. Sartre está citado en mi libro, y hasta con énfasis, no sé si cinco o seis veces" ("Respuesta de Adolfo Prieto," *Ciudad* 2 [1959]: 102).

11. Prieto, *Borges y la nueva generación*, p. 89.

12. Juan José Sebreli, "El escritor argentino y su público," *Revista centro* 3, no. 7 (1954): 27.

13. David Viñas, "Benito Lynch: la realización del *Facundo*," *Contorno* 5/6 (1955): 19.

14. Sartre, *Literature & Existentialism*, pp. 62–63.

15. Noé Jitrik, "*Adán Buenosayres:* la novela de Leopoldo Marechal," *Contorno* 5/6 (1955): 44.

16. Adolfo Prieto, *Sociología del público argentino* (Buenos Aires: Leviatán, n.d.), p. 12, arrives at this conclusion on the basis of a survey of reader preferences and attitudes conducted by Gino Germani.

17. Noé Jitrik, *El escritor argentino: dependencia o libertad* (Buenos Aires: Ediciones del Candil, 1967), pp. 20, 31.

18. David Viñas, *Dar la cara* (Buenos Aires: Jamcana, 1966), p. 600.

19. Noé Jitrik, "Algunos libros, algunas mujeres," *Contorno* 5/6 (1955): 46.

20. Juan José Hernández Arregui, *Imperialismo y cultura (la política en la inte-*

ligencia argentina) (Buenos Aires: Amerindia, 1957), p. 140, quotes Victoria Ocampo's statement of 1931.

21. Victoria Ocampo states: "Lo que desde ya sabemos afirmar de América es que estamos enamorados extrañamente de ella. Y ese amor, como todo gran amor, es una prueba. Prueba que arroja sobre nuestras incapacidades e imperfeccioines una luz resplandeciente y cruel. Ese amor se dirige a lo que está más allá de nosotros y parte de lo que está más allá de nosotros. Tener conciencia de ello, sufrir por ello es saludable. . . ." ("Carta a Waldo Frank" *Sur* 1 [1931]: 18). In an interview printed in *La nación*, 10 November 1970, Ocampo would state: "Pero la difusión de la cultura no parece ser el camino elegido por la mayoría de la turbulenta juventud contemporánea. *Sur* no conoce otro."

22. Oscar Masotta, "*Sur* o el antiperonismo colonialista," *Contorno* 7/8 (1956), pp. 39–45. In *Contorno* 3 (1954): 1–2, Adelaida Gigli also addressed the cultural role of *Sur* in the article, "Victoria Ocampo: V. O."

23. D. Viñas, "Benito Lynch," p. 20.

24. León Rozitchner, "Comunicación y servidumbre: Mallea," *Contorno* 5/6 (1956): 30.

25. Roberto Hosne, "El desconformismo de la nueva generación," *Gaceta literaria* 4 (1956): 11.

26. In "Terrorismo y complicidad," the short introductory essay which prefaces the combination 5/6 issue of their journal, the *Contorno* staff called attention to this comment printed in a recent issue of *Marcha*.

27. Emir Rodríguez Monegal, writing about David Viñas in *Narradores de esta América*, emphasizes only the negative side of that critical endeavor when he states that "Vista a más de una década de distancia, buena parte de la labor de demolición emprendida por los parricidas parece hoy superflua. . . ." Vol. 2 (Buenos Aires: Alfa, 1974), p. 314.

28. Francine Masiello, "Argentine Literary Journalism: The Production of a Critical Discourse," *Latin American Research Review* 20, no. 1 (1985): 39.

29. Ismael Viñas and Noé Jitrik, "Enrique Larreta o el linaje," *Contorno* 5/6 (1955): 14.

30. Prieto, *Borges y la nueva generación*.

31. Jitrik, "Algunos libros," p. 46.

32. Jitrik, "Algunos libros," p. 2.

33. I. Viñas, "Traición de los hombres honestos," p. 3.

34. Rozitchner, "Mallea," p. 35.

35. Rodríguez Monegal, *Juicio*.

36. Rodríguez Monegal, *Juicio*.

Chapter 4. From Perón to Frondizi

1. Marvin Goldwert, *Democracy, Militarism, and Nationalism in Argentina, 1930–1966: An Interpretation* (Austin: University of Texas Press, 1972), p. 144ff., provides a thorough analysis of the different factions within the army, the spectrum of political parties, and the distinct groups within the labor movement during this contradictory period.

2. The novels published by David Viñas during the *Contorno* period are: *Cayó sobre su rostro* (1955), which received the Primer Premio Municipal and the Gerchunoff Prize; *Los años despiadados* (1956): *Un dios cotidiano* (1957), which won the Kraft prize; and *Los Dueños de la tierra* (1959), which won a Losada prize and is considered his most important fictional work. The major studies treating

David Viñas's fiction written during this period are: Fernando Alonso and Arturo Rezzano, *Novela y sociedad argentinas* (Buenos Aires: Paidos, 1971), pp. 172–209; John S. Brushwood, *The Spanish American Novel: A Twentieth Century Survey* (Austin: University of Texas Press, 1975), pp. 228–301; David William Foster and Virginia Ramos Foster, *Modern Latin American Literature*, vol. 2 (New York: Frederick Ungar, 1975), pp. 429–32; Noé Jitrik, *Seis novelistas argentinos de la nueva promoción* (Mendoza: Biblioteca Pública General, 1959); Rodríguez Monegal, "David Viñas en su contorno," in *Narradoes de esta América*, vol. 2, pp. 310–30; and Juan Carlos Portantiero, *Realismo y realidad en la narrativa argentina* (Buenos Aires: Ediciones Procyón, 1961), pp. 83–106. See the appendix for a more complete bibliography of studies treating Viñas's works.

3. Rodolfo Borello, in an interview with the author, May 1979.

4. Martin S. Stabb, "Argentine Letters and the Peronato: An Overview," *Journal of Inter-American Studies and World Affairs* 12, nos. 3–4 (1971): 437, describes the "Peronization" of the universities which the Romero intervention attempted to undo.

5. The *Contorno* staff's reactions to the university intervention were recorded in "Resollando por la herida," *Contorno cuadernos* 1 (1957): 22–23.

6. Juan José Sebreli's recent essay, *Los deseos imaginarios del peronismo* (Buenos Aires: Legasa, 1983), contradicts this widely held assumption by arguing that among the middle class Perón had wide support.

7. Ernesto Goldar, states about R. Walsh and others, presumably including the *Contorno* group: "Hay algunos lúcidos que parecen convencidos ser los destinatarios de la sana razón. Son los que quieren salvar al peronismo del peronismo. Lo conciben inferiorizado, como fenómeno paria negado de la excelencia del marxismo verbal. Se trata de intelectuales nimbados por la 'ideología revolucionaria' que se acercan al peronismo para examinarlo, extirparle males endémicos y orientarlo por la buena senda" (*El peronismo en la literatura argentina*, pp. 138–39).

8. See Julio Mafud, *Argentina desde adentro* (Buenos Aires: Americalee, 1979), whose introductory chapters describe the significant social, economic, and demographic changes since 1930 and how they contributed to Argentina's increasingly disadvantageous position within the British commercial empire.

9. See Angel Rama, "La tecnificación narrativa," in *La novela en América Latina: panoramas. 1929–1980* (Colombia: Instituto Colombiano de Cultura, 1982), p. 294–360.

10. See Andre Malraux, "The 'New Left' Can Succeed!" *Yale French Studies* 15 (1954–1955): 49–60.

11. Johnson, *Political Change in Latin America.*

12. Prieto, *Literatura y subdesarrollo* p. 186.

13. D. Viñas, "Generación traicionada," p. 14.

14. The most coherent description of the *Contorno* plan for government, although hardly specific with regard to the structural changes envisioned, is found in Ismael Viñas, "Un prólogo sobre el país," *Contorno cuadernos* 1 (1957): 1–4.

15. Osiris Troiani, "Examen de conciencia," *Contorno* 7/8 (1956): 9.

16. Troiani, "Examen de conciencia," p. 9.

17. Ismael Viñas, "Miedos, complejos y mal entendidos," *Contorno* 7/8 (1956):15.

18. León Rozitchner, "Experiencia proletaria," p. 3, states that "al fin de cuentas el proletariado, víctima de la loca pero necesaria aventura, fue el único que no lucró con el peronismo . . . sin solicitar . . . el aumento paralelo en la

cuenta del banco." However, Goldwert, *Democracy,* p. 147, quotes James W. Rowe, *Argentina's Durable Peronists: A Twentieth Anniversary Note:* "Despite vagueness and debate over statistics, the best evidence is that even by late 1955 the wages of Argentine skilled and unskilled workers had more than outpaced the inflated cost-of-living when compared with 1943, not to mention the fringe benefits amounting to some 40 to 50 per cent of wage costs."

19. Rozitchner, "Experiencia proletaria," p. 4.

20. See Sebreli, *Deseos imaginarios del peronismo,* that the author characterizes as a work of self-criticism.

21. Juan José Sebreli, "Aventura y revolución peronista: testimonio," *Contorno* 7/8 (1956): 46.

22. Sebreli, "Aventura," p. 48.

23. Sebreli, "Aventura," p. 49.

24. Sebreli, "Aventura," p. 47.

25. Rozitchner, "Experiencia proletaria," p. 8.

26. David Viñas, "Tres o cuatro cosas," *Revista de derecho y ciencias sociales* 3 (1956–1957): 13.

27. I. Viñas, "Prólogo," p. 1.

28. I. Viñas, "Prólogo," p. 1.

29. D. Viñas, "Generación traicionada," p. 14.

30. David Viñas, "Leopoldo Lugones: mecanismo, contorno y destino," *Revista centro* 3, no. 5 (1953): 7.

31. Troiani, "Examen de conciencia," p. 9.

32. Rodolfo Mario Pandolfi, "17 de octubre; trampa y salida," *Contorno* 7/8 (1956): 22.

33. Pandolfi, "17 de octubre;" Adolfo Prieto, "Peronismo y neutralidad," *Contorno* 7/8 (1956): 28–31; Rozitchner, "Experiencia proletaria."

34. "Terrorismo y complicidad" (editorial), *Contorno* 5/6 (1955): 2.

35. Sebreli, "Aventura," p. 45.

36. Sebreli, "Aventura," p. 46.

37. Sebreli's *sui generis* conclusion is that Perón, through his demagoguery, won over the working-class masses and thus converted a potentially futile rebelliousness into authentic revolutionary action. Perón therefore succeeded where the Socialists had failed, in spite of the latters' pretense of possessing the correct interpretation of national reality. As stated in the text, his 1985 book, *Los deseos imaginarios del peronismo,* largely refutes this earlier analysis.

38. Rozitchner, "Experiencia proletaria," p. 2.

39. Troiani, "Examen de conciencia," p. 9.

40. I. Viñas, "Miedos, complejos y malosentidos," p. 12.

41. D. Viñas, "Historia excluída," p. 16.

42. José Luis Romero, "Los elementos de la realidad espiritual argentina," *Realidad* 1, no. 2 (1947): 6.

43. Rodolfo Kusch, "Inteligencia y barbarie," *Contorno* 3 (1954): 6.

44. Kusch, "Inteligencia y barbarie," p. 7.

45. D. Viñas, *Dar la cara* pp. 44, 177.

46. D. Viñas, "Generación traicionada," p. 14.

47. I. Viñas, "Prólogo," p. 4.

48. León Rozitchner, "Lucha de clases, verificación de laicismo," *Contorno cuadernos,* 1 (1957): 20.

49. Rozitchner, "Lucha de clases," p. 21.

50. Hernández Arregui, *Formación de la conciencia nacional,* pp. 463–79.

51. D. Viñas, in *Dar la cara,* p. 581, captures this spirit of optimism. One

character states, "A mí no me interesa la lucha aquí. . . . La lucha política, la que se está abriendo con tantas posibilidades . . . A mí me gustan los problemas, me gusta la gente, acercarme a la gente, saber qué piensa, qué quiere. . . ."

52. Ramón Alcalde, "La iglesia argentina: instrucciones para su uso," *Contorno cuadernos* 1 (1957): 7.

53. Alcalde, "Iglesia," p. 9.

54. Rozitchner, "Experiencia proletaria," p. 6.

55. Hosne, "Desconformismo," p. 11.

56. Juan Carlos Portantiero, "La joven generación literaria," *Cuadernos de cultura* 7, no. 29 (1957): 30.

57. "Peronismo . . . ¿y lo otro?" p. 2.

58. Prieto, *Borges y la nueva generación*, p. 19.

59. I. Viñas, "Miedos, complejos y malosentendidos," p. 13; Rozitchner, "Experiencia proletaria," p. 8.

60. Karl Mannheim, "The Problem of the Intelligentsia: An Inquiry Into its Past and Present Role," *Essays on the Sociology of Culture* (London: Routledge & Kegan Paul, Ltd., 1956), pp. 91–171, refers to the classic works of Max Weber concerning the "apartness" of the intelligentsia in Western societies, especially since 1848.

61. D. Viñas, "Generación traicionada," p. 14.

62. Rozitchner, "Experiencia proletaria," p. 6.

63. I. Viñas, "Miedos, complejos y malosentendidos," p. 13.

64. Troiani, "Examen de conciencia," p. 10.

65. This was the general criticism of José Chiaramonte, "*Contorno* y el peronismo," *Gaceta literaria* 8 (1956): 15; Osvaldo Seiguerman and Pedro Orgambide, "Encrucijada y rebeldía," *Gaceta literaria* 15 (1958): 1, 15–17; and Portantiero, "Joven generación literaria," p. 30.

66. Goldwert, *Democracy*, p. 178, quotes the *New York Times*, 12 November 1958.

67. Rozitchner, "Experiencia proletaria," p. 5.

68. The shallowness of this general attack on "bourgeois values" only becomes clear in the light of the "dirty war" of the 1970s and early 1980s. A 26 June 1983 article of the *Buenos Aires Herald* ("Cambiaso Case Casts a Long Shadow") demonstrates scorn for Police Chief Verplaetsen (who, it must be assumed, participated widely in the governmental campaign of disappearances, murders, and tortures against leftists, or at least shared the mentality and values system of its militants) for a purported " 'bourgeois morality'—on occasion a synonym for legality. . . ." It is apparent that Rozitchner's understanding of a despicable "bourgeois mentality," however contradictory, pretentious, or hypocritical, was far superior to what replaced it as a mentality of the state.

69. Troiani, "Examen de conciencia," p. 10.

70. Pandolfi, "17 de octubre," p. 27.

71. I. Viñas, "Miedos, complejos y malosentendidos," pp. 11, 13.

72. Sebreli, "Aventura," p. 47.

73. Halperín Donghi, "Del fascismo al peronismo," *Contorno* 7/8 (1956): 18.

74. Rozitchner, in "Lucha de clases," p. 8, criticized the writers of *Azul y blanco* who called the *Contorno* writers "un pequeñño grupo de pseudo-intelectuales fuboides"—in reference to their previous affiliation with FUBA, the federation of students at the Universidad Nacional de Buenos Aires. However, a year later, even the *Contorno* writers themselves would admit the shortcomings of their analysis during this period, and the failure in political action to which it led.

75. "Peronismo . . . ¿y lo otro?" p. 2.

Chapter 5. The Explosion of the Frondizi Illusion and the Demise of *Contorno*

1. Frondizi would fulfill these promises: his general amnesty came immediately after his election in May 1958, but he postponed the "normalization" of the CGT until 1961 and did not restore the Peronist party to legality until early in 1962. See Donald C. Hodges, *Argentina, 1942–1976: The National Revolution and Resistance* (Albuquerque: University of New Mexico Press, 1976), p. 35.
2. Gary W. Wynia, *Argentina in the Post-War Era: Politics and Economic Policy Making in a Divided Society* (Albuquerque: University of New Mexico Press, 1978), pp. 83–90.
3. D. Viñas, "Generación traicionada."
4. León Rozitchner, "Un paso adelante, dos atrás," *Contorno* 9/10 (1959): 1, 3.
5. Ismael Viñas, "Orden y Progreso," *Contorno* 9/10 (1959): 61.
6. Rozitchner, "Un paso adelante," p. 7.
7. Viñas, "Orden y progreso," p. 65.
8. Rozitchner, "Un paso adelante," p. 8.
9. I. Viñas, "Orden y progreso," p. 70.
10. I. Viñas, "Orden y progreso," pp. 65–66.
11. Ramón Alcalde, "Imperialismo, cultura y literatura nacional," *Contorno* 5/6 (1955): 57–60; Masotta, "*Sur* o el antiperonismo colonialista," pp. 39–45; Juan José Sebreli, "Aventura," pp. 45–49.
12. I. Viñas, "Orden y progreso," p. 68.
13. Recent writings by the *Contorno* participants on the topic of cultural dependency include: León Rozitchner, "Persona, cultura y subdesarrollo," *Revista de la Universidad de Buenos Aires*, fifth epoch, 6, no. 1 (1961): 75–98; Prieto, *Literatura y subdesarrollo*; Jitrik, *El escritor argentino*; Juan José Sebreli, *Historia argentina y consciencia de clase* (Buenos Aires: Editorial Perrot, 1957), in addition to several other works; and David Viñas, *Literatura argentina y realidad política: de Sarmiento a Cortázar* (Buenos Aires: Siglo XXI, 1971). I analyze these and other writings in "The Argentine Generation of 1955 and the Problematic of Cultural Dependency," in "Argentine Generation," pp. 348–82.
14. Rozitchner, "Un paso adelante," p. 10.
15. Tulio Halperín Donghi, "El espejo de la historia," *Contorno* 9/10 (1959): 77.
16. Halperín Donghi, "Espejo de la historia," p. 81.
17. Rozitchner, "Un paso adelante," p. 13.
18. See Note 13.
19. Portantiero, "Joven generación," pp. 27–44.
20. Goldar, *Peronismo en la literatura argentina*, p. 142.
21. Juan José Hernández Arregui, *Imperialismo y cultura (la política en la inteligencia argentina)*, rev. ed. (Buenos Aires: Hachea, 1961), pp. 270–99.
22. I. Viñas, "Orden y progreso," pp. 70–71.
23. I. Viñas, "Orden y progreso," p. 72.
24. Rozitchner, "Un paso adelante," p. 13.
25. I. Viñas, "Orden y progreso," p. 75.
26. I. Viñas, "Orden y progreso," p. 72.
27. Rozitchner, "Un paso adelante," p. 3.
28. I. Viñas, "Orden y progreso," p. 28.
29. Halperín Donghi, "Espejo de la historia," pp. 79, 81.
30. Rozitchner, "Un paso adelante," p. 11.
31. Rozitchner, "Un paso adelante," p. 14.
32. Rozitchner, "Un paso adelante," p. 11.

Chapter 6. Conclusion

1. Early studies written about the *Contorno* writers in relation to a nation-wide generation are the following (a more comprehensive listing can be found in the bibliography): D. Viñas, "La historia excluída," pp. 10–16; Rodríguez Monegal, "Juicio"; Juan Carlos Ghiano, "La generación argentina de 1945," *Comentario* 5, no. 18 (1958): 29–35; I. Viñas, "Generación argentina de 1945," pp. 35–44; Pedro G. Orgambide, "Izquierda y facilidad," *Gaceta Literaria* 3, no. 19 (1959): 1, and D. Viñas, "Generación traicionada."

2. More recent critical writings that treat the *Contorno* group in a generational context are: Luis Gregorich, "La nueva generación de izquierda y el peronismo," *Cuadernos de crítica* 2 (1965): 1–13; Portantiero, "Joven generación," pp. 27–44; and Arturo Cambours Ocampo, *El problema de las generaciones literarias (esquema de las últimas promociones argentinas)* (Buenos Aires: A. Peña Lillo, 1963). Fernando Alonso and Arturo Rezzano classified David Viñas and others as among the writers of "El 50 literario" in *Novela y sociedad argentinas*, pp. 172–209. Gustavo Valadez bestowed the title "Generation of 1955" in "David Viñas y la generación del 55," *Vórtice* (Stanford University) 1, no. 1 (1974): 93–102; as did Katra, "Argentine Generation."

3. Rodolfo Walsh, Francisco Urondo, and Juan Carlos Portantiero, "La literatura argentina del siglo XX," in Emmanuel Carballo et al., *Panorama de la actual literatura latinoamericana* (Madrid: Fundamentos, 1971). This emphasis on *Contorno*'s role in anticipating the period following the fall of Perón is also present in the deliberations of María Luisa Bastos, "*Contorno, Ciudad, Gaceta literaria*: tres enfoques de una realidad," *Hispamérica* 4/5 (1973): 49–64; and Masiello, "Argentine Literary Journalism," pp. 27–60.

4. Gregorich, "La nueva generación," pp. 1–13.

5. I am aware that my use of the term "generation" in this hemispheric context stretches the meaning of the term and that "spirit of the epoch" might be more appropriate for some readers. See Adolfo Prieto, "Conflictos de generaciones," in *América latina en su literatura*, ed. Fernández Moreno, pp. 406–23.

6. Luis Ricardo Furlán, *Generación poética del cincuenta* (Buenos Aires: Ediciones Culturales Argentinas, 1974), copies from a broad list of commentators in characterizing the spirit of the time and how these ideological currents affected the sensitivities and literary project of the "1950 writers" (although concentrating on Argentine writers, he indicates influences that are primarily continental in scope).

7. Angel Rama, "Medio siglo de narrativa latinoamericana (1922–1972)," *La novela en América Latina*, p. 158.

8. Furlán, *Generación poética*, p. 17, quotes Emma de Cartosio.

9. "Peronismo . . . ¿y lo otro?" p. 2.

10. David Viñas, in "Nacionalismos: del integral al populista," *El periódico de Buenos Aires* 1 (15–21 September 1984): 9, calls attention to the observation of Robert A. Potash, in *Perón y el G.O.U.: los documentos de una logia secreta* (Buenos Aires: Sudamericana, 1984), that a similar form of populist nationalism to what the country knew under Perón is entirely unlikely, given that no source of funding is available that would compare with the abundant capital available to Perón that was accumulated during the Second World War.

11. See Antonio L. Geist, "El neo-romanticismo: evolución del concepto de compromiso en la poesía española (1930–1936)," *Ideologies & Literature* 7, no. 15 (1981): 94–119.

Current Bibliographies of the *Contorno* Writers

Contorno and the Argentine Literary Tradition

Alonso, Fernando, and Arturo Rezzano. *Novela y sociedad argentinas*, pp. 172–209. Buenos Aires: Paídos, 1971.

Bastos, María Luisa. "*Contorno, Ciudad, Gaceta literaria*: tres enfoques de una realidad." *Hispamérica* 2, no. 4/5 (1973): 49–64.

Bianchi, Julio. "Panorama actual de la novela argentina." *Gaceta literaria* 4, no. 20 (1960): 28–29.

Bloch, Jean Richard. *Sociología y destino del teatro*. Buenos Aires: Siglo XX, 1957.

Brushwood, John S. *The Spanish American Novel: A Twentieth Century Survey*. Austin: University of Texas Press, 1975.

Cambours Ocampo, Arturo. *El problema de las generaciones literarias: esquema de las últimas promociones argentinas*. Buenos Aires: A. Peña Lillo, 1963.

Carnevale, Jorge. "Literatura argentina actual o la máscara del coraje." *Cero* (Buenos Aires) 2 (1964).

Castagnino, Raúl H. *Sociología del teatro argentino*. Buenos Aires: Nova, 1963.

Chiaramonte, José. "*Contorno* y el peronismo." *Gaceta literaria* 1, no. 8 (1956): 15.

Dellepiane, Angela B., "La novela argentina desde 1950 a 1965." *Revista iberoamericana* 66 (1968): 237–82.

Diego, Celia de. "La sinrazón razonada de los parricidas." *Ficción* 12 (1958): 90–99.

Facultad de Filosofía y Letras, Instituto de Letras, Adolfo Prieto, editor. *Encuesta: la crítica literaria de la Argentina*. Santa Fe: Universidad Nacional del Litoral, 1963.

Fayt, Carlos S. *Naturaleza del peronismo: confrontaciones*, pp. 192–200. Buenos Aires: Viracocha, 1967.

Fernandez Moreno, César. "Las revistas literarias en la Argentina." *Revista hispánica moderna* 29 (1963): 46–54.

———. *La realidad y los papeles: panorama y muestra de la poesía argentina contemporánea*, pp. 344–49. Madrid: Aguilar, 1967.

Furlán, Luis Ricardo. *La generación poética del cincuenta*. Buenos Aires: Ediciones Culturales Argentinas, 1974.

Ghiano, Juan Carlos. *La novela argentina contemporánea 1940–1960*. Buenos Aires: Dirección General de Relaciones Culturales, Ministerio de Relaciones Exteriores y Culto, n.d.

———. "Riesgos de la novela argentina." *Ficción* 6 (1957): 117–23.

————. "La generación argentina de 1945." *Commentario* 5, no. 18 (1958): 29–35.

Giudici, Ernesto, et al. "¿Qué es la izquierda?" *Cuadernos de cultura* 50 (1960); reprinted as *¿Qué es la izquierda?* Buenos Aires: Documentos, 1961.

Goldar, Ernesto. *El peronismo en la literatura argentina.* Buenos Aires: Freeland, 1971.

Gregorich, Louis. "La nueva generación de izquierda y el peronismo." *Cuadernos de crítica* 2 (1965): 1–13.

————. ed. *La generación del 55: los narradores.* Buenos Aires: Centro Editor de América Latina, 1968.

Hernández Arregui, Juan José. *Imperialismo y cultura (la política en la inteligencia argentina).* Buenos Aires: Amerindia, 1957. Rev. and enl. ed. Buenos Aires: Hachea, 1961.

————. *La formación de la conciencia nacional (1930–1960).* 2d ed., enl. Buenos Aires: Hachea, 1970.

Hosne, Roberto. "El disconformismo de la nueva generación." *Gaceta literaria* 4 (1956): 11.

Jitrik, Noé. *Seis novelistas argentinos de la nueva promoción.* Mendoza: Ediciones Biblioteca San Martín, 1959.

————. *Escritores argentinos: dependencia o libertad.* Buenos Aires: Ediciones del Candil, 1967.

Katra, William H. "The Argentine Generation of 1955: Politics, the Essay, and Literary Criticism." Ph.D. diss., University of Michigan, 1977.

Lafleur, Héctor René, Sergio D. Provenzano, and Fernando P. Alonso. *Las revistas literarias argentinas 1893–1967.* 2d ed. expanded. Buenos Aires: Centro Editor de América Latina, 1968.

Lagmanovich, David. "La narrativa argentina de 1960 a 1970." *Nueva narrativa hispanoamericana* 2, no. 1 (1972): 99–117.

Martínez, Tomás Eloy. "El nuevo cine argentino." *Lyra* 19, no. 186–188 (1962).

Masiello, Francine. "Argentine Literary Journalism: The Production of a Critical Discourse." *Latin American Research Review,* 20, no. 1 (1985): 27–60.

Montserrat, Santiago. *Sentido y misión del pensamiento argentino.* Córdoba: Universidad Nacional de Córdoba, Dirección General de Publicaciones, 1963.

Orgambide, Pedro. "Izquierda y facilidad." *Gaceta literaria* 19 (1959): 1–3, 6–7.

Peltzer, Federico. "Panorama de la literatura argentina contemporánea." *Señales* 12, no. 121 (1960): 5–11.

Perriaux, Jaime. *Las generaciones argentinas.* Buenos Aires: EUDEBA, 1970.

Pezzoni, Enrique. "Literatura." In *Argentina 1930–1960,* edited by Jorge A. Paita pp. 413–19. Buenos Aires: Sur, 1961.

Portantiero, Juan Carlos. "La joven generación literaria." *Cuadernos de cultura* 29 (1957): 27–44.

————. *Realismo y realidad en la narrativa argentina.* Buenos Aires: Procyón, 1961.

————. "La literatura argentina después del 43: algunas notas previas." *Lyra* 20, no. 189–191 (1963).

Prieto, Adolfo. *Borges y la nueva generación.* Buenos Aires: Letras Universitarias, 1954.

————. *Literatura y subdesarrollo: notas para un análisis de la literatura argentina.* Rosario: Biblioteca, 1968.

Rest, Jaime. "En busca de una definición." *Señales* 12, no. 129 (1961): 11–16.

Rodríguez Monegal, Emir. "El juicio de los parricidas: la nueva generación argentina y sus maestros." *Marcha* (30 December 1955 to 10 February 1956). Reprinted as *El juicio de los parricidas: la nueva generación argentina y sus maestros.* Buenos Aires: Editorial Deucalión, 1956.

Salvador, Nelida. "Las revistas de una época literaria: *Florida-Boedo.*" *Testigo* 3 (1966): 40–44.

Sarlo Sabajanes, Beatriz. "Novela argentina: códigos de los verosimil." *Los libros* 3, no. 25 (1972): 18–19.

———. "Los dos ojos de *Contorno.*" *Punto de vista* 4, no. 13 (1974): 93–102.

Stabb, Martin S. "Argentina's Quest for Identity." In his *In Quest of Identity,* pp. 146–81. Chapel Hill: University of North Carolina Press, 1967.

Torchia Estrada, Juan Carlos. *La filosofía en la Argentina.* Washington, D.C.: Pan American Union, 1961.

Vanasco, Alberto. "Un nuevo frente de la novela argentina." *Contemporánea* 2 (1957): 3, 7.

Verbitsky, Bernardo. "Proposiciones para un mejor planteo de nuestra literatura." *Ficción* 12 (1958): 3–20.

Viñas, David. "Una generación traicionada." *Marcha* 21, no. 992 (31 December 1959): 12–15, 20; no. 993 (15 January 1960): 22–23.

———. *Literatura argentina y realidad política.* Buenos Aires: Jorge Alvarez, 1964. Revised and expanded: *Literatura argentina y realidad política: de Sarmiento a Cortázar* (Buenos Aires: Siglo Veinte, 1971).

Viñas, David, et al. *Contorno: selección.* Edited with prologue by Carlos Mangone and Jorge Warley. Buenos Aires: Centro Editor de América Latina, 1981.

Viñas, Ismael. "Algunas reflexiones en torno a las perspectivas de nuestra literatura: autodefensa de un supuesto parricida." *Ficción* 15 (1958): 6–21.

———. "La generación argentina de 1945." *Comentario* 5, no. 18 (1958): 35–44.

Waismann, Abraham. "Correnti spirituali nell'Argentina d'oggi." *Filosofia* 17 (1966): 75–91.

Wapnir, Salomón. *La crítica literaria argentina.* Buenos Aires: Acanto, 1956.

Ramón Alcalde
(1922)

BOOKS AND ARTICLES

Hermann Hesse: su vida y su obra. Buenos Aires: Universitaria, 1953.

"Teoría y práctica de un teatro argentino." *Buenos Aires literaria* 2, no. 17 (1954): 1–22.

"Imperialismo, cultura y literatura nacional." *Contorno* 5/6 (1955): 57–60.

"*Ayer, hoy, mañana,* de Mario Amadeo" (book review). *Contorno* 7/8 (1956): 55–57.

"La iglesia argentina: instrucciones para su uso." *Contorno cuadernos* 1 (1957): 4–7.

"La integracion cultural en los estudios técnicos." Conferencia pronunciada el 15 de septiembre de 1959 en la Facultad de Ingeniería Química. Santa Fe: Universidad Nacional de Litoral, 1959.

Alcalde, Ramón, et al. *Estrategia en la universidad*. Buenos Aires: Editorial del Movimiento de Liberación Nacional, 1964.

TRANSLATION

Carter, Jimmy. *Camino al triunfo*. Ramón Alcalde and Luis Justo, trans. Buenos Aires: Marymar, 1976.

Regina Gibaja

"Sobre lo femenino." *Centro* 4 (1952).

"La mujer: mito porteño." *Contorno* 3 (1954).

"Ernesto L. Castro y la novela social." *Contorno* 5/6 (1955): 26.

El público de arte: encuesta en el Museo Nacional de Bellas Artes. Buenos Aires: Editorial de la Universidad de Buenos Aires, Instituto Torcuato di Tella, 1964.

"Aspectos sociales y culturales de la modernización." *Revista latinoamericana de sociología* 1, no. 1 (1965): 111–14.

"Actitudes hacia la familia entre obreros industriales argentinos." *Revista latinoamericana de sociología* 3, no. 3 (1967): 411–32.

Las ciencias sociales en la escuela: supuestos epistemológicos y pedagógicos del texto de sexto grado. Mexico: UNAM, 1979.

Adelaida Gigli
(1929)

"El único rostro de Jano [R. Arlt]." *Contorno* 2 (1954): 13–14.

"Victoria Ocampo: V. O." *Contorno* 3 (1954): 1–2.

"La poesía de Martínez Estrada: oro y piedra para siempre." *Contorno* 4 (1954): 17–19.

"Unos libros, algunas mujeres." *Contorno* 5/6 (1955): 45–48.

Tulio Halperín Donghi
(1925)

BOOKS

El pensamiento de Echeverría. Buenos Aires: Sudamericana, 1951.

Los moriscos del reino de Valencia (1520–1609). Ph.D. diss., Facultad de Filosofía y Letras, Universidad de Buenos Aires, 1954.

El Río de la Plata al comenzar el siglo XIX. Buenos Aires: Universidad Nacional de Buenos Aires, Facultad de Filosofía y Letras, 1961.

Tradición política española e ideología revolucionaria de Mayo. Buenos Aires: EUBA, 1961.

Historia de la Universidad de Buenos Aires. Buenos Aires: EUBA, 1962.

Argentina en el callejón. Montevideo: ARCA, 1964.

Estudios latinoamericanos desde perspectiva norteamericana. Montevideo: Universidad de la República, Facultad de Humanidades y Ciencias, 1969.

Historia contemporánea de América Latina. Madrid: Alianza, 1969. 2d ed. and enl.: Madrid: Alianza, 1970. French trans. *Histoire contemporaine de l'Amérique latine.* Paris: Payot, 1972.

El revisionismo histórico argentino. Mexico: Siglo Veintiuno, 1971.

Argentina: de la revolución de independencia a la confederación rosista. Buenos Aires: Paídos, 1972.

Argentina: la democracia de masas. Buenos Aires: Paídos, 1972.

Hispanoaméraica después de la independencia: consecuencias sociales y económicas de la emancipación. Buenos Aires: Paídos, 1972. *The Aftermath of Revolution in Latin America.* Translated by Josephine de Bunsen. New York: Harper and Row, 1973.

Historia argentina. Buenos Aires: Paídos, 1972.

Revolución y guerra: formación de una élite dirigente en la Argentina criolla. Buenos Aires: Siglo Veintiuno, 1972. *Politics, Economics, and Society in Argentina in the Revolutionary Period.* Translated by Richard Southern. New York: Cambridge University Press, 1975.

El ocaso del orden colonial en Hispanoamérica. Buenos Aires: Sudamericana, 1978.

Un conflicto nacional: moriscos y cristianos viejos en Valencia. Madrid: Institutición Alfonso el Magnánimo, 1980.

La cuantificación histórica: trayectoria y problemas. Buenos Aires: Instituto Nacional de Antropología e Historia, Departamento de Investigaciones Históricas, 1980.

Proyecto y construcción de una nación: Argentina, 1846–1880. Caracas: Biblioteca Ayacucho, 1980.

Guerra y finanzas en la formación del estado argentino (1791–1850). Buenos Aires: Belgrano, 1982.

Una nación para el desierto. Buenos Aires: Centro Editor de América Latina, 1982.

José Hernández y sus mundos. Buenos Aires: Sudamericana and Instsituto Torcuato di Tella, 1985.

Reforma y disolución de los imperios ibéricos, 1750–1850. Madrid: Alianza, 1985.

Tradición política española e ideología revolucionaria de Mayo. Buenos Aires: Centro Editor de América Latina, 1985.

COLLABORATIONS

Cortés Conde, Roberto, Tulio Halperín Donghi, and Haydee Gorostegui de Torres. Part 1 of *Evolución del comercio exterior argentino: exportaciones 1864–1964.* Buenos Aires: Facultad de Filosofía y Letras, 1965.

Instituto de Investigaciones Históricas. *Jornadas de historia y economía argentinas en los siglos XVIII y XIX.* Buenos Aires-Rosario: Facultad de Filosofía de Rosario and IDES, 1964).

Tella, Torcuato S., and Tulio Halperín Donghi, ed. *Los fragmentos del poder de la oligarquía a la poliarquía argentina.* Buenos Aires: Jorge Álvarez, 1969.

Halperín Donghi, Tulio, ed. *El ocaso del orden colonial en Hispano-américa.* Buenos Aires: Sudamericana, 1978.

ARTICLES

"Tradición y progreso en Esteban Echeverría." *Cuadernos americanos* 49 (1950): 203–15.

"Panorama della storiografia argentina." *Revista storica italiana* 64 (1952): 596–607.

"Martí, novelista del fin de siglo." *Archivo Jose Marti* 6 (La Habana: 1953): 400–402.

"Las cartas de una peruana." *Sur* 221 (1953): 94–102.

"Positivismo historiográfico de José María Ramos Mejía." *Imago mundi* 1, no. 5 (1954): 56–64.

"Rosismo y restauración europea en los informes del consul sardo en Buenos Aires, Baron Henri Picolet d'Hermillen (1835–1848)." *Revista de historia de América* (Mexico) 37/38 (1954): 205–54.

"La historiografía argentina en la hora de la libertad." *Sur* 237 (1955): 114–21.

"Juan Álvarez, historiador." *Sur* 232 (1955): 27–32.

"Del fascismo al peronismo." *Contorno* 7/8 (1956): 15–21.

"Crisis de la historiografía y crisis de la cultura." *Imago mundi* 11/12 (1956).

"Vicente Fidel López, historiador." *Revista de la Universidad de Buenos Aires* 1, no. 3 (1956): 365–74.

"El espejo de la historia." *Contorno* 9/10 (1959): 76–81.

"Historia y larga duración: examen de un problema." *Cuestiones de filosofía* (Buenos Aires) 1, no. 2/3 (1962): 74–96. Also as "Histoire et longue durée. (Examen d'un probleme)" in *Cah. V. Pareto* 15, no. 68 (1968): 109–33.

"Para un balance de la situación actual de los estudios de historia económica argentina." *Universidad* (Santa Fe) 62 (1964): 79–90.

"Storia e storiografia della'America coloniale spagnola." *Revista storia italiana* 64–76 (1964): 5–37.

"Algunas observaciones sobre Germani, el surgimiento del peronismo y los migrantes internos." *Desarrollo económico* 14, no. 56 (1975): 765–81.

"Estudios recientes sobre el pensamiento político de Rosas." *Criterio* 49, no. 1736 (1976): 137–45.

"¿Para qué la inmigración? Ideología y política immigratoria y aceleración del proceso modernizador: el caso argentino, 1810–1914." *Jahrbuch für Geschichte von Staat, Wirtschaft und Gesellschaft Lateinamerikas* 13 (1976): 437–88.

"Cincuenta años de historia latinoamericana." *Criterio* 50, no. 1777–1778 (1977): 706–14.

"Sarmiento: su lugar en la sociedad argentina post-revolucionaria." *Sur* 341 (1977): 121–35.

"Carlos Real de Azúa, 1916–1977." *Hispanic American Historical Review* 58, no. 4 (1978): 697–99.

"José Luis Romero y su lugar en la historiografía argentina." *Desarrollo económico* 20, no. 78 (1980): 249–74. Also in José Luis Romero, *Las ideologías de la cultura nacional y otros ensayos*, Luis Alberto Romero, ed., pp. 187–236. Buenos Aires: Centro Editor de América Latina, 1982.

"Nueva narrativa y ciencias sociales hispanoameicanas en la década del sesenta." *Hispamérica* 9, no. 27 (1980): 3–18.

BOOK REVIEWS

"Clara Vilaseca: *Biografía de una época. Cartas de Mariquita Sánchez.*" *Sur* 219/220 (1953): 135–39.

"José Luis Lanuza: *Estaban Echeverría y sus amigos.*" *Sur* 219/220 (1953): 139–40.

"Felix Lizaso: *Proyección humana de Martí.*" *Sur* 228 (1954): 113–15.

"Enrique Anderson Imbert: *Estudios sobre escritores de América.*" *Sur* 233 (1955): 93–95.

"Jean Sarrailh: *L'Espagne éclairée de la seconde moitiée du XVIIIe siècle.*" *Sur* 236 (1955): 98–102.

"Ezequiel Gallo: *Farmers in Revolt: The Revolution of 1893 in the Province of Santa Fe, Argentina.*" *Revista internacional de bibliografía* 28, no. 1 (1978): 74–75.

"Manuel Moreno Fraginales: *The Sugarmill: The Social Complex of Sugar in Cuba, 1760–1860.*" *Revista internacional de bibliografía* 28, no. 1 (1978): 78–80.

"Lucía Sala de Tuourón, Nelson de la Torre, and Julio C. Rodríguez: *Artigas y su revolución agraria, 1811–1820.*" *Hispanic American Historical Review* 59, no. 2 (1979): 324–25.

About Tulio Halperín Donghi

Burghi, Hilda. Review of *Tradición española*. *Sur* 275 (1962): 94–97.

Fisher, John R. Review of *Politics, Economics and Society in Argentina in the Revolutionary Period* by Tulio Halperín Donghi, translated by Richard Southern. *Bulletin of Hispanic Studies* 54, no. 2 (1977): 168–69.

Lynch, John. Review of *Politics, Economics and Society in Argentina in the Revolutionary Period* by Tulio Halperín Donghi. *Journal of Latin American Studies* 9, no. 1 (1977): 161–62.

McGavin, Thomas F. Review of *Politics, Economics and Society in Argentina in the Revolutionary Period* by Tulio Halperín Donghi. *Hispanic American Historical Review* 57, no. 2 (1977): 340–42.

Pérez Brignoli, Héctor. "¿Historia política o historia del poder? Reflecciones sobre un libro reciente de Tulio Halperín Donghi." *Estudios sociales centroamericanos* 4, no. 10 (1975): 125–39. Bibliography.

Noé Jitrik
(1928)

BOOKS ON LITERARY CRITICISM, THEORY, HISTORY AND POLITICS

Haracio Quiroga: una obra de experiencia y riesgo. Buenos Aires: Ediciones Culturales Argentinas, 1959. 2d ed. Montevideo: Arca, 1967.

Seis novelistas argentinos de la nueva promoción. Mendoza: Cuadernos de Versión, 1959.

Leopoldo Lugones, mito nacional. Buenos Aires: Palestra, 1960.

Procedimiento y mensaje en la novela. Cordoba: Universidad Nacional de Córdoba, 1962.

El escritor argentino: dependencia o libertad. Buenos Aires: Ediciones del Candil, 1967.

Echeverría y la realidad nacional. Buenos Aires: Centro Editor de América Latina, 1967.

Horacio Quiroga. Buenos Aires: Centro Editor de América Latina, 1967.

Muerte y resurreccción de "Facundo." Buenos Aires: Centro Editor de América Latina, 1968.

El 80 y su mundo: presentación de una época [with anthology]. Buenos Aires: Jorge Alvarez, 1968. 2n ed. called *El mundo del 80.* Buenos Aires: Centro Editor de América Latina, 1982.

Tres ensayos sobre Esteban Echeverría. Besançon (France): Les Annales de l'Université de Besançon, 1969.

Ensayos y estudios de la literatura argentina. Buenos Aires: Galerna, 1970.

La revolución del noventa. Buenos Aires: Centro Editor de América Latina, 1970.

El fuego de la especie: ensayos sobre seis escritores argentinos. Buenos Aires: Siglo Veintiuno, 1971.

José Hernández. Buenos Aires: Centro Editor de América Latina, 1971.

Sarmiento. Buenos Aires: Centro Editor de América Latina, 1971.

José Martí. Buenos Aires: Centro Editor de America Latina, 1971.

La novela futura de Macedonio Fernández. Caracas: Universidad Central de Venezuela, Ediciones de Biblioteca, 1973.

El no existente caballero (ensayo sobre la forma del "personaje" en la literatura latinoamericana). Buenos Aires: Megápolis, 1975.

Producción literaria y producción social. Buenos Aires: Sudamericana, 1975.

Las contradicciones del modernismo: productividad poética y situación sociológica. Mexico: Colegio de México, 1978.

El modernismo. Buenos Aires: Centro Editor de América Latina, 1980.

La memoria compartida. Mexico: Editorial Veracruzana, 1982.

La lectura como actividad. Mexico: Premia, 1982.

Los dos ejes de la cruz. Puebla: U.A.P., 1983.

Las armas y las razones: ensayos sobre el peronismo, el exilio, la literatura (1975–1980). Buenos Aires: Sudamericana, 1984.

El melódico perplejo (ensayos heterodoxos). Mexico: Universidad Autónoma Metropolitana, 1985.

Temas de teoría: crítica literaria, trabajo crítico. Mexico: Premia, in press.

La vibración del presente. Buenos Aires: C.E.A.L., in press.

CREATIVE WRITING

Feriados (poetry). Buenos Aires: Contorno, 1956.

El año que se nos viene y otros poemas. Buenos Aires: Alpe, 1959.

Addio a la mamma. Buenos Aires: Zona de la Poesía Americana, 1965.

La fisura mayor (stories). Buenos Aires: Sudamericana, 1967.

Llamar antes de entrar (stories). Caracas: Síntesis Dosmil, 1972.

Comer y comer: poemas, 1965–1970. Buenos Aires: Ediciones de la Flor, 1974.

Del otro lado de la puerta: rapsodia. Buenos Aires: Megápolis, 1974.

Viajes (textos-objetos reconstruidos). Mexico: UNAM, 1979.

El ojo de jade (short novel). Mexico: Premia Ediotr, 1980.

Fin del ritual. Mexico: Joaquín Mortiz, 1981.

Díscola cruz del sur, guíame (Poems). Mexico: premia, in press.

A Oídos sordos (criticism-fiction). Buenos Aires: Bruguera, in press.

Los lentos tranvías. Buenos Aires 1930–1943. Mexico: Joaquín Mortiz, in press.

COLLABORATIONS AND WORKS EDITED

Jitrik, Francisco Urondo, and Cesar Fernández Moreno, eds. *Antología interna, 1950–1965.* Buenos Aires: Zona de la Poesía Americana, 1965.

Echeverría, Esteban. *La cautiva, El matadero y otros escritos.* Edited by Noé Jitrik. Buenos Aires: Centro Editor de América Latina, 1967.

La vuelta a Cortázar en nueve ensayos. Buenos Aires: Carlos Pérez, 1968.

Los viajeros: antología. Buenos Aires: Jorge Alvarez, 1969.

El nacimiento del lenguaje nacional. Vol. 1 (anthology). Buenos Aires: Estudio Entelman, 1972.

El nacimiento del lenguaje nacional. Vol. 2 (anthology). Buenos Aires: Estudio Entelman, 1973.

Jitrik and César Fernández Moreno, eds. *El nacimiento del lenguaje nacional.* Vol. 3 (anthology). Buenos Aires: Estudio Entelman, 1974.

García Márquez, Gabriel. *"El coronel no tiene quien le escriba" y "La increíble y triste historia de la cándida Eréndira y su abuela desalmada."* Edited and prologue by Noé Jitrik. Buenos Aires: Librería del Colegio, 1975. Prologue reprinted as "La escritura y la muerte," *Memoria compartida,* pp. 215–54.

Barrenechea, Ana Marí, Noé Jitrik, Jaime Rest, et al. *La crítica literaria contemporánea.* Edited by Nicolás Rosa. Buenos Aires: Centro Editor de América Latina, 1981.

ARTICLES

"Tres nuevas revistas porteñas." *Centro* 3, no. 5 (1953): 33–37.

Viñas, Ismael, and Noé Jitrik. "E. Larreta o el linaje." *Contorno* 5/6 (1955): 13–14.

"Adán Buenosayres: la novela de Leopoldo Marechal." *Contorno* 5/6 (1955): 38–45.

"Los comunistas (Manauta, Barletta, Yunque, Varela)." *Contorno* 5/6 (1955): 48–51.

"Guibert: un poeta con geografía." *Contorno* 7/8 (1956): 52–55.

"Cambaceres: adentro y afuera." *Boletín de literaturas hispánicas* 2 (Rosario, 1960). Also in *Ensayos y estudios,* pp. 35–54.

"Un novelista oblicuo [H. A. Murena]." *Ficción* 23 (1960): 52–71.

"Bipolaridad en la historia de la literatura argentina." *Boletín de Literatura Argentina* (Córdoba, 1961). Also in *Ensayos y estudios,* pp. 222–49.

"El proceso de nacionalización de la literatura argentina." *Humanidades* 5 (1962): 37–57. Also in *Ensayos y estudios,* pp. 179–99.

"Poesía argentina: aislamiento y esperanza." *Los andes* (Mendoza, 22 October 1962): 35–41. Also in *Escritor argentino,* pp. 35–46.

"Poesía argentina entre dos radicalismos." *Zona* 1 (1963). Also in *Ensayos y estudios,* pp. 200–221.

"La crítica literaria en la argentina." In *Encuesta: la crítica literaria en la Argentina,* edited by Adolfo Prieto. Rosario: Facultad de Filosofía y Letras, 1963. Also in *Escritor argentino,* pp. 53–58.

"Los desplazamientos de la culpa en las obras 'sociales' de Manuel Gálvez." *Duquesne Hispanic Review* 2 (1963): 143–66. Also in *Ensayos y estudios*, pp. 55–80.

"1926, año decisivo para la narrativa argentina." *El mundo* (4 July to 1 August 1965). Also in *Escritor argentino*, pp. 83–88.

"Cuaderno de notas." *Alcor* 39/40 (Asunción, 1966): 25–28.

"El escritor argentino: condena o salvación." *Marcha* 1301 (1966). Also in *Escritor argentino*, pp. 11–22.

"Soledad y urbanidad. Ensayo sobre la adaptación del romanticismo en la Argentina." *Boletín de literatura argentina* 2 (1966): 27–61. Also in *Ensayos y estudios*, pp. 139–78.

"Arlt, *El juguete rabioso*." *El mundo*. Also in *Escritor argentino*, pp. 89–94.

"*Don Segundo Sombra*, Ricardo Güiraldes." *El mundo*. Also in *Escritor argentino*, pp. 95–101.

"*Zogoibi*, de Enrique Larreta." *El mundo*. Also in *Escritor argentino*, pp. 103–8.

"Guillermo Tell." *Casa de las Américas* 7, no. 43 (1967). Also in *Fisura mayor*.

"Participación de la juventud en la literatura." *Revista de la Universidad Nacional de Córdoba* 9, no. 5 (1968): 875–99.

"Estructura y significación en *Ficciones*, de Jorge Luis Borges." *Casa de las Américas* 53 (1969): 50–62. Also in *La nouvelle critique* (1968): *contra Borges*, Buenos Aires: Galerna, 1978; and *Fuego de la especie*, pp. 129–50.

"Sobre el tema del canto en el *Martín Fierro*, de José Hernández." *Unión* 9, no. 3 (1970): 105–28. Also in *Fuego de la especie*, pp. 13–46.

"Destrucción y formas en las narraciones." In *América Latina en su literatura*, edited by César Fernández Moreno, pp. 219–42. Mexico: Siglo XXI, 1972. Also in *Producción literaria*, pp. 139–72. Also as "Destruction and Forms in Fiction," in *Latin America in its Literature*, edited by César Fernández Moreno, Julio Ortega, and Iván A. Schulman, pp. 155–79. New York: Holmes & Meier, 1980.

" 'Jugar su papel dentro del sistema'." *Hispamérica* 1 (1972): 17–29.

"Retrato discontinuo de Macedonio Fernández." *Crisis* 3 (1973): 44–49. Also in *Novela futura*, pp. 5–34.

"Crítica satélite y trabajo crítico en 'El perseguidor' de Julio Cortázar." *Nueva revista de filología hispánica* 23, no. 2 (Mexico: 1974); 337–68. Also in *Producción literaria*, pp. 82–129.

"Escritura y dictadura" (about Roa Bastos). *Excelsior* (Mexico: October 1974).

"Arte, violencia, ruptura." *La palabra y el hombre* 14 (1975): 19–27. Also in *Producción literaria*, pp. 65–81.

"Battista, entre la investigación y el juego." Prologue to *Como tanta gente que anda por ahí*, by Vicente Battista. Barcelona: Planeta, 1975.

"Blanco, negro, ¿mulato? Una lectura de *El reino de este mundo*, de Alejo Carpentier." *Texto crítico* 1, no. 1 (1975): 32–60. Also in *Memoria compartida*, pp. 175–214.

"En los comienzos de la represión en la Argentina: ojeada contemporánea sobre la vida cultural." *Cambio* 1, no. 1 (Mexico: 1975). Also as "Propuestos para discutir la actual situación argentina" in *Armas y las razones*, pp. 76–121.

"Una lectura anti-narcisista: *Matar a Título* de Arturo Cerretani." *Revista de crítica literaria latinoamericana* 1, no. 1 (1975): 151–56. Also in *Siempre* (Mexico: 1975), and in *Eco* (Bogotá: First Semester, 1975).

"Yo, El Supremo: la escritura en el centro del infierno." *El nacional* (Caracas: 7 September 1975).

"En las manos de Borges el corazon de Arlt" (about R. Piglia, *Moneda Falsa*). *Cambio* 3 (1976).

"Entre el dinero y el ser: lectura de *El juguete rabioso* de Roberto Arlt." In *The Analysis of Hispanic Texts.* Edited by Lisa E. Davis and Isabel Taran, pp. 256–99. Ann Arbor: Bilingual Press, 1976. Also in *Escritura* 1 (Caracas, 1976): 3–39; *Dispositio* 1, no. 2 (1976): 100–33; and *Memoria compartida*, pp. 79–122.

"Soledad: huraña, desdén, timidez." In *Aproximaciones a Quiroga*, edited by Angel Flores, pp. 37–61. Caracas: Monte Avila, 1976.

" 'Alturas de Macchur Picchu': una marcha piramidal a través de un discurso poético incesante." *Nueva revista de filología hispánica* 26, no. 2 (1977): 510–55. Also in *Memoria compartida*, pp. 123–74.

"Las dos traducciones" (about Sonnet X of Mallarmé). *Revista de la Universidad de México* 32, no. 2 (1977): 26–36. Also in *Point of Contact* 2 (1976).

"La enseñanza de la literatura a nivel medio y superior." *Colección pedagógica universitaria* 2 (Xalapa, 1977).

"El *Facundo:* la gran requeza de la pobreza." Introduction to *Facundo: civilización y barbarie*, by Domingo Faustino Sarmiento, pp. ix–lii. Caracas: Biblioteca Ayacucho, 1977. Also in *Memoria compartida*.

"The Future Novel." Translated by William Clamuro. *Review* 21/22 (1977): 137–48. Also in Spanish in *Novela futura*, pp. 39–86.

"Hacer algo con el texto." *Cuadernos de literatura* 2, no. 5 (Mexico, 1977).

"Entre el corte y la continuidad: una escritura crítica" (about J. J. Saer, *El limonero real*). *Revista iberoamericana* 44, nos. 102/103 (1978): 99–109. Also in *Vibración del presente*.

"La perifrástica productiva en *Cien años de soledad.*" In *Mèlanges offertes à André Joucla-Ruau*, pp. 813–48. Aix-en-Provence: Univ. de Aix-en-Provence, 1978. Also in *Producción literaria*, pp. 19–47.

"Primeros tanteos: literatura y exilio." *Nueva sociedad* (Caracas) 35 (1978): 48–55. Also as "Mirar hacia adentro: literatura y exilio," in *Armas y las razones*, pp. 122–46.

"Nuevas precisiones sobre trabajo crítico." *Literatura y linguística* (Xalapa: 1978). Also in *Temas de teoría*.

"La palpitación de un proyecto (notas sobre textos de Julieta Campos)." Presentation of a record by J.C., edited by "Voz viva de Mexico" of the U.N.A.M., 1979. Also in *Vibración del presente*.

"Diario de viaje." *Diálogos* (Mexico) 15, no. 85 (1979): 20–22. Also in *Viajes*.

"Literatura e integración latinoamericanas." *Latino américa* 2 (1979): 311–23. Also as "La integración latinoamericana en su literatura" in *Armas y las razones*.

"*Paradiso* entre desborde y ruptura." *Texto crítico* 5, no. 13 (1979): 77–89. Also as "A propos de *Paradiso* de J. Lezama Lima," in *Littérature latino-americaine d'aujourd'hui*. Paris: Colloque de Cerisy, 1980; also in *Vibración del presente*.

"Presencia y vigencia de Roberto Arlt." Prologue to *Antología*, by Roberto Arlt, pp. 7–35. Mexico: Siglo XXI, 1980. Also in *Literatura boletín* (Buenos Aires) 1, no. 1 (1982); also in *Vibración del presente*.

"Las desventuras de la crítica." *Marcha* (Mexico: 2d epoch). Also in *Armas y las razones*, pp. 193–228.

"Acción textual/acción sobre los textos." In *El lenguaje: problemas y reflexiones actuales.* Puebla: Ediciones de la U.A.P., 1980. Also in *Revista iberoamericana* 114/115 (1981):149–65; and in *Temas de teoría.*

"Literatura y psicoanálisis ¿o psicoanálisis y literatura?" In *Trabajos del psicoanálisis.* Mexico: Instituto Mexicano de Psicoanálisis, 1981. Also in *Temas de teoría.*

"Ritmo y espacio: de la anemia perniciosa a la demografía desbordante." *Revista de bellas artes* (Mexico) 3 (1981). Also in *Iberoamericana.* Frankfurt: 1983; and in *Vibración del presente.*

"Sentiments complexes sur Borges." *Les temps modernes* 420. Also in Spanish in *Unomasuno* (Mexico) 185 (1981); and in *Vibración del presente.*

"Arguedas: reflexiones y aproximaciones." *Revista iberoamericana* 122 (1982). Also in *Vibración del presente.*

"Doce asedios y una coda final para entrar en la poesía" (sobre Tomás Segovia). *Crítica y creación* 7 (1982). Also in *Crítica* (San Diego) 1, no. 1 (1984): 120–35; also in *Vibración del presente.*

"En torno a la poética modernista." *Semiosis* (Xalapa) 9 (1982).

"Lenguaje e ideología." *Apuntes de extensión académica* (Mexico: U.N.A.M., 1982).

"Las Malvinas: un sustituto peligroso." *Le monde diplomatique* (Mexico: June, 1982).

"Papeles de trabajo: notas sobre vanguardismo latinoamericano." *Revista de crítica literaria latinoamericana* (Lima) 8, no. 15 (1982). Also in *Armas y las razones;* pp. 167–92. and in *Vibración del presente.*

"Le vécu, le théorique, la coïncidence. Esquisse sur les rapports entre deux littératures." *Lendemains* (Berlin) 227 (1982). Also in Spanish in *Cuadernos americanos* 43, no. 2 (1984); also in *Armas y las razones,* pp. 147–66.

"Escritura y trabajo crítico: una perspectiva productiva para la textualidad latinoamericana." *Acta poética* (Mexico) 4/5 (1982–1983). Also in *Temas de teoría.*

"Lectura de Vasconcelos." *Unomasuno* (21 April–21 July 1983). Also in *Vibración del presente.*

"Literatura política en el imaginario social." *Discurso: cuadernos de teoría y análisis* (Mexico) 2, no. 6 (1985): 47–68.

"El asombro y la escritura, la ropa. Desnudos, cobardes, esclavos. El sexo omitido." In *Homenaje a Ana María Barrenechea.* Forthcoming.

"La poesía gauchesca: su evolución." In *Historia de la literatura latinoamericana.* Barcelona: RBA, Proyectos Editoriales, forthcoming.

"José Hernández." In *Historia de la literatura lationoamericana.*

"Rubén Dario." In *Historia de la literatura latinoamericana.*

POEMS, STORIES, AND MISCELLANEOUS TEXTS

"Dichterliebe," *Casa de las Américas* 5, no. 31 (1965).

"Guillermo Tell." *Casa de las Américas* 7, no. 43 (1967).

"La rectificación." *La palabra y el hombre* (Xalapa) 42 (1967): 303–308. Also in *Fisura mayor.*

"La inacción. Toda carne. Gnoseología." *La palabra y el hombre* 45 (1968): 31–33.

"Textos" ("Égloga felina y satánica," "Égloga filosofúnebre," "Égloga maligna y con datos científicos," "Elegía oprobiosa," "Epístola a los copernicanos,"

"Epístola que se vuelve contra sí misma," "Oda renacida y frágil," "Profecía número uno"). *Punto de Contacto/Point of Contact* 1, no. 1 (1975): 19–31.

"Elegía simple al esbozo de un amor que pudo ser más ancho y en cambio fue muy breve." *La palabra y el hombre* 19 (1976): 19–21.

"Poemas." *Revista nacional de cultura* (Caracas) 35, no. 224 (1976): 107–11.

"Poemas." *Excelsior* (Mexico: October, 1976).

"Poema." *Zaguán* (Mexico: March, 1977).

"Entrevista sobre *Décade de Cerisky.*" *Eco* (Bogota) 205 (1978).

"Bucólica aparte." *Unomasuno* (30 June 1979).

"Cuento de una tarde de mayo." *Diálogos* (Mexico) 82 (1979).

"Lamento por la muerte de Roland Barthes." *Unomasuno* (19 April 1980).

"El callejón y las salidas" (series of texts). *Unomasuno* (14 June–15 December 1980).

"Bucólica extrema ('Oda a una historia personal,' 'Elegía discepoliana')," *Eco* 232 (1981): 409–14.

"A la manera criolla de un Proust." *Crítica y creación* (Mexico) 6 (1982).

"Desde el desprecio al respeto." *Los universitarios* (Mexico) 202 (1982).

"En una ocasión tan ruda: palabras con motivo de la obtención del Premio Villarrutia." *Unomasuno* (18 February 1982).

"Las pequeñas especies singulares." *Revista de bellas artes* 10 (1982).

"Soy soldado de levita." *Revista de bellas artes* (Mexico) 2 (1982).

"Cortázar: crear algo entre dos." *México en el arte* 5 (1984).

"Poemas." *Estaciones* (Monterrey) 1, no. 2 (1984).

"Lecturas eróticas." *La jornada* (Mexico: 1985).

BOOK REVIEWS

"Reseña: *Otras inquisiciones*, de Jorge Luis Borges." *Revista centro* 3, no. 5 (1953): 35–37.

"*Historia prodigiosa*, de Adolfo Bioy Casares." *Lyra* 186/88 (1962).

"Reseña de *Tiempo pasado: semblanzas de escritores argentinos* de Bernardo González Arrili." *Nueva revista de filosofía hispánica* 25, no. 2 (1976): 444.

"Reseña de Josefina Ludmer: *Onetti: los procesos de construcción del relato.*" *Nueva revista de filología hispánica* 27, no. 1 (1978): 165–67.

"Reseña de *La autonomía literaria* de Renato Prada Oropeza." *Revista iberoamericana* 112/113 (1980): 669–71.

"Reseña de *Leer Borges* de Gerardo Mario Goloboff." *Revista iberoamericana* 112/113 (1980): 667–69.

"Sobre *Crítica en marcha*, de Jorge Ruffinelli." *Diálogos* (Mexico) 16 (1980): 48–49.

"Notas sobre libros en 'Panorama Editorial' de Radio U.N.A.M. de febrero a setiembre de 1981." *Unomasuno* (June–October 1981).

"Sobre *Recuerdo de la muerte*, de Miguel Bonasso," *La jornada* (Mexico: 1985).

ABOUT NOÉ JITRIK

Foster, David William. "Noé Jitrik: *Facundo*, and the uses of Literary Stylistics." *Chasqui* 5, no. 1 (1975): 15–27.

————. "Not the Same Old Wine in New Bottles (Review of *Producción literaria y producción social*)." *Chasqui* 5, no. 2 (1976): 66–75.

————. "Noe Jitrik: Literary Criticism vs. Trabajo Crítico." *Revista/Review interamericana* 8, no. 1 (1978): 148–75.

————. "Jitrik: 'crítica literaria' vs. 'trabajo crítico.' " *Texto crítico* 24/25 (Jalapa: 1982).

Katra, William H. "Noé Jitrik: Critical Artisan in Search of Literature's *significación*." In "The Argentine Generation of 1955: Politics, the Essay, and Literary Criticism," pp. 269–308. Ph.D. diss., University of Michigan, 1977.

Rodolfo Kusch
(1922–1959)

ESSAYS

La ciudad mestiza. Buenos Aires: 1952.

La seducción de la barbarie: análisis heretico de un continente mestizo. Buenos Aires: Raigal, 1953.

Tango y credo rante. Buenos Aires: Talía, 1959.

La muerte de El Chacho. La leyenda de Juan Moreira, con poesía de Goly Bernal. Buenos Aires: Stilcograf, 1960.

América profunda. Buenos Aires: Hachette, 1962.

De la mala vida porteña. Buenos Aires: Peña Lillo, 1966.

Indios, porteños y dioses. Buenos Aires: Stilcograf, 1966.

El pensamiento indígena americano. Puebla, Mexico: J. M. Cajica, Jr., 1970. 2d ed. enl. *El pensamiento indígena y popular en América*. Buenos Aires: Hachette, 1977.

La negación en el pensamiento popular. Buenos Aires: Cimarrón, 1975.

Geocultura del hombre americano. Buenos Aires: F. García Cambeiro, 1976.

Esbozo de una antropología filosófica americana. Buenos Aires: Castañeda, 1978.

ARTICLES

"Inteligencia y barbarie." *Contorno* 3 (1954): 4–7.

"Lo superficial y lo profundo en Martínez Estrada." *Contorno* 4 (1954): 5–8.

Oscar Masotta
(1930–1979)

BOOKS

Roberto Arlt. Buenos Aires: Universidad de Buenos Aires, Facultad de Filosofía y Letras, 1959.

Sexo y traición en Roberto Arlt. Buenos Aires: Jorge Alvarez, 1965.

Happenings. Buenos Aires: Jorge Alvarez, 1967.

El "pop-art." Buenos Aires: Columbia, 1967.

Conciencia y estructura. Buenos Aires: Jorge Alvarez, 1969.

La historieta en el mundo moderno. Buenos Aires: Paídos, 1970.

Introducción a la lectura de Jacques Lacan. Buenos Aires: Proteo, 1970.

Temas de Jacques Lacan. Buenos Aires: Ediciones Nueva Visión, 1971.
Ensayos lacanianos. Buenos Aires: Anagrama, 1976.
El modelo pulsional. Buenos Aires: Altazor, 1980.

ARTICLES

"Denuncias sin testigo." *Contorno* 3 (1954): 14–15.
"*Sur* o el antiperonismo colonialista." *Contorno* 7/8 (1956): 39–45.
"Explicación de *Un dios cotidiano* [by David Viñas]." *Comentario* 5, no. 20 (1958): 78–88. Reprinted in his *Conciencia y estructura.*
"Leopoldo Lugones y Juan Carlos Ghiano: antimercantilistas." *Centro* 12 (1959): 146–62. Reprinted as *Leopoldo Lugones y Juan Carlos Ghiano, antimercantilistas.* Buenos Aires: Libreros y Editores del Polígono, 1983.
"¿Qué es el psicoanálisis?" *Los libros* 1, no. 5 (1969): 15, 21.
"Aclaraciones en torno a Jacques Lacan." *Los libros* 2, no. 10 (1970): 6–7.

ABOUT MASOTTA

Germán García. *Oscar Masotta y el psicoanálisis en Argentina.* Buenos Aires: Argonauta, 1980.

Adolfo Prieto
(1928)

BOOKS

El sentimiento de la muerte a través de la literatura española (siglos XVI y XV). Ph.D. diss., Facultad de Filosofía y Letras, Universidad de Buenos Aires, 1953.
Borges y la nueva generación. Buenos Aires: Letras Universitarias, 1954.
Sociología del público argentino. Buenos Aires: Leviatán, 1956.
La literatura autobiográfica argentina. Rosario: Facultad de Filosofía y Letras, Universidad Nacional del Litoral, 1962.
El martinfierrismo. Montevideo: Universidad de la República, Facultad de Humanidades y Ciencias, 1967.
Diccionario básico de literatura argentina. Buenos Aires: Centro Editor de América Latina, 1968.
La fantasía y lo fantástico en Roberto Arlt. Buenos Aires: Tiempo Contemporáneo, 1968.
Literatura y subdesarrolo: notas para un análisis de la literatura argentina. Buenos Aires: Biblioteca, 1968.
Estudios de literatura argentina. Buenos Aires: Galerna, 1969.

IN COLLABORATION:

La literatura argentina y su público. Santa Fe: Universidad Nacional del Litoral, 1959.
Proyección del rosismo en la literatura argentina. Rosario: Facultad de Filosofía y Letras, Universidad del Litoral, 1959.

Las claves de Adán Buenosayres y tres artículos de Julio Cortázar, Adolfo Prieto, Graciela de Sola. Mendoza: Azor, 1966.

BOOKS EDITED

Encuesta: la crítica literaria en la Argentina. With Prologue. Rosario: Facultad de Filosofía y Letras, Universidad del Litoral, 1963.

Antología de Boedo y Florida. Cordoba: Universidad Nacional de Córdoba, 1964.

El ensayo romántico: textos de Esteban Echeverría, Juan María Gutiérrez y Juan Bautista Alberdi. Buenos Aires: Centro Editor de América Latina, 1967.

El periódico "Martín Fierro." Buenos Aires: Editorial Galerna, 1968.

José Hernández. *Prosas y oratoria parlamentaria.* Prologue by A. Prieto, pp. 9–22. Rosario: Biblioteca, 1974.

José Ramos Mejía. *Las multitudes argentinas.* Prologue by A. Prieto, pp. 9–19. Rosario: Biblioteca, 1974.

Los años de la emancipación política. Prologue by A. Prieto, pp. 9–20. Rosario: Biblioteca, 1974.

Las guerras civiles: el rosismo. Prologue by A. Prieto. Rosario: Biblioteca, 1974.

Roberto Arlt. *Los Siete Locos. Los Lanzallamas.* Prologue, Notes, Vocabulary, and Chronological Tables by A. Prieto. Caracas: Biblioteca Ayacucho, 1978.

Holmberg. *Relatos.* Prologue by A. Prieto. Buenos Aires: El Ateneo, 1979.

El discurso criollista en la formación de la Argentina moderna. Buenos Aires: Sudamericana, 1987.

ARTICLES

"Borges, el ensayo crítico." *Revista centro* 3, no. 7 (1953): 9–19.

"*Los ídolos de Mujica Laínez.*" *Contorno* 1 (1953): 5.

"Sobre la indiferencia argentina." *Ciudad* 1, no. 1 (1955): 8–15.

"Peronismo y neutralidad." *Contorno* 7/8 (1956): 28–31.

"Habla la nueva generación." *Polémica literaria* 3 (1957).

"Los dos mundos de Adán Buenosayres." *Boletín de literaturas hispánicas* 1 (1959): 57–74. Also in *Claves de 'Adán Buenosayres'*, pp. 34–49, with articles by Leopoldo Marechal, Julio Cortázar, and Graciela Maturo. Mendoza: Editorial Azor, 1966. Also in *Interpretaciones y claves de 'Adán Buenosayres'*, pp. 33–54. Montevideo: Acalí, 1977.

"La literatura de izquierda. El grupo Boedo." *Fichero* 2 (1959): 17–20.

"El martinfierrismo." *Revista de literatura argentina e iberoamericana* (Mendoza) 1 (1959): 9–31. Reprinted in Montevideo: Facultad de Filosofía y Humanidades, Universidad de la República, 1968.

"Respuesta de Adolfo Prieto." *Ciudad* 2 (1959): 101–6.

"El sentimiento de la muerte en la literatura español medieval, siglos XIV y XV." *Revista de literaturas modernas* (Mendoza) 2 (1960): 115–70.

"La literatura autobiográfica." *Revista de historia* (Rosario) 5 (1960): 72–97.

"Una curiosa revista de orientación futurista." *Boletín de literaturas hispánicas* (Rosario) 3 (1969). Also in *Los vanguardismos en la América Latina*, edited by Oscar Colla, pp. 49–60. Barcelona: Península, 1977.

"La fantasía y lo fantástico en Roberto Arlt." *Boletín de literaturas hispánicas* 5 (1963). Also as Prologue to Roberto Arlt, *Viaje terrible*. Buenos Aires: Tiempo Contemporáneo, 1968.

"Gálvez: *El mal metafísico.*" *Duquesne Hispanic Review* 2 (1963): 119–28. Also in *Estudios de literatura argentina*, pp. 8–27.

"La prosa romántica;" "El ensayo en la época romántica;" "Domingo Faustino Sarmiento." In *Historia de la literatura argentina*, pp. 256–336. Buenos Aires: Centro Editor de América Latina, 1967.

"La generación del ochenta: las ideas y el ensayo;" "La generación del ochenta: la imaginación." In *Historia de la literatura argentina*, pp. 433–80. Buenos Aires: Centro Editor de América Latina, 1967.

"Conflictos de generaciones." In *América latina en su literatura*, edited by César Fernández Moreno, pp. 406–23. Mexico: UNESCO-Siglo XXI, 1972.

"Borges y la nueva generación." In *Contra Borges*, edited by Juan Flo. Buenos Aires: Galerna, 1978.

"Los sesenta: balance crítico." *Revista iberoamericana* 125 (1983): 889–901.

"Daniel Moyano: una literatura de la expatriación." In *Cuadernos hispanoamericanos* 416 (1985): 189–95.

"Encuentros con Angel Rama." *Texto crítico* 31/32 (Xalapa, 1985): 33–38.

"Argentina: la primera literatura de masas." In *Augusto Roa Bastos y la producción cultural americana*, pp. 213–31. Buenos Aires: Ediciones de la Flor-Ediciones Folios, 1986.

ABOUT PRIETO

Borello, Adolfo. "Adolfo Prieto: literatura y sociedad en la Argentina." *Cuadernos hispanoamericanos* 214 (1967): 133–46.

Foster, David William. "Adolfo Prieto: Profile of a Parricidal Literary Critic." *Latin American Research Review* 13, no. 3 (1978): 125–45.

Katra, William H. "Adolfo Prieto: Autobiography and 'crítica totalizadora.' " In "The Argentine Generation of 1955: Politics, the Essay, and Literary Criticism," pp. 309–44. Ph.D. diss., University of Michigan, 1977.

León Rozitchner
(1924)

BOOKS

Persona y comunidad: ensayo sobre la significación ética de la afectividad de Max Scheler. Buenos Aires: EUBA, 1962.

Moral burguesa y revolución. Buenos Aires: Procyón, 1963.

Ser judío. Buenos Aires: Ediciones de la Flor, 1967.

Freud y los límites del individualismo burgués. Buenos Aires: Siglo Veintiuno, 1972.

Freud y el problema del poder. Buenos Aires: Folios Ediciones, 1982.

Las Malvinas: de la guerra "sucia" a la guerra "limpia." Buenos Aires: Centro Editor de América Latina, 1985.

Perón, entre la sangre y el tiempo: lo inconsciente y la política. Buenos Aires: Centro Editor de América Latina, 1985.

ARTICLES

"A propósito de *El juez* de H. A. Murena." *Centro* 4, no. 8 (1954): 16–30.
"Communicación y servidumbre: Mallea." *Contorno* 5/6 (1955): 27–35.
"Experiencia proletaria y experiencia burguesa." *Contorno* 7/8 (1956): 2–8.
"Lucha de clases, verificación del laicismo." *Contorno cuadernos* 1 (1957): 8–21.
"Un paso adelante, dos atrás." *Contorno* 9/10 (1959): 1–15.
"Ensayo sobre la moral burguesa (a propósito de Playa Girón)." *Universidad de la Habana* 27 (1960): 7-141.
"Persona, cultura y subdesarrollo." *Revista de la Universidad de Buenos Aires* 6, no. 1 (1969): 75–98.

Juan José Sebreli
(1930)

BOOKS

Historia argentina y conciencia de clase. Buenos Aires: Perrot, 1957.
Martínez Estrada: una rebelión inútil. Buenos Aires: Palestra, 1960.
Buenos Aires: vida cotidiana y alienación. Buenos Aires: Siglo Veinte, 1964.
Eva Perón: ¿aventurera o militante? Bueos Aires: Siglo Veinte, 1966.
La cuestión judía en Buenos Aires. Buenos Aires: Tiempo Contemporáneo, 1968.
Mar del Plata: el ocio represivo. Buenos Aires: Tiempo Contemporáneo, 1970.
Los oligarcas. Buenos Aires: Centro Editor de América Latina, 1971.
La teoría de la novela. Buenos Aires: Edhasa, 1971.
Apogeo y ocaso de los Anchorena. Buenos Aires: Siglo Veinte, 1972.
Tercer mundo: mito burgués. Buenos Aires: Siglo Veinte, 1975.
Viñas, David, Ismael Viñas, Juan José Sebreli. *Contorno: selección.* Prologue by Carlos Mangone and Jorge Warley. Buenos Aires: Centro Editor de América Latina, 1981.
Fútbol y masas. Buenos Aires: Galerna, 1981.
De Buenos Aires y su gente: antología. Buenos Aires: Centro Editor de América Latina, 1982.
Los deseos imaginarios del peronismo. Buenos Aires: Legasa, 1983.
El riesgo de pensar: ensayos 1950–1984. Buenos Aires: Sudamericana, 1984.
La saga de los Anchorena. Buenos Aires: Sudamericana, 1985.
Las señales de la memoria. Buenos Aires: Sudamericana, 1987.

ARTICLES

"Posición del hombre en el caos moderno." *Existencia* 1, no. 1 (1949).
"Celeste y colorado." *Sur* 217/218 (1952).
"A propósito de *Entre mujeres solas.*" *Sur* 221 (1953): 115–20.
"El escritor argentino y su público." *Revista centro* 3, no. 7 (1953): 24–29.
"Inocencia y culpabilidad de Roberto Arlt." *Sur* 223 (1953): 109–19.

"Los 'martinfierristas': su tiempo y el nuestro." *Contorno* 1 (1953): 1–2.

"La acción de Sarmiento y la razón de Alberdi." *Sur* 230 (1954): 74–78.

"Alberto Girri: *Misantropos*" (Book review). *Sur* 226 (1954): 96–99.

"H. A. Murena: *El juez*" (Book review). *Centro* 4, no. 8 (1954): 43–46.

"Manuel Gálvez y el sainete histórico." *Contorno* 3 (1954): 2–4.

"Martínez Estrada o el alma encadenada." Capricornio 8 (1954): 15–23.

"Ramón Ferreira: *Tiburrón y otros cuentos*" (Book review). *Sur* 227 (1954): 97–98.

"Rodolfo Kusch: *La seducción de la barbarie*" (Book review). *Sur* 228 (1954): 115–18.

"Ernesto Palacio: *Historia de la Argentina 1515–1938*" (Book review). *Sur* 234 (1955): 101–104.

"Miguel Angel Speroni: *Las arenas*" (Book review). *Sur* 234 (1955): 104–106.

"El moralismo y la utilización imperialista de la pequeña burguesía." *Izquierda* (Buenos Aires) 2 (1955).

"Testimonio [el peronismo]." *Contorno* 7/8 (1956): 45–49.

"Martínez Estrada y el fatalismo telúrico." *Gaceta literaria* 3, no. 20 (1960): 19–20.

"Hector Raurich, un pensador maldito." *Capricornio* 1, no. 1 (1965): 1–6.

"Raices ideológicos del populismo." In *El populismo en la Argentina*. By Osvaldo Bayer et al. Edited by Jose Isaacson, pp. 153–84. Buenos Aires: Plus Ultra, 1974.

"El joven Masotta." *Arte nova* 5 (1980).

F. J. Solero

NOVELS

El dolor y el sueño. Buenos Aires: Schapire, 1953.
La culpa. Buenos Aires: Doble P., 1956.

ESSAYS

Solero, F. J., ed. *Las narraciones más extraordinarias*. Buenos Aires: Schapire, 1953.
¿Qué es América? Literatura y contorno. Buenos Aires: Ámbito, 1972.

ARTICLES

Review of *Desde esta carne. Sur* 223 (1953): 139–40.

"Roberto Arlt y el pecado de todos." *Contorno* 2 (1954): 6–7.

"Eduardo Mallea en su laberinto." *Contorno* 3 (1954): 13.

"E. Cambaceres, primer novelista argentino." *Contorno* 5/6 (1955): 55.

"Eugenio Cambaceres y la novela argentina." *Ficción* 3 (1956): 105–24.

POEMS

"Responso." *Contorno* 3 (1954): 5–7.

"Matrimonio secreto; poeta desocupado." *Sur* 300 (1966): 84–87.

David Viñas
(1927)

BOOKS (ESSAYS)

Literatura argentina y realidad política. Buenos Aires: Jorge Álvarez, 1964.

Del apogeo de la oligarquía a la crisis de la ciudad liberal: Laferrere. Buenos Aires: Jorge Álvarez, 1967; Siglo Veinte, 1975.

Argentina: ejército y oligarquía. La Habana, 1967.

Literatura argentina y realidad política: de Sarmiento a Cortázar. Buenos Aires: Siglo Veinte, 1971.

Rebeliones populares argentinas: de los montoneros a los anarquistas. Buenos Aires: Carlos Pérez, 1971.

Grotesco, inmigración y fracaso: Armando Discépolo. Buenos Aires: Corregidor, 1973.

Literatura argentina y realidad política: la crisis de la ciudad liberal. Buenos Aires: Siglo Veinte, 1973.

Literatura argentina y realidad política: apogeo de la oligarquía. Buenos Aires: Siglo Veinte, 1975.

Qué es el fascismo en Latinoamerica. Barcelona: Gaya Ciencia, 1977.

Indios, ejército y frontera. Buenos Aires: Siglo Veintiuno, 1982.

Los anarquistas en América latina. Mexico: Katún, 1983.

COLLABORATIONS

Viñas, David, et al. *Más allá del boom: literatura y mercado.* Mexico: Marcha Editores, 1981.

NOVELS

Cayó sobre su rostro. Buenos Aires: El Doble, 1955.

Los años despiadados. Buenos Aires: Letras Universitarias, 1956.

Un dios cotidiano. Buenos Aires: Kraft, 1957.

Los dueños de la tierra. Buenos Aires: Losada, 1958.

Dar la cara. Buenos Aires: Jamcana, 1962.

En la semana trágica. Buenos Aires: Jorge Álvarez, 1966.

Los hombres de a caballo. La Habana: Casa de las Américas, 1967.

Cosas concretas. Buenos Aires: Tiempo Contemporáneo, 1969.

Jaurí. Buenos Aires: Granica, 1974.

Carlos Gardel. Madrid: Montal, 1979.

Cuerpo a cuerpo. Mexico: Siglo XXI, 1979.

Ultramar. Madrid: Edialsa, 1980.

STORIES

"Los desorientados" (fragment). *Centro* 2 (1952): 27–45.

"Milonga." *Contorno* 1 (1953): 4–5.

"Solamente los huesos" (fragment). *Centro* 10 (1955): 51–71.

"¡Paso a los héroes!" *Contorno* 7/8 (1956): 31–39.

"Un poco de bondad." *Ficción* 7 (1957): 3–11.

"Un solo cuerpo mudo." *Ficción* 14 (1958): 32–38.

"Los dueños de la tierra" (fragment). Espiral (Bogota) 77 (1960): 76–85.

"Entre delatores." *Ficción* 35/37 (1962): 50–58.

Las malas costumbres. Buenos Aires: Jamcana, 1963.

"Gabriela me llama" (fragment from *Los hombres de a caballo*). *Casa de las Américas* 7, no. 41 (1967): 80–83.

"Santificar las fiestas." In *Los diez mandamientos*. Buenos Aires: Jorge Álvarez, 1967.

"Barba azul." In *Cuentos recontados*. Buenos Aires: Tiempo Contemporáneo, 1968.

SCREENPLAYS (all from Viñas's narratives)

El jefe, directed by Fernando Ayala, 1957.

El candidato, directed by Fernando Ayala, 1959.

Dar la cara, directed by José M. Suárez, 1961.

PUBLISHED PLAYS

Sara Goldmann, mujer de teatro. First performance: Gente de Teatro, Buenos Aires, 1958. Directed by Alberto Rodríguez Muñoz.

Lisandro. Buenos Aires: Merlín, 1971. First performance: 22 April 1972. Directed by Luis Macchi in the Chacabuco Theatre.

Tupac Amaru, Dorrego, Maniobras. Buenos Aires: Cepe, 1974. First performance of *Tupac Amaru*: 22 May 1973. Directed by Fernando Ayala in the Licco Theatre.

MISCELLANEOUS

Historia de América latina. Tomo 4: México y Cortés. Madrid: Hernando, 1978.

Historia de América latina. Tomo 6: Expansión de la conquista. Madrid: Hernando, 1978.

Viñas, David, and Emilio Miguel. *Monstruario* (Four wood engravings by Emilio Miguel, with texts selected by David Viñas). *Iberoamericana*, 4, no. 9 (1980): 35–41.

"Trece preguntas a David Viñas" (Interview), *Voz fronteriza* (San Diego) 1, no. 2 (1976).

ARTICLES

"Comentario a la novela de James Jones, *De aquí a la eternidad*." *Las ciento y una* 1 (1953): 2.

"F. J. Solero: *El dolor y el sueño*" (book review). *Sur* 224 (1953): 157–59.

"Leopoldo Lugones: mecanismo, contorno y destino." *Centro* 3, no. 5 (1953): 3–22.

"Tres nuevas revistas porteñas." *Centro* 3, no. 5 (1953): 33–35.

"Quiroga: el mito de Anteo." *Espiga* (Buenos Aires) 7, no. 18/19 (1953–54): 7.

"Arlt y los comunistas" [pseudonym: Juan José Gorini]. *Contorno* 2 (1954): 8.

"Arlt—un escolio" [pseudonym: Diego Sánchez Cortés]. *Contorno* 2 (1954): 11–12.

"Benito Lynch y la pampa cercada." *Cultura universitaria* (Caracas) 46 (1954): 40–53.

"*Doña Bárbara* y la libertad futura." *Liberalis* (Buenos Aires), 30 (1954): 4–14.

"La historia excluída: ubicación de Martínez Estrada." *Contorno* 4 (1954): 10–16.

"Manuel Mujica Laínez." *Contorno* 3 (1954): 8.

"Los ojos de Martínez Estrada" [pseudonym: Raquel Weinbaum]. *Contorno* 4 (1954): 1.

"Onetti: un novelista que se despide." *Contorno* 3 (1954): 13.

"Tres novelistas argentinos por orden cronológico: Bernardo Verbitsky (1907), J. Carlos Onetti (1909), José Bianco (1915)." *Centro* 4, no. 8 (1954): 11–15.

"Benito Lynch: la realización del *Facundo*." *Contorno* 5/6 (1955): 16–21.

"Los dos ojos del romanticismo" [pseudonym: Raquel Weinbaum]. *Contorno* 5/6 (1955): 2–5.

"Prieto, *Borges y la nueva generación*" (book review). *Liberalis* 31/32 (1955): 66–72.

"*Donde haya Dios* por Alberto Rodríguez" (book review). *Comentario* (Buenos Aires) 3, no. 10 (1956): 89–91.

"Hemingway: tres etapas de su vida nortoamericana." *Comentario* 4, no. 13 (1956): 94–97.

"Tres o cuatro cosas." *Revista de derecho y ciencias sociales* (Buenos Aires) 3 (1956–1957): 13–14.

"Escribe David Viñas." *Gaceta literaria* 3, no. 17 (1959): 15.

"Una generación traicionada." *Marcha* 22, no. 992 (1959): 12–15, 20; no. 993 (1960): 22–23.

"Repaso y balance de la literatura argentina (1900–1960)." *Humanidades* (Mérida, Venezuela) 2, no. 7/8 (1960): 397–406.

"*Gauchos judíos* y xenofobia." *Revista de la Universidad de Mexico* 18, no. 3 (1962): 14–19.

"Prólogo" to *En la sangre*, by Eugenio Cambaceres, pp. 5–11. Buenos Aires: EUDEBA, 1967.

"Mirada de clubman y arquitectura teatral." In *La crítica moderna*, by Rodolfo A. Borello, pp. 99–116. Buenos Aires: Centro Editor de América Latina, 1968.

"Armando Discépolo: grotesco, inmigración y fracaso." Prologue to *Obras escogidas*, by Armando Discépolo, vol. 1, pp. vii–lxvi. Buenos Aires: Jorge Álvarez, 1969.

"Después de Cortázar: historia y privatización." *Cuadernos hispanoamericanos* 234 (1969): 734–39.

"Sábato y el bonapartismo." *Los libros* 1, no. 12 (1970): 6–8. Also in *Literatura argentina y realidad política: de Sarmiento a Cortázar*, pp. 110–21.

"Cortázar y la fundación mitológica de Paris." *Nuevos aires* 3 (1971): 27–34. Also in *Literatura argentina y realidad política: de Sarmiento a Cortázar*, pp. 122–32.

"*La vorágine*: Crisis, populismo y mirada." *Hispamérica* 3, no. 8 (1974): 3–21. Also in *Literatura argentina y realidad política: apogeo de la oligarquía*, pp. 57–70.

"Entre Fidel y Allende: situación del escritor en América latina." Oral presentation at the MLA Convention, San Francisco, 1975.

"Poderes de la literatura y literatura del poder: trabajadores, burócratas y francotiradores." *Caravelle* 25 (1975): 153–59.

"Una hipótesis sobre Borges: de Macedonio a Lugones." *Revista de crítica literaria latinoamericana* 2, no. 4 (1976): 139–42.

"La iglesia entre el Vaticano y Pinochet," *Cuadernos para el diálogo* (1976): 38–39.

"El teatro rioplatense (1880–1930: un circuito y algunas hipótesis." *Ideologies and Literature* 1, no. 1 (1976–77): 69–72.

"Prólogo." In *Teatro rioplatense (1886–1930)*, by E. Gutiérrez et al., edited by Jorge Lafforgue, pp. ix–xliv. Caracas: Biblioteca Ayacucho, 1977.

"Una hipótesis sobre Borges." *La palabra y el hombre* 29 (1979): 32–35.

"Manuel Rojas en perfil (y sin retoques)." *Casa de las Américas* 21, no. 121 (1980): 88–92.

"Pareceres y disgresiones en torno a la nueva narrativa latinoamericana." *Iberoamericana* 4, no. 10 (1980): 9–35. Also in *Más allá del boom*, David Viñas, et al., pp. 13–50.

"Déjenme hablar de Walsh." *Casa de las Américas* 22, no. 129 (1981): 147–49. Also in *Plural*, 2d epoch, 10, no. 118 (1981): 17–19.

"Onetti: de la evasión al exilio." *Plural*, 2nd epoch, 10, no. 114 (1981): 31–34.

"Malouines: de la crise au desastre." *Les temps modernes* 39, no. 437 (1982): 1039–63.

"Demonios no, Platón: sobre dos falsas simetrías." *El mundo* (Cordoba: 4 September 1984).

"Nacionalismos: del integral al populista." *El periodista de Buenos Aires* 1 (15–21 September 1984): 9.

"Alonso: el conjuro o el rito." *Casa de las Américas* 150 (1985): 165–66.

SELECTED ESSAYS TREATING DAVID VIÑAS

Agosti, Hector P. "Viñas: política y literatura." In *La milicia literaria*, pp. 163–66. Buenos Aires: Sílaba, 1969.

———. "Viñas." In *Cantar opinando*, pp. 120–25. Buenos Aires: Boedo, 1982.

Alonso, Fernando, y Arturo Rezzano. "David Viñas." In *Novela y sociedad argentinas*, pp. 193–209. Buenos Aires: Paídos, 1971.

Becco, Horacio Jorge. "Los años despiadados." *Revista iberoamericana* 22, no. 43 (1957).

Borello, Rodolfo. "Sobre la literatura de protesta en la Argentina." *Eidos* (Madrid) 34 (1971): 96–110.

———. "Texto literario y contexto histórico-generacional: Viñas y los escritores liberales argentinos." In *Texto/contexto en la literatura iberoamericana*, pp. 33–40. Madrid: Instituto Internacional de Literatura Iberoamericana, 1980.

Bottone, Mireye. "Del libreto cinematográfico a la novela: *Dar la cara*." In his *La literatura argentina y el cine*, pp. 27–31. Rosario: Universidad Nacional del Litoral, 1964.

Brushwood, John S. *The Spanish American Novel: A Twentieth Century Survey.* Austin: University of Texas Press, 1975.

———. "Las novelas de David Viñas: mensaje y significación." *Taller Literario* 1, no. 1 (1980): 1–10.

Cano, Carlos J. "Épica y misoginia en *Los hombres de a caballo.*" *Revista iberoamericana* 42, no. 96/97 (1976): 561–65.

Castagnino, Raúl H. "Otros caminos de la estilística: Las 'formas de relieve' por via tipográfica en la técnica de algunos novelistas argentinos contemporáneos." *Humanidades* 36 (1960): 123–48.

———. *Márgenes de los estructuralismos,* pp. 148–56. Buenos Aires: Nova, 1975.

——— (unsigned). "Condena a las dictaduras: jornadas de intelectuales latinoamericanos exilados en España." *Presencia argentina* (1979): 13.

Cresta de Leguizamón, Marí Luisa. *Algunos novelistas de la actualidad.* Cordoba: Universidad Nacional de Córdoba, 1962.

Fajardo, Diogenes. "La novelista de David Viñas." Ph.D. diss., University of Kansas, 1981.

Foster, David William. "*Literatura argentina y realidad política:* David Viñas and Sociological Literary Criticism in Argentina." *Ibero Amerikanisches Archiv* 1, no. 3 (1975): 253–77.

———. "David Viñas: Deconstructive and Corrective Readings of Argentine Sociocultural History." In press.

Foster, David William and Virginia Ramos Foster. *Modern Latin American Literature,* vol. 2., pp. 427–32. New York: Frederick Ungar, 1975.

Goldar, Ernesto. *El peronismo en la literatura argentina,* pp. 101–103. Buenos Aires: Freeland, 1971.

González Echeverría, Roberto. "David Viñas y la crítica literaria: *De Sarmiento a Cortázar.*" *Eco* 35, no. 216 (1979): 588–606. Also in his *Isla a su vuelta fugitiva: ensayos críticos sobre literatura hispanoamericana,* pp. 103–22. Madrid: Porrúa Turanzas, 1983.

Gramuglio, Marí Teresa. "La actitud testimonial en David Viñas." *Setecientosmonos* (Rosario) 4, no. 9 (1967).

Grossi, Héctor. "Angry Young Argentina: David Viñas Speaks His Mind." *Américas,* 12, no. 1 (1960): 14–17.

Heker, Liliana. "*Dar la cara;* novela de David Viñas." *El escarabajo de oro* 4, no. 17 (1963): 19–22.

Herrera, Francisco. "David Viñas." In *Enciclopedia de la literatura argentina.* Buenos Aires: Sudamericana, 1970.

Jitrik, Noé. "David Viñas." In *Seis novelistas argentinos de la nueva promoción,* pp. 68–72. Mendoza: Cuadernos de Versión, 1959.

Katra, William H. "David Viñas: Toward a Dialectical Criticism." In "The Argentine Generation of 1955: Politics, the Essay, and Literary Criticism," pp. 230–69. Ph.D. diss., University of Michigan, 1977.

———. "The Political Commentary of David Viñas: The Resemanticization of a 'Borgean' Reality." In *Proceedings of the Pacific Coast Council on Latin American Studies,* edited by Thomas Wright, vol. 12 (1985). San Diego: San Diego University Press, 1986.

Kerr, Lucille. "La geometría del poder: *Los hombres de a caballo* de David Viñas." *Revista de crítica literaria latinoamericana* 5, no. 9 (1979): 69–77.

Lapeyre, Albert. "Histoire et société dans *Los dueños de la tierra*." Ph.D. diss., Université de Bordeaux, 1981.

Larra, Raúl. "David Viñas o el terrorismo literario." In his *Mundo de escritores*, pp. 23–27. Buenos Aires: Sílaba, 1973.

López Morales, Eduardo E. "De levita (de esos de caballería)" [*Los hombres de a caballo*]. *Casa de las Américas* 46 (1968): 186–92.

Lyon, Ted. "El engaño de la razón: Quiroga, Borges, Cortázar, Viñas." *Texto crítico* 2, no. 4 (1976): 116–26.

Magis, Carlos H. "Novela, realidad y malos entendidos (sobre *Los hombres de a caballo*)." *Revista de la Universidad de México* 25, no. 6 (1971): 10–17.

Masotta, Oscar. "Explicación de *Un dios cotidiano*." *Comentario* 5, no. 20 (1958): 78–88. Also in his *Conciencia y estructura*. Buenos Aires: Jorge Álvarez, 1968.

Mattarollo Benasso, Rodolfo. "Para una crítica de la crítica (sobre *Literatura argentina y realidad política: de Sarmiento a Cortázar)*." *Revista latinoamericana* 1, no. 1 (1972): 137–40.

McBride, Cathryn Ann. "Referents in Discourse: A Study of Narrative Cohesion in the Spanish Originals and English Translations of Three Latin American Novels: Carlos Fuentes, David Viñas, María Luisa Bombal." *DAI* 38 (1977): 1371A–72A.

"Once preguntas concretas a David Viñas." *El grillo de papel* 1, no. 2 (1959–60): 24.

Orgambide, Pedro, y Roberto Yahni, ed. *Enciclopedia de la literatura argentina*, pp. 625–26. Buenos Aires: Sudamericana, 1970.

Peltzer, Federico. "Dios en la literatura argentina." *Señales* 12, no. 126/127 (1960): 7–14.

Pereira, Teresinka Alves. *"Tupac Amaru."* In her *La actual dramaturgia latinoamericana*, pp. 31–36. Bogotá: Tercer Mundo, 1979.

Portantiero, Juan Carlos. "Viñas: la quiebra de la ilusión." In his *Realismo y realidad en la narrativa argentina*, pp. 91–96. Buenos Aires: Procyón, 1961.

Rasi, Humberto M. "David Viñas, novelista y crítico comprometido." *Revista iberoamericana* 42, no. 95 (1976): 259–65.

Rodríguez Monegal, Emir. "Los parricidas crean: David Viñas, *Un dios cotidiano*." *Marcha* 20, no. 931 (1958): 23.

———. Review of *Dar la cara*. *El país* (Montevideo) (11 February 1963).

———. "David Viñas en su contorno." *Mundo nuevo* 18 (1976): 75–84. Also in his *Narradores de esta América*, vol. 2, pp. 310–30. Montevideo: Alfa, 1974.

Rosa, Nicolás. "Literatura argentina y David Viñas." *Setecientos monos*, 1, no. 5 (1965): 9–13.

———. "Sexo y novela: David Viñas." In his *Crítica y significación*, pp. 7–99. Buenos Aires: Galerna, 1970.

———. "Viñas: La evolución de una crítica." *Los libros* 2, no. 18 (1971): 10–14.

Senkman, Leonardo. *La identidad judía en la literatura argentina*, pp. 293–94, 317–18. Buenos Aires: Pardes, S.R.L., 1983.

Sirusky, Jaime. "El ejército como última estructura sobreviviente del liberalismo oligárquico hoy sólo tiene como ideología el antipensamiento. Entrevista con David Viñas." *Marcha* 3/4 (1967): 102–14.

Solero, Francisco Jorge. Review of *Cayó sobre su rostro. Ficción* 1 (1956): 180–85.

Sosnowski, Saúl. *"Los dueños de la tierra* de David Viñas: cuestionamiento e impugnación del liberalismo." *Caravelle* 25 (1975): 57–75.

————. *"Jauría* de David Viñas; continuación de un proyecto desmitificador." *Revista de crítica literaria latinoamericana* 4, no. 7/8 (1978): 165–72.

Szichman, Mario. "Entrevista: David Viñas." *Hispamérica* 1, no. 1 (1972): 61–67.

Tealdi, Juan Carlos. *Borges y Viñas (literatura e ideología)*. Madrid: Orígenes, 1983.

Timossi, Jorge. *"Literatura argentina y realidad política:* se abre la polémica." *Casa de las Américas* 7, no. 41 (1967): 125–27.

Valadez, Gustavo. "David Viñas y la Generación del 55." *Vórtice* (Stanford) 1, no. 1 (1974): 93–102. Bibliography.

Vázquez Rossi, Jorge. "David Viñas y la crítica literaria argentina." *La lagrimal trifurca* (Rosario) 2 (1968): 14–22, 39–43.

Ismael Viñas
(1925)

BOOKS (ESSAYS)

Orden y progreso: la era del frondizismo. Buenos Aires: Palestra, 1960.

El radicalismo. Buenos Aires: Centro Editor de América Latina, Colección Polémica, 1970.

La reacción nacionalista. Buenos Aires: Centro Editor de América Latina, Colección Polémica Num. 56, 1971.

Capitalismo, monopolios y dependencia. Buenos Aires: Centro Editor de América Latina, 1972.

La organización del despojo económico. Buenos Aires: Centro Editor de América Latina, Colección Transformaciones en el Tercer Mundo, no. 11, 1973.

Tierra y clase obrera. Buenos Aires: Achaval, 1973.

Las transnacionales. Buenos Aires: Centro Editor de América Latina, Colleción Transformaciones en el Tercer Mundo, no. 15, 1974.

La liberación nacional. Buenos Aires: Orientación Socialista, 1975.

El papel de los intelectuales. Buenos Aires: Orientación Socialista, 1975.

Historia del movimiento obrero. Buenos Aires: Centro Editor de América Latina, Colección Siglomundo, 1982.

Viñas, Ismael, and Moshe Ben Porat. *La clase obrera israeli.* Jerusalem: Moked, 1982.

BOOKS (POEMS)

El libro de Juan Fernández. Buenos Aires: Contorno, 1955.

Esto sabemos. Buenos Aires: Contorno, 1957.

COLLABORATIONS (ESSAYS)

Viñas, Ismael et al. *Las izquierdas en el proceso político argentino.* Buenos Aires: Palestra, 1961.

Alcalde, Ramón et al. *Estrategia en la universidad*. Buenos Aires: Liberación Nacional, 1964.

Vazeilles, José et al. *Los sindicatos*. Buenos Aires: Liberacion Nacional, 1965.

Viñas, Ismael, and Eugenio Gastiazoro. *Economía y dependencia*. Buenos Aires: Carlos Perez, 1968.

Ansaldi, Waldo, and Ismael Viñas. *Estructura social y política argentina*. Córdoba: Universidad Nacional de Córdoba, 1972.

Viñas, Ismael et al. *El peronismo*. Montevideo: Cuadernos de Marcha, 1974.

ARTICLES

"Eduardo Mallea." *Revista centro* 3, no. 6 (1953): 6–13.

"La traición de los hombres honestos." *Contorno* 1 (1953): 2–3.

"Una expresión, un signo [R. Arlt]." *Contorno* 2 (1954): 2–5.

"Reflexión sobre Martínez Estrada." *Contorno* 4 (1954): 2–4.

Viñas, Ismael, and Noé Jitrik. "Enrique Larreta o el linaje." *Contorno* 5/6 (1955): 13–14.

"Miedos, complejos y malosentendidos." *Contorno* 7/8 (1956): 11–15.

"Un prólogo sobre el país." *Contorno cuadernos* 1 (1957): 1–4.

"Algunas reflexiones en torno a las perspectivas de nuestra literatura: autodefensa de un supuesto parricida." *Ficción* 15 (1958): 6–21.

"La generación de 1945." *Comentario* 5, no. 18 (1958): 6–21.

"Una opción: subordinación, independencia, desarrollo." *Contorno cuadernos* 2 (1958): 1–2.

"Alrededor de *Sarmiento* (de Ezequiel Martínez Estrada)." *Cuidad* 1, no. 1 (1959): 30–34.

"Brujas en la Argentina." *Revista centro* 13 (1959): 3–7.

"Esquema para la actual literatura argentina." *Revista del mar dulce* (October 1959).

"Orden y progreso." *Contorno* 9/10 (1959): 15–75.

"Krieger Vasner o el desarrollismo en el poder." *Marcha* (1967): 6–8.

"Romero, Puiggros, o la historia sin clases." *Los libros* 2, no. 12 (1970): 16–18.

"Las carnes en la economía argentina." *Los libros* (1971): 10–13

"Claves del antisemitismo en la Argentina" (in Hebrew). *Dispersión y unidad* (Jerusalem) 81/82 (1977): 135–47.

"Judíos en la Argentina" (in Hebrew). *dispersión y unidad* 83/84 (1977): 132–53. (Reprinted in English in *Forum* 3, 1977.: 101–19.

"Capital y periferia." *Testimonio* (Jerusalem) 2 & 3 (August & November 1978): 26–38.

"La guerra del Líbano y los intereses de clase." *Encuentro* (Jerusalem-Buenos Aires) 19 (1982): 13–14.

"Los judíos y la sociedad argentina—un análisis clasista." *Controversia* (Buenos Aires) 83/84 (1983): 70–111.

"La crisis mundial y el endeudamiento de los estados en la actualidad." *Nueva presencia* (7 December 1984): 11–13

"La formación social israeli y la idea nacional." *Encuentro* 31, 32, 33 (July–December 1984): 55–63, 53–62, 55–62.

"La narrativa lationamericana: ausencias, excluídos y expulsados." *Hispamérica* 40 (1985): 89–96.

"Israel-Latinoamérica: ¿pragmatismo o relaciones internacionales subrogadas?" *Dispersión y unidad* (Jerusalem) 2d epoch, 3 (1986): 205–24.

POEM PUBLISHED

"Engañado Adanita." *Contorno* 3 (1954): 9.

General Sources

Agosti, Héctor P. "La 'crisis' del marxismo." In *¿Qué es la izquierda?*, edited by Ernesto Guidici et al. pp. 51–66. Buenos Aires: Documentos, 1961.

Brombert, Victor. "Raymond Aron and the French Intellectuals." *Yale French Studies* 16 (1955–56): 13–23.

Busch, Thomas W. "Sartre's Use of the Reduction: *Being and Nothingness* Reconsidered." In *Jean-Paul Sartre: Contemporary Approaches to His* Philosophy, edited by Hugh J. Silverman and Frederick A. Elliston. Pittsburgh, Dusquesne University, 1980.

Camus, Albert. *The Rebel.* Translated by Anthony Bower. New York: Alfred A. Knopf, 1957.

Cândido, António. "Literatura y subdesarrollo." In *América latina en su literatura*, edited by César Fernández Moreno, pp. 335–53. Madrid: Siglo Veintiuno, 1971.

Desan, Wilfred. *The Marxism of Jean-Paul Sartre.* Glouster, Mass.: Peter Smith, 1974.

Fanon, Frantz. *The Wretched of the Earth.* Translated by Constance Farrington. Preface by Jean-Paul Sartre. New York: Grove, 1963.

Fell, Joseph P., III. *Emotion in the Thought of Sartre.* New York and London: Columbia Universiity Press, 1965.

Flynn, Thomas R. *Sartre and Marxist Existentialism: The Test Case of Collective Responsibility.* Chicago: University of Chicago Press, 1984.

Geist, Antonio L. "El neo-romanticismo: evolución del concepto de compromiso en la poesía española (1930–36)." *Ideologies & Literature* 7, no. 15 (1981): 94–119.

Girard, René. "Existentialism and Criticism." *Yale French Studies* 16 (1955–56): 45–52.

Giudici, Ernesto, ed. *¿Qué es la izquierda?* Buenos Aires: Documentos, 1961.

Golder, Ernesto. *El peronismo en la literatura argentina.* Buenos Aires: Freeland, 1971.

Goldwert, Marvin. *Democracy, Militarism, and Nationalism in Argentina, 1930–1966: An Interpretation.* Austin: University of Texas Press, 1972.

Goonatilake, Susantha. *Crippled Minds: An Exploration into Colonial Culture.* Delhi: Vikas Publishing House, 1982.

Hernández Arregui, Juan José. *Imperialismo y cultura (la política en la inteligencia argentina),* rev. ed. Buenos Aires: Hachea, 1961.

———. *La formación de la conciencia nacional (1930–1960).* 2d ed. enlarged. Buenos Aires: Hachea, 1970.

Hirch, Arthur. *The French Left.* Montreal: Black Rose Books, 1982.

Hodges, Donald C. *Argentina, 1942–1976: The National Revolution and Resistance.* Albuquerque: University of New Mexico Press, 1976.

Jeanson, Francis. *Sartre and the Problem of Morality.* Introductiion by Robert V. Stone. Bloomington: Indiana University Press, 1980.

Johnson, John J. *Political Change in Latin America: The Emergence of the Middle Sectors.* Stanford: Stanford University Press, 1958.

Lee, Edward N., and Maurice Mandelbaum, eds. *Phenomenology and Existentialism.* Baltimore: Johns Hopkins Press, 1967.

Mafud, Julio. *Argentina desde adentro.* Buenos Aires: Americalee, 1979.

Malraux, Andre. "The 'New Left' Can Succeed!" *Yale French Studies* 15 (1954–55): 49–60.

Mannheim, Karl. "The Problem of the Intelligentsia: An Inquiry Into its Past and Present role." In *Essays on the Sociology of Culture,* pp. 91–171. London: Routledge & Kegan Paul, Ltd., 1956.

McCarthy, Patrick. *Camus.* New York: Random House, 1982.

Merleau-Ponty, Maurice. *Les Adventures de la dialectique.* Paris: Gallimard, 1956.

Morán, Fernando. *Novela y semidesarrollo (una intepretación de la novela hispanoamericana y española).* Madrid: Taurus, 1971.

Novak, George, ed. *Existentialism Versus Marxism: Conflicting Views on Humanism.* New York: Delta Press, 1966.

Ocampo, Victoria. "Carta a Waldo Frank." *Sur* 1 (1931): 17–18.

Rama, Angel. *La novela en América Latina: panoramas. 1929–1980.* Colombia: Instituto Colombiano de Cultura, 1982.

Romero, José Luis. "Los elementos de la realidad espiritual argentina." *Realidad* 1, no. 2 (1947): 1–13.

———. *Las ideologías de la cultura nacional y otros ensayos.* Edited by Luis Alberto Romero. Buenos Aires: Centro Editor de América Latina, 1982.

Royle, Peter. *The Sartre-Camus Controversy: A Literary and Philosophical Critique.* Ottowa: University of Ottowa Press, 1982.

Sartre, Jean-Paul. *Anti-Semite and Jew.* Translated George J. Becker. New York: Schocken Books, 1948.

———. *Existentialism and Humanism.* Translated by Philip Mairet. London: Methuen, 1948.

———. *The Transcendence of the Ego.* Translated by Forrest Williams and R. Kirkpatrick. New York: Farrar, Straus and Giraux, 1957.

———. *Critique de la raison dialectique.* Vol. 1. Paris: Gallimard, 1960.

———. *Literature & Existentialism.* Translated Bernard Frechtman. New York: Citadel, 1962.

———. *Search for a Method.* Translated by Hazel Barnes. New York: Random House, 1963.

———. "Materialism and Revolution." In *Literary and Political Essays,* translated by Annette Michaelson. New York: Collier Books, 1965.

———. *Being and Nothingness.* Translated by Hazel E. Barnes. New York: Washington Square Press, 1969.

———. *Situations.* Vol. 2. Paris: Gallimard, 1947–76.

Satre, Jean-Paul, David Rousset, and Gerard Rosenthal. *Entretiens sur la politique.* Paris: Gallimard, 1949.

Senkman, Leonardo. *La identidad judía en la literature argentina.* Buenos Aires: Pardes, S.R.L., 1983.

Stabb, Martin S. "Argentine Letters and the Peronato: An Overview." *Journal of Inter-American Studies and World Affairs* 12, nos. 3–4 (1971): 434–55.

Walsh, Rodolfo, Francisco Urondo, and Juan Carlos Portantiero. "La literatura argentina del siglo XX." In *Panorama de la actual literatura latinoamerciana,* edited by Emmanuel Carballo et al. Madrid: Fundamentos, 1971.

Wynia, Gary W. *Argentina in the Post-War Era: Politics and Economic Policy Making in a Divided Society.* Albuquerque: University of New Mexico Press, 1978.

Index